AN INTRODUCTION TO LOGIC

UNIVERSITY OF BRISTOL
PHILOSOPHY DEPARTMENT
WOODLAND RD,
TOL
TE

An Introduction to Logic

THE CRITICISM OF ARGUMENTS

PETER ALEXANDER
Reader in Philosophy, University of Bristol

London
GEORGE ALLEN AND UNWIN LTD

PRINTED IN GREAT BRITAIN
in 10 *on* 11*pt Times Roman*
AT THE PITMAN PRESS
BATH

Preface

This is an elementary textbook of logic intended for the student who does not necessarily expect to study logic to an advanced level but who wishes to know something about its various branches and who, above all, would welcome some help from logicians in the understanding of the nature of arguments which are actually used in the pursuit of those activities where argument has a place. There are many excellent textbooks of logic and a new one requires a special defence. The most usual reason for producing a new textbook is that the subject has developed and it is important that the student should not be introduced to outdated ideas. Although I hope that I have avoided such ideas and reported some new ones, my main defence is different. This book is intended to differ from others in the field largely in emphasis.

Most recent textbooks of logic appear to have as their main aim the introduction of the student to logic as an autonomous and highly technical subject. They stress the systematic character of logic and hence its likeness to pure mathematics rather than its connections with everyday forms of reasoning. They usually explicitly avoid philosophical problems or reduce discussion of them to a minimum, and one effect of this is to reduce to a minimum the discussion of the applications of logic and its connections with everyday discourse, since this is where most philosophical problems arise. Students who do not propose to devote their lives to the study of logic are inclined to find that approach frustrating. I believe that a balanced view of logic which will avoid this frustration is best achieved if the student becomes acquainted with its limitations as well as its powers from the very beginning.

I shall attempt to emphasize the connection of the logician's concepts with the logical conceptions implicit in everyday English, both non-technical and technical, in the hope of encouraging the student to develop some sensitivity to the character and power of the arguments he meets in other fields. I shall largely be discussing formal matters in an informal way. Because I think it is important for an introductory book to range widely over the subject I shall be unable to deal fully with the philosophical problems that arise but I hope, at least, to draw attention to them and to encourage their further study.

For the same reason, I shall not go deeply into any one branch of logic, but shall hope to arouse the student's interest in the more specialized books to which I refer. The book is intended to stand on its own as an introduction to the subject but its most successful use will be as a prolegomenon or an adjunct to these excellent works. Some familiarity with the techniques of formal logic such as can be gained from them will help to exhibit the point of the informal discussions in this book and I hope that these informal discussions will help to exhibit the rationale of those techniques.

It will be obvious to the expert that, in this connection I am greatly indebted to the following books, as well as those to which reference is made elsewhere.

E. J. LEMMON, *Beginning Logic* (London, 1965)

BENSON MATES, *Elementary Logic* (New York, 1965)

P. SUPPES, *Introduction to Logic* (Princeton, N.J., 1957)

W. V. QUINE, *Elementary Logic* (revised edition, New York, 1965)

W. V. QUINE, *Mathematical Logic* (revised edition, Cambridge, Mass., 1951)

W. V. QUINE, *Methods of Logic* (London, 1952)

P. F. STRAWSON, *Introduction to Logical Theory* (London, 1952)

W. C. and M. KNEALE, *The Development of Logic* (Oxford, 1962)

I am grateful to Professor Stephan Körner and Mr David Hirschmann, of the University of Bristol, for helpful comments, to Mrs Yvonne Kaye and Miss Bridget Baker for typing and to my wife for help with proof-reading.

Contents

PREFACE

Chapter I   THE NATURE OF THE SUBJECT
1. Reasoning and Logic   1
2. Sentences, Statements and Propositions   7
3. Meaning and Truth   12
4. Inference and Implication   15
5. Truth and Validity   17
6. Factual Truth and Logical Truth   19
7. Language and Reasoning   21
8. Support   22
9. The Logic of Non-Statements   28

Chapter II   SOME TYPES OF ARGUMENT
1. Scheme of Classification   30
2. Conclusive Arguments   31
3. Non-Conclusive Arguments   46
   a. Inductive Arguments   48
   b. Arguments from Particular to Particular   58
   c. Interpretative Arguments   59

Chapter III   LANGUAGE AND ITS FORMALIZATION
1. General   62
2. Key Words
   a. The Verb 'to be'   67
      (i) The 'is' of existence   67
      (ii) The 'is' of identity   69
      (iii) The 'is' of predication   70

   b. 'All' and 'Some': Universal, Particular and
      Singular Statements
      (i) 'All' and 'Some' in everyday discourse and in
          Logic   73
      (ii) Singular Statements   77
      (iii) Existential Import   79
      (iv) Quantifiers   84

c. Compound Statements
   (i) General Considerations   90
  (ii) Conjunction: 'and'   91
 (iii) Disjunction and Alternation: 'either . . . or'   98
 (iv) Denial: 'not' and 'no'
     (a) The Denial of Simple Statements   101
     (b) The Denial of Compound Statements   109
       (1) Conjunctive Statements   110
       (2) Disjunctive Statements   112
       (3) Alternative Statements   113
  (v) Implication: 'If . . . then'   114

Chapter IV   SOME PRINCIPLES OF INFERENCE

1. Introductory   135
2. Immediate Inferences   135
  a. Conversion   140
  b. Obversion   143
  c. Contraposition   146
  d. Inversion   147
3. Classes   154
4. Logical Properties of Relations   158
5. Relations between Classes   160
6. The Syllogism   168
7. Criticisms of Syllogistic Theory   179
  a. The Syllogism as Relating Propositions   183
  b. The Syllogism as Relating Classes   186
  c. The Syllogism as Relating Predicates   192
8. The Testing of Validity by Truth Tables   201
9. Validity and Invalidity   218

Chapter V   SYSTEMS AND PROOFS

1. General Considerations   222
2. Axiomatic Systems
  a. Propositional Calculus   229
  b. Predicate Calculus   236
3. Systems of Natural Deduction   246
  a. Propositional Calculus   248
  b. Predicate Calculus   256
4. Some Applications   265

5. Further Steps   270

APPENDIX: A Note on Other Systems   273

INDEX   275

CHAPTER I

The Nature of the Subject

1. REASONING AND LOGIC

Almost everyone engages in reasoning but not everyone engages in logic; to use a logical argument is not necessarily to engage in logic. This is a point which the title of this book is intended to make. It is a book on logic regarded as the criticism of arguments and to use a logical argument is not the same as to criticize or assess an argument from the logical point of view. There would be no place for the development of logic by a handful of experts if most of us did not use arguments in the course of our everyday activities and if we did not respect some types of argument and reject other types. Crudely, we can say that logic rests on the everyday acceptance and rejection of different types of argument and attempts to exhibit the principles upon which such acceptance and rejection rest, could rest, or ought to rest.

Logic is sometimes regarded as a branch of philosophy, and as such is taught in the philosophy departments of universities. On the other hand, it is sometimes regarded as closely related to mathematics, and as such is taught in mathematics departments. This division corresponds to a wider and a narrower conception of logic. In its narrower conception it is sometimes called 'foundations of mathematics' and is concerned with the principles and the general structure of mathematical reasoning. In this aspect it has become a highly specialized and technical subject and has contributed to such branches of mathematics as set theory and the theory of computers. In its wider conception, as a branch of philosophy, logic can be said to include the assessment or criticism of all types of arguments, whatever their subject-matter and wherever they occur. This may include the consideration of arguments in both informal and formal ways as we shall see.

This book is concerned mainly with the wider conception of logic and will do no more than glance obliquely at the narrower conception. It should not be supposed, however, that these two conceptions are independent or can be sharply separated. Logic, of whatever sort, springs from an analysis of the conceptions of everyday discourse in

1

so far as that discourse is rational, where everyday discourse is understood as the discourse in which we engage both in the course of our ordinary lives as citizens and members of families and in our professional lives as scientists or craftsmen or scholars. Wherever, in our daily pursuits, we reason or argue or infer we use the conceptions upon which logic is based or which the logician studies.

It is an essential feature of rational discourse that we have reasons, or that there be reasons, for accepting or rejecting statements or arguments. We may reject statements because they are false and this involves matters of fact rather than matters of logic. When we reject an *argument* because it is invalid or not a sound argument we do so, if we are being rational, on the basis of some principle, either explicit or implicit. This is a matter of logic because it involves, usually, not a particular subject-matter but the features of the linguistic framework within which we can talk about many different subject-matters. Putting this as simply as possible, we use certain conceptions in our discourse which impose on that discourse, whatever the subject matter, certain powers and restrictions; these conceptions are represented in English by such words as 'and', 'or', 'if', 'not' and 'therefore' which figure largely in arguments and whose use is governed by rules[1] which in turn help to determine which arguments we accept or reject.

Logic, of whatever sort, begins with the analysis of those types of argument which we accept or reject, in an attempt to describe precisely the conceptions which govern this acceptance and rejection and to isolate patterns of argument which differ as between these two broad classes. Having abstracted from our discourse these controlling conceptions the logician is able to work with these, ignoring all possible subject-matters, in such a way as to exhibit the relations between these various conceptions. We thus find the logician working with abstract systems the purpose of which is to exhibit in the most general way possible the various logical conceptions with which we normally work in rational discourse.

We may illustrate the fundamental point here by a very simple example. The statement

> Some apples are red

is true, but that it is true is something we know from our knowledge

[1] Some philosophers would argue that there are no rules, only regularities; but some of the regularities we find in language and reasoning we regard as precedents and therefore as rules governing future procedures. For opposing views see P. Ziff, *Semantic Analysis* (Ithaca, N.Y., 1960) and P. F. Strawson, *Introduction to Logical Theory* (London, 1952). See also, L. Wittgenstein, *Philosophical Investigations* (Oxford, 1953).

of certain matters of fact concerning the apples we have seen or heard about. It is a truth which is specifically about apples and knowledge about apples is essential to our ability to say that it is true. It may be called a 'factual truth'. The statement

All apples are either red or not red

is also true but for a different reason. We can know it to be true without knowing anything about apples and it would be true if we substituted the name of any other objects for 'apples'. Such truths are called 'logical truths'. This one depends upon the properties of the words 'either—or' and 'not', or rather the conceptions which these words stand for, and not on any particular subject-matter.

Philosophy is not an exact science issuing in firm and universally acceptable conclusions. Neither is it an inexact science. In the modern sense of the word, it is not a science at all. It does not aim to establish truths about matters of fact by empirical investigation as the sciences do; it does not aim to establish laws governing, or theories explaining, occurrences in the natural world. This is not to say that it is a vague and indefinite subject in which anything is acceptable. The idea of reasonableness or rationality is of the utmost importance to it. Philosophers regard their activity as essentially involving the rational supporting of statements; they accept that any assertion they make must be supported by reasons and must be defended against reasoned criticism. They deal in matters of interpretation and opinion but only when these are rationally supported. They are thus necessarily concerned about reasoning and the nature of rational support, and being inclined to take as little as possible for granted, they are also concerned to give as clear an analysis of rational support as they can. It is of particular importance for the philosopher to know how different kinds of statement differ, especially in respect of the kind of support which is possible and appropriate for them. Viewed in the most general way, this is the subject matter of logic.

Philosophy is sometimes said to be a 'second-order' activity, that is, an activity which has as its subject-matter another activity, which may be called a 'first-order' activity. We are familiar with many activities which may be classified in this way. If baking a cake is a first-order activity, then judging the result in an exhibition is a second-order activity; if driving a car is a first-order activity then explaining the point of each of the movements involved in driving is a second-order activity. In relation to the poet's activity, the literary critic's assessment of his poems is a second-order activity. In each case, the second-order activity depends upon the first-order activity

3

and involves such things as judging, describing, analysing, praising and explaining it.

Much philosophy may be regarded as a second-order activity which takes as its subject-matter certain first-order human activities such as describing the world scientifically, engaging in political activity, acting morally or acting on religious beliefs. There is, of course, a certain relativity about this idea. If we regard B as a first-order activity then, in relation to B, C may be a second-order activity. But there may be another activity A in relation to which B is a second-order activity and C a third-order activity. Thus, we might regard some branches of philosophy as third-order activities. For example, if we regard ethics as the study of the nature of moral judgment we might say that the first-order activity is people's behaviour towards one another, the second-order activity is the judging of that behaviour ('He ought not to have done that') and the third-order activity is the consideration of the meanings of such judgments (' "Ought" used in this way means . . .'). It is not important, here, to decide on the correctness of the various possible classifications but it is important to see that philosophy is at least not always a first-order activity. It often involves the analysis and evaluation of other activities with a view to understanding them. A great many of these are, or involve, linguistic activities and may be studied through a study of linguistic activities.

Logic may be said to be a second-order activity in relation to the first-order activity of reasoning. A great many of our everyday activities, whether undertaken for business or pleasure, involve reasoning. This is true of chess-playing, investigating the properties of matter, forecasting the state of the weather or the stock-market, constructing a theology and generally trying to decide what to do in a great many situations. We may say that the logician is interested in investigating reasoning of any sort and wherever it occurs. However, reasoning is a complex business with various aspects and others besides logicians investigate it. It is studied by the psychologist in so far as it may be influenced by emotional and motivational factors and by the linguist in so far as it is verbal. We may accept a conclusion not because there are good reasons for accepting it but because we desperately wish it to be true; we may put forward a bad argument, as it were by accident, because we have constructed our sentences badly. These matters concern the psychologist and the linguist respectively.

In any piece of reasoning it should be possible to discern what may be called the 'argument', that is, the statement intended as the conclusion and the statements taken to support it. In this sense, the argument may be regarded as a publicly accessible component of a piece of reasoning, a component which can be represented symbolically, in words or other symbols, written down, understood by many people and examined by them for soundness or validity. The logician is concerned to examine the similarities in and differences between arguments about different subject-matters, to generalize as far as possible about them and to point to those features which make them good or bad, sound or unsound, acceptable or unacceptable, valid or invalid. That is, he is concerned to unearth and state, as far as possible, the principles which govern the soundness or unsoundness of arguments.

A basic idea in all this is that of *support*. This is a wide term, but not necessarily a vague one. As I am using it, it is a relation between statements which goes some way towards justifying our drawing one statement as a conclusion from others. It is not an absolute 'all or none' relation, by which I mean that statements may support one another completely or strongly or weakly. Support may be conclusive or inconclusive and inconclusive to various degrees. Conclusive support is the upper limit of a whole scale of degrees of support.

The logician is likely to be good at distinguishing good arguments from bad ones because he has spent much time studying the criteria by which we judge arguments. But he does not, ultimately or usually, make or invent these criteria; he is not a kind of dictator or super-human law-giver. Ultimately he must take as his data the consensus of opinion of rational argument-users on what is a sound or an unsound argument. This he will not do by conducting surveys and sending out questionnaires but by examining the kinds of argument that people accept and reject when they are reasoning in various fields in which they are competent. We might say that he examines the generally accepted and the generally rejected arguments and extracts from this mass the criteria or principles upon which people, on the whole, appear to judge arguments. It may sometimes look as if he legislates rather than discovers, but this is merely an appearance. If he says, for example, that we must avoid contradictions in our reasoning this is because we do not normally admit that reasoning which leads to or contains contradictions is good reasoning. We may even say that it is not reasoning at all but something else, since one of the essential aims of reasoning is to lead us to specific conclusions rather than others, that is, to rule out some of the possibilities, and it can be shown that from two contradictory statements anything whatever follows.

This does not mean that logic cannot be *normative* in character, that is, that it cannot involve judgments of value. Nothing I have said precludes the logician from saying that one type of argument in general use is better than another type of argument in general use or from inventing a new way of arguing which is better than an established way. Nevertheless in making these judgments, his criteria of value will bear some close relation to what rational men value, to what they hope to achieve by rational argument and to what they will admit as reasonable.

We may say, in summary, that the logician's first aim is to achieve clarity about the soundness of the various kinds of arguments we use and about the basis on which they may be criticized. This involves a great deal of analysis of types of argument actually in use and the abstraction from them of logical principles and logical conceptions which are generally acceptable. Most logicians then go on to study these principles and conceptions in a more abstract way and to build coherent *systems* of inference which exhibit the relations between these various conceptions. As we shall see, when we are faced with arguments in everyday discourse there are often alternative ways of giving logical analyses of them; the same argument may be seen in more than one way, each way embodying different logical conceptions. The argument itself, we may say, is neutral between different interpretations which may be given of it. Depending upon which conceptions we choose to concentrate on, we may construct different logical systems covering the same ranges of arguments and these systems may be strictly alternatives or they may be incompatible. It may, however, be impossible to make a firm choice and say, 'This system is clearly the right one and the others wrong'. This sort of judgment may be just inappropriate at this level; one system may show up certain features of those arguments it embraces while another shows up other, equally interesting, features. There is still room for interpretation and a certain freedom of choice between different systems. This sort of consideration has led to the idea that we may study the nature of systems as such, comparing and contrasting different systems on a purely abstract level in the way in which a geometer might compare one system of non-Euclidean geometry with another. His aim will not have to do with possible applications of the systems but with the relations between their own internal structures and between their respective powers.

There is a possible misconception about logic and logicians which should perhaps be mentioned at this point. Logicians are sometimes pictured as being hostile to any kind of discourse which is not subject to the principles and rules in which they deal or as demanding that every kind of discourse be controlled by those rules and principles. It is thought, for example, by some of those who have this picture, that the importance of poetry and certain brands of theology provides the basis of some kind of argument against the whole of the logician's activity. Logicians may differ in their attitudes to these matters but nothing in the conception of logic implies that it must be regarded as an all-embracing theory of discourse. Logic covers, or aims to cover, any kind of discourse in which reasoned argument occurs or is appropriate but is silent about other kinds of discourse. Nothing in the conception of logic commits the logician to despising or ignoring poetry or to including it within his subject-matter; nothing in it commits him to regarding a high content of reasoned argument as the only criterion of value for discourse. There are many kinds of discourse having markedly different features and the different kinds cannot ultimately be sharply separated. The better we understand one kind of discourse the better equipped we are to understand the others. The poet and the logician make different uses of the same language; metaphors can be appreciated only in relation to literal uses.

2. SENTENCES, STATEMENTS AND PROPOSITIONS

I have briefly and provisionally characterized logic as the examination of the relations between statements, or kinds of statements, by virtue of which some statements are regarded as supporting others. The aim is to discover, as far as possible, general principles of reasoning. There is here an analogy between logic and the sciences. Just as the scientist attempts to bring as many different kinds of phenomena as possible under as few general laws as possible, so the logician hopes to show that many different inferences (or arguments) which appear superficially to be different, in fact fall under the same general principles. Caution is of course necessary. It is important that we should not allow our enthusiasm for generalization to lead us to distort the character of arguments in the attempt to fit them to a principle. This is a trap into which logicians have frequently fallen; if we keep actual arguments constantly in our minds this may help to avoid it.

I have from time to time mentioned 'statements' and it is important to say something more about the way in which I am using the word. Distinctions have been drawn between sentences, statements and propositions and the value of these distinctions as well as the possible ways of drawing them have been the subject of much controversy.[2] I

---

[2] See art. 'Propositions, Judgments, Sentences and Statements' in *Encyclopedia of Philosophy* (New York, 1967), Vol. 6.

can do no more here than attempt to make my use of these terms intelligible without claiming to do justice to the controversial issues at stake.

The problems in this area begin at a very early stage; there are great difficulties even in saying what a sentence or a word is. It is tempting to say that a sentence in a given language is a combination of words of that language which is complete in itself and which obeys the grammatical rules of that language. Immediately we may ask what 'complete in itself' means; the combinations of words 'Shut up!' and 'Holy Moses!' and 'Well done!' are complete in themselves but it is difficult to decide whether they are sentences or not and whether they obey or disobey grammatical rules. However, we are all able to recognize many sentences and it will be enough for my purpose if it can be agreed that whatever definition is adequate it will certainly contain the idea that a sentence is a collection of words, spoken or written.

The next thing to note is that every word and so every sentence may be characterized as a word or a sentence of, or in, some particular language. There are no words or sentences which are neutral as between all the different languages. The same shape or the same sound may appear as a written or spoken word in two different languages but even if they can be said to mean the same there are difficulties about saying that the same *word* appears in both languages; thus it makes perfectly good sense to distinguish between the *English word* 'art' and the *French word* 'art'.

We would all, I think, accept the following groups of words as English sentences.

    (1) Birds fly.
    (2) Cats fly.
    (3) Cats are carnivorous.
    (4) Where is the screwdriver?
    (5) Shoulder arms.
    (6) I shouldn't do that if I were you.

We would also probably accept that each of these has a normal use or that each would usually be used in doing a particular sort of thing. The first three would usually be used to state or assert something, the fourth to ask a question, the fifth to issue a command and the sixth to give advice. There are various other things we use sentences to do such as making requests, issuing warnings or prohibitions, commending, appraising, and so on.[3]

[3] See, e.g. J. L. Austin, *How to do things with Words* (Oxford, 1962).

8

The fact that the six sentences quoted have uses to which they are usually put should not be allowed to obscure the fact that the same sentence may be used to do different things, either at the same time or at different times, and that different sentences may be used to do the same thing. 'There is a bull' might be used both to convey information (state) and to warn. I may use the sentence 'I have a pain' to inform someone of a matter of fact, to express a feeling in order to relieve it, as I might say 'Ouch', or to plead for sympathy. I may convey the same fact to someone by saying 'Cats are carnivorous' or by saying 'Cats eat meat'.

Moreover, any sentence may be used as an illustration in the course of making a grammatical point about the English language or in the course of explaining a logical principle. In this connection, the distinction is sometimes made between *use* and *mention*; I use a sentence when, for example, I make a statement or issue a command with it, I mention it when I take it as an example and talk about it. This is quite a useful rough-and-ready distinction but it is doubtful if it can be sustained; clearly, there is a sense in which when we mention a sentence we are using it for a special purpose.

Another interesting feature of sentences is that the same sentence may be used at one time to say something true and at another time to say something false. For example, I may say 'It is raining' this morning when it is true and say it again this afternoon when it is false.

In view of these various facts about the ways in which sentences may be used it clearly will not do to say that *sentences* can be true or false. Of course, the most common uses of the examples 4, 5 and 6 in the above list have nothing to do with truth and falsity; questions of truth and falsity simply do not arise when we ask questions, issue commands and give advice. In connection with 1, 2 and 3 it is not the *sentences* which may be true or false. If one sentence may be used at one time to state something, where the question of truth or falsity does arise, and at another time to express an emotion, where such questions do not arise, then it cannot be the sentence itself that is true or false. We shall say that it is the *statements* or *assertions* which sentences may be used to make which are true or false. Whenever a sentence is used to make a statement or an assertion questions of truth or falsity arise.[4]

---

[4] It should be noted that a statement may be an assertion or it may not. There are contexts in which it is appropriate to distinguish. 'He asserted that the novel is dead' suggests a polemical intention or tone which 'He stated that the novel is dead' or 'He said that the novel is dead' does not. On the other hand, it is sometimes useful to say that someone asserted something to make it clear that he did more than just consider it for the sake of argument and then we may say that he stated it.

It follows that we must regard logical relations as holding between statements rather than between sentences. If a sentence is used to make a statement then this statement will imply others, contradict others, and so on; if the same sentence is used to issue a warning or to give advice the same implications may not be involved; but, if anything is implied, it will be the warning or the advice and not the sentence used to give it which does the implying.

When it is not misleading, I shall sometimes, for the sake of brevity, talk of a sentence as a statement instead of using the location 'the statement which this sentence is (or *may be*) used to make'.

It is important to stress here that, although a sentence is necessarily tied to a particular language, since it must be an English sentence or a French sentence or a sentence in some other language, a statement is not so tied. It does not make sense to talk of an English or French *statement*. The sentences 'It is raining' and '*Il pleut*' would both normally be used to make the same statement. Since these two sentences would normally be said to have the same meaning it is tempting to identify the statement and the *meaning* of the sentence. This, however, is misleading since the same sentence used for different purposes may be said to have different meanings corresponding to these uses. Moreover, we may use a sentence to make different statements at different times and, in doing so, rely on the sentence having a constant meaning. It is because the sentence 'I have red hair' has one clear and relatively constant meaning in English that it can be used by me to make one statement, about myself, a false one, and by someone else to make another statement about himself, a true one.[5]

Since logical relations hold between statements and since statements are not tied to particular languages we may say that in studying logic we are not studying something which depends upon the particular language in which we are working. I am not here, for example, writing about English logic rather than French or German logic. Thus when I talk of a logical relation depending upon the use of 'and' or 'if-then' this is an elliptical way of talking about the logical relations which depend upon or govern the uses of any words which have the same function in any other language as well. We are here relying on the assumption that any argument expressed in English could be translated, without any important loss from the point of view of reasoning, into any other language. Even if there is no synonym for the word 'and', for instance, in some language it may very well be that there is some element of sentence-structure which performs the same function in that language as 'and' does in English.

[5] See P. F. Strawson, *Introduction to Logical Theory* (London, 1952), esp. Chap. 1.

Sentences may be simple or compound and I shall use this same terminology of statements. A *simple* sentence is one which cannot be broken up into parts, all of which are either sentences or words which merely link sentences; a *compound* sentence is one which can be so analysed. Thus, 'It is raining' is a simple sentence whereas 'It is raining and the wind is blowing' is compound since it can be broken up into the sentences 'It is raining' and 'The wind is blowing' with the merely linking word 'and'. There are, of course, various familiar ways of compounding sentences as we shall see.

The simple sentences with which we shall usually be concerned are of the kind most appropriate for making statements, that is, the kind which the grammarians call 'indicative'. Logicians are inclined to call statements made with these simple sentences, and some of their compounds, 'categorical', meaning that they state or assert explicitly and unconditionally.

One branch of logic has come to be known as 'the propositional calculus' and I shall use this term, and talk of propositions in doing so, just because this terminology is fairly widely accepted. It is based on the view, which has been much criticized, that propositions are the entities between which logical relations hold. One reason for the criticisms which have been levelled against the notion of propositions is that it has been used in connection with a theory of meaning which has come in for considerable criticism in its own right.

It seems inescapable that inferences involve not merely sets of marks on paper or spoken sounds but also what these mean. What a sentence means is in one sense independent of that particular sentence since the same may be meant by other sentences in the same language and by sentences in different languages. Logicians hope, as I have said, to study principles of reasoning which are independent of any particular language in which they happen to carry out their researches. The term 'proposition' has been widely used to name the meaning of a sentence. According to this usage it was correct to say that an indicative sentence 'expresses' a proposition and the same proposition as any sentence in any other language into which the first sentence could be correctly translated. The proposition was also said to correspond to the facts, and so to be true, or to fail to correspond to the facts, and so to be false. Thus propositions were sometimes conceived as whatever it is that can be true or false. Clearly, sentences used to ask questions and issue commands, and other non-indicative sentences could not be said to express propositions.

What is the difference between propositions and statements as I have said this latter term is to be used? Clearly, they are being used partly to serve the same sort of function. A statement, however, is something a sentence may be used to make; a sentence does not make a statement, but people make statements using sentences in various languages. Propositions, however, were regarded as being *expressed* by sentences, as if they were essentially tied to sentences rather than their uses and in such a way as to minimize the possibility of a sentence being used in different ways for different purposes.

This way of talking encouraged people to think of meanings as mysterious entities somehow necessarily attached to sentences and controlling rather than controlled by the uses to which the sentences were put. Putting it in another way, it was likely to suggest that whenever anyone used a particular indicative sentence it expressed a particular proposition. It is surely more accurate to regard indicative sentences as being used in various ways, sometimes to make statements but sometimes to do other things.

One of the difficulties attached to the conception of propositions which I have outlined is that they were regarded as both the meanings of sentences and what was true or false. There is, however, some incoherence here since it is odd to say that the *meaning* of the sentence 'It is raining' is true or false; it seems more sensible to say that the statement it is used to make, on some occasions, is true or false. The reservation 'on some occasions' is necessary because the particular sentence may sometimes be used in such a way as to make us doubtful about saying that a statement was being made and to make us hesitate to ask whether it was true or false, for example, in a novel or in a stage play.[6]

The term 'proposition' is now perhaps more often used in a more neutral way to mean simply what is asserted in the making of a statement. In this use it is perhaps not very different from 'statement' used in the way I am using it. In an attempt to avoid confusion as far as possible I shall on the whole regard logical relations as holding between statements but sometimes, in deference to convention, especially in the last chapter, I shall talk of propositions.

3. MEANING AND TRUTH

It is important that we observe certain distinctions between meaning and truth. In everyday discourse we are sometimes careless about the distinction. For example, we sometimes say that an utterance is meaningless when strictly we should say that it is false. We use 'meaningless' as an emphatic version of 'false' for we sometimes say

---

[6] See J. L. Austin, 'Truth' *Proc. Arist. Soc.*, Supp. Vol. XXIV (1950) reprinted, along with criticisms, in *Truth*, ed. G. Pitcher (Englewood Cliffs, 1964). See also David Mitchell, *An Introduction to Logic* (London, 1962), esp. Chap. 5.

that an utterance is meaningless because it is obviously and flagrantly in conflict with the facts.

We can say that a sentence is meaningful if, and only if, it obeys the rules of our language and meaningless if it does not. This is not simply a matter of grammar since we sometimes hold that perfectly grammatical sentences are meaningless and ungrammatical sentences meaningful. For example, 'Democracy is triangular' would be said by most English speakers to be grammatical but we would not, except in special circumstances, regard it as meaningful. The special circumstances might be that it is used in a poem or in an elaborate metaphor. On the other hand, 'Pigs fly' is both grammatical and meaningful, though usually false.

It would be nice to be able to say that any collection of words which does not obey the grammatical rules of some language is not meaningful, so cannot be used to make a statement. However, this brings us sharply up against the awkward facts that it is very difficult to say what the grammatical rules of any natural language are and that people do understand one another even when they speak in sentences which they regard as ungrammatical. It is, however, probably safe to say that if a sentence is regarded as ungrammatical by a group of people it will be understood by them only if the departures from their conception of grammaticalness is not extreme. When we understand someone who says 'We was going to the cinema' we take them to be intending what we would intend by 'We were going to the cinema' but a greater departure from grammaticalness, such as 'He didn't get no marks' might give us pause and an even greater one, such as 'The gangster was the policeman shooting' might leave us completely bewildered.[7]

Fortunately, it is not essential here that we make up our minds about how words and sentences are to be correctly characterized or what exactly constitutes meaningfulness. It is enough that we can usually recognize sentences as such and say whether they are meaningful or not. This is sufficient to enable us to draw and use rough and ready distinctions between sentences and statements and to say something about their differences.

There is a sense in which we can say that meaningfulness is prior to truth and falsity. An utterance must be understandable, and must probably be an utterance of a sentence, before we can even consider whether it is intended to be a statement and so before we can consider whether it is true or false. If someone said, with every appearance of sincerity, 'Democracy is triangular' and sought our

[7] For some of the problems see *The Structure of Language*, ed. J. A. Fodor and J. J. Katz (Englewood Cliffs, 1964).

agreement, we should be inclined to say 'That's just meaningless'. If he were now able to explain to us what he meant by it we should consider it appropriate to enquire whether it was true or false. That would depend upon its having the appropriate relation to the facts; our original doubts depended upon our inability to see what facts to consider in relation to it, to see what would count in favour of, or against, its being true. There is a perfectly good sense in which we originally did not know what was being stated or even whether anything was being stated so we were not able to say whether it was true or false.

It seems, then, that anything that is true or false must be a statement or an assertion, otherwise the question of truth or falsity does not arise. Further, a statement or an assertion must involve the use of a meaningful sentence and this in turn probably involves grammaticalness or near-grammaticalness. However, we must beware of saying that every grammatically correct indicative sentence can be used to make a statement for then we shall be faced with such difficult examples as 'Democracy is triangular'. The fact is that meaningfulness depends upon more than formal arrangements of words, which is what rules of grammar concern. Languages involve conventions about which words appropriately go together and this is a matter of content and context rather than form. This in turn concerns the way in which words and sentences connect with or 'hook on to' the facts or states of affairs. Because we do not regard 'democracy' as referring to something which has a shape in a literal sense, we don't regard it as sensible to say that it has that particular shape to which we refer by 'triangular'.

However, it is important that we do not go too far in the opposite direction and adopt a 'referential' theory of meaning. I am not here concerned to discuss the various theories of meaning that have been canvassed but it is worth issuing a warning against this particular variety. When we say 'This book is a best-seller' we are *referring* to a specific book; some theories of meaning have said, or implied, that the meaning of 'this book' is the object to which it refers. There has been much controversy about how referring is to be understood[8] but there is fairly general agreement that referential theories of meaning are unacceptable.[9]

Theories according to which the meaning of an expression is identical with the state of affairs to which it is used to refer are open

[8] See, e.g. B. Russell, 'On Denoting', *Mind*, XIV (1905), and P. F. Strawson, 'On Referring', *Mind*, LIX (1950).

[9] For a brief account of some difficulties see Gilbert Ryle, 'The Theory of Meaning', *British Philosophy in the Mid-Century*, ed. C. A. Mace (London, 1957) and J. L. Austin, 'The Meaning of a Word' in *Philosophical Papers* (Oxford, 1961).

to a number of objections, an important one being that this could only account for the meaning of sentences used to make statements. Moreover, and worse, it is difficult to say that universal statements such as 'All men are vertebrates' or negative statements such as 'John is not tall' or false statements, or statements about mythical creatures such as unicorns are used to *refer* to states of affairs. Further, even when we do use a sentence to refer to some particular thing in making a statement it does not seem correct to say that the particular thing to which it refers is its meaning. The theory appears to make the erroneous assumption that all words function in the same way as proper names.

It is probably better to regard the meaning of an expression as the set of rules or linguistic conventions which govern its (correct) use. This leaves open the possibility that the expression in question may sometimes be used to refer to something and at other times not to refer to something and that in either case it may be used to make a statement or for some other purpose.

A sentence may thus have various meanings corresponding to various different uses and it must have such a meaning that it can be used to make statements before questions of truth or falsity become relevant. When these do become relevant they are questions about the truth or falsity of the statements which it is, or can be, used to make. Thus to say that a statement is true or that it is false is to imply that certain sentences which can be used to make it are meaningful; to say that a sentence or a string of words is meaningless is to imply that no question of truth or falsity can arise in connection with its utterance.

4. INFERENCE AND IMPLICATION

Logicians regard it as a vulgar error to confuse inference and implication although there is considerable looseness to be found on this matter in common speech. Literally, the two terms mean quite different things which it is valuable to keep separate. Inferring is drawing a conclusion from a statement or set of statements; implication is a relation between statements. Only people infer; only statements imply.[10] We infer when we accept a statement and draw a conclusion from it; in inferring, the *making* or *accepting* of statements is involved. Statements may imply one another without anyone's actually making or accepting these statements.

---

[10] For our present purpose it can be argued that we can infer from other things besides statements, e.g. from commands, and that other things besides statements imply, e.g. moral judgments, but we can ignore that here. The central point is that it is not people who imply but it is people who infer.

For example, the statement which would normally be made with the sentence

> John is a bachelor

implies the statement which would normally be made with the sentence

> John is unmarried.

If I were told, and accepted, that the first statement was true I should be able to infer the truth of the second statement. In fact it is just the relation of implication between these two statements which justifies my inferring one from the other.

It is true that we sometimes say such things as 'What are you implying?', which suggests that people as well as statements may imply, but strictly the question means 'What does the statement you have just made imply?' Even in common speech it is a vulgar error to say 'What are you inferring?' instead of 'What are you implying?'

Implication does not involve truth or falsity, except in a purely hypothetical way. If one statement p implies another statement q then q would necessarily be true if p were true, but in saying that this is so we are not saying that either p or q is in fact true. On the other hand, in inferring p from q we are accepting, or supposing, p to be true, and as a consequence of this and the relation of implication between them, accepting, or supposing, q to be true. If I say that q may be inferred from p I mean that if it is correct to accept p then it follows that it is correct to accept q and this is to draw attention to the relation of implication between p and q.

When we are considering an argument from the logical point of view we may set it out in such a way as to draw attention to a type or pattern of inference, or a possible inference, or we may set it out in such a way as to draw attention to an implication-relation upon which such an inference or inference-pattern is based. For example, the argument

> All men are mortal
> Socrates is a man
> ∴ Socrates is mortal

is here set out as an inference-pattern. (I say an 'inference-pattern' rather than an 'inference' because I am not here concerned to say whether the statements involved are true or false.) The sign for 'therefore' indicates that we are supposing that the first two statements are accepted as true, and in consequence, that the third statement is accepted as true. If I now uttered these three sentences outside the context of a logical discussion and with every sign of conviction and sincerity I should be making an inference or repeating an inference I had already made. We may, however, represent the implication upon which this inference depends by writing

> *If* all men are mortal
> *and* Socrates is a man
> *then* Socrates is mortal.

This makes it quite clear that we are not accepting any of the statements, or even *making* them, but only drawing attention to a relation between them. In logic we are concerned primarily to study implications because we are concerned to discover the relations between statements upon which inferences depend.

5. TRUTH AND VALIDITY

Statements may be true or false but only arguments may be valid or invalid. In everyday speech we sometimes refer to valid statements and what we mean by this is either that the statements are true or that they are the conclusions of valid arguments. The first of these uses is, strictly speaking, a misuse.

What it is that determines the truth or falsity of statements raises many difficult questions but for our purpose it is sufficient to say that when we make a statement we assert that some state of affairs exists and the statement is true if that state of affairs does indeed exist, false if it does not. It is sometimes said that a statement is true if it *corresponds* to some state of affairs, false if it does not. Problems arise when we enquire into what, precisely 'corresponds to' means, and if this were a book on epistemology we should have to spend a great deal of time discussing this. For our present purpose, that of distinguishing truth from validity, the idea is perhaps intuitively clear enough.

Validity is different. Provisionally we can say that whether an argument is valid or not does not depend upon some relation it bears to external states of affairs but does depend upon the relations between the various statements which it contains, that is, upon the form or structure of the argument itself. Using 'validity' in its widest sense we may say that an argument is valid if the statements taken to support the conclusion do in fact support it to the extent claimed. The statements taken to support the conclusion will henceforth be called the *premisses* of the argument.

This is a wide sense of the word 'validity' which not every logician would accept because of the varying degrees of support for which it allows. The fullest possible support may be called *conclusive support* and we find it in such arguments as

(1) $2 + 2 = 4$
(2) $3 + 1 = 4$
(3) $\therefore 2 + 2 = 3 + 1$

where (1) and (2) are the premisses and (3) is the conclusion. This argument is such that given the premisses the conclusion necessarily follows. No other conclusion from (1) and (2) which conflicts with (3) is possible. The validity of arguments in which support is conclusive will be called *deductive validity* and the arguments, according to custom, *deductive arguments*. To say that an argument is deductively valid is to say that if the premisses are true then the conclusion must be true or, more accurately, that if the premisses were true then the conclusion would necessarily be true. It should be noted that validity does not depend upon the actual truth or falsity of the premisses; hence the use of the subjunctive mood in the more accurate formulation. It is clear that validity depends upon the relations between the statements.

Some logicians would restrict validity to what I am calling 'deductive validity'. There is, however, no harm in using the term in a wider sense if we are clear about what we are doing. We frequently draw conclusions from evidence which does not give conclusive support to them and we regard ourselves as perfectly justified in doing so. We may say that such arguments are valid if we recognize that their conclusions must be regarded as more or less tentative or provisional, depending upon the strength of the support, and that the validity we are talking about is not deductive validity. When we say that an argument of this sort is valid we are saying something like 'If the premisses are true then the conclusion is likely to be true' and the strength of the likelihood depends on the strength of the support. This notion of strength of likelihood is usually a comparative rather than a quantitative notion. Thus, given that each of the statements *a*, *b* and *c* gives some support to statement *x* then the support given by *a*, *b* and *c* together is stronger than that given by one of them alone but we cannot give a numerical value to this 'stronger than' except possibly in very special circumstances.

The question whether or not an argument is deductively valid is independent of the question whether the statements composing it are actually true. The logician's business is with validity rather than truth; he is concerned to distinguish in general between sound and unsound arguments. It is sometimes possible to say that any argument having some specific structure is sound, or valid, just in virtue of that structure and irrespective of the subject-matter to which it is applied. If an argument of this given structure is used then, whatever the subject-matter, its conclusion will be true as long as its premisses are true.

Of course, anyone who uses arguments hopes, in doing so, to reach true conclusions. To say that the logician is interested in validity rather than in truth is to say something about his professional interest as a logician; it is not to say that in no capacity is he interested in truth nor to say that he does not hope that the statements he makes about arguments and their validity will be true. If he decides that an argument having some specific structure is valid then he is saying that whether the true statements used as premisses are statements in geology or statements in physics, the conclusion will be a true statement in geology or physics respectively. It is not his business to decide that they are true but the business of geologists and physicists.

This implies that there is a certain class of arguments used in many different contexts from which it is possible to abstract a specific common structure upon which the validity or invalidity of the original argument depends. Some logicians are inclined to think that this is true of all arguments but others are less optimistic about this, holding that some arguments, at least, can be understood and assessed only in relation to the particular contexts in which they are used. The distinction is sometimes drawn between formal logic, based on the assumption of common and isolable structures, and informal logic, based on the assumption of the indispensability of contexts.

I am inclined to think that something of interest, but not necessarily everything, can be learnt about some types of argument by formal methods but that some arguments, and perhaps some aspects of all arguments, will not yield to formal treatment. Moreover, and perhaps most importantly, the application of conclusions in formal logic to actual arguments always involves some informal logical analysis of those arguments. Some reasons for saying these things have already been touched on and further reasons will emerge in the sequel.[11]

6. FACTUAL TRUTH AND LOGICAL TRUTH

In the last section truth was considered as involving a relation between statements and matters of fact or states of affairs. This notion of truth may be called 'factual truth' to distinguish it from

[11] See Gilbert Ryle, *Dilemmas* (Cambridge, 1954), Chap. VIII.

another, to be called 'logical truth', which I just mentioned in Section 1.

Few, if any, speakers of English would deny that the statement

> All married men are men

is true. Many would no doubt be inclined to say that it is trivial but not that it is false. Now it is clear that the truth of this statement does not depend upon matters of fact or states of affairs, except perhaps matters of linguistic fact. In order to see that it is true we do not have to examine married men to see whether they are indeed men. In this it is contrasted with

> All married men are happy

since to establish whether this is true or not we would have to examine married men. The first of these statements may be said to be *logically true* while the second is factually true, if it is true, factually false, if it is false.

How we are to account for or describe logical truth is a controversial question but we can at least say that it has to do with relations internal to statements, between words or ideas, rather than relations between statements and something else. An analysis of the statement itself in relation to the context of ideas with which it is connected will show whether it is logically true or not. Logical truths are for this reason sometimes called *analytic* statements, in contrast to factual statements which are called *synthetic*. One rather unsatisfactory way of making the distinction is to say that in analytic statements the subject term 'contains' the predicate term whereas in synthetic statements it does not. This seems plausible in relation to our statement

> All married men are men,

but must be elaborated to deal with such statements as

> All bachelors are unmarried

which would be regarded by many as analytic and by some as logically true. Here it is not obvious that the subject *term* 'contains' the predicate *term* although it seems clear that the *meaning* of 'bachelor' involves the *meaning* of 'unmarried'.

Perhaps the most important property of logically true statements is that their denials are self-contradictory. Thus we can deny

> All bachelors are unmarried

by saying

> Some bachelors are married

and this is self-contradictory just because of what we mean by 'bachelor' and 'married'. If however we similarly deny

> All bachelors are unhappy

by saying

> Some bachelors are happy

this statement is not self-contradictory. To discover which of these statements is true we have to investigate bachelors.

The logician is particularly interested in logical truth because any valid deductive argument can in fact be regarded as based on a logical truth and has the property that the combination of the premisses and the denial of the conclusion is self-contradictory. Thus the argument

> All men are mortal
> Socrates is a man
> ∴ Socrates is mortal

is based on the logical truth

> 'All men are mortal and Socrates is a man'
> implies 'Socrates is mortal'

and the statement

> All men are mortal, Socrates is a man and Socrates is not mortal

is self-contradictory.

This is yet another topic which is fraught with difficulties but it will be enough for our purpose if we can recognize logical truths even if we cannot give a full and adequate account of them. It will help if we say that a logical truth is a statement that is true whatever the state of extra-linguistic facts and whose denial is self-contradictory.

7. LANGUAGE AND REASONING

I have said that I should like everything I say in this book to be related as far as possible to our everyday use of arguments, whether in the sciences, theology, mathematics, history or merely in our day-to-day transactions with families and friends. I want to avoid even the appearance that logic is necessarily an abstract study having little connection with our daily lives. This is an appearance which many books on logic unintentionally give; it is a misleading appearance which often produces dissatisfaction in the minds of students in the initial stages.

Because of this I wish to stress the connection of various symbolic systems in logic with the language of everyday discourse. However, this is a more fundamental matter than it may at first sight appear. In the first place, the soundness or unsoundness of arguments couched in ordinary English depends almost entirely upon the proper and precise use of certain ordinary English words; fallacies can usually be traced to some misuse of these words which everyone who has a clear understanding of the language should be able to avoid. There are, of course, certain subtleties which we often miss when we learn our language and it is part of the logician's job to point these out but what he points out when he does this is something about the properties of our language.

In the second place, the features of the English language which are important here are not peculiar to the English language but are features shared by most, perhaps all, natural languages in one way or another. This is indicated by the fact that arguments can, on the whole, be freely translated from language to language. The most abstruse and abstract system of logic has its roots somewhere in natural languages, including their 'technical' parts, in that its concepts have been developed out of, or abstracted from, some aspect of the structure of these natural languages.

My aim will be, as far as possible, to provide the basic links between various systems of logic and features of the English language from which they spring, in the belief that the same could be done for other natural languages. Thus we shall be implicitly studying common ways of looking at the world and commonly accepted principles of reasoning which are enshrined in different languages of which English is one example. Thus remarks about English usages are intended to have a wider application than to the merely peculiar and accidental features of one language.

8. SUPPORT

I now wish to lead up to the detailed analysis of arguments by considering some ways in which statements support one another, illustrating some of the points I have already made in a general way.

Consider the following pairs of statements.

A (1) All undergraduates are human.
    (2) This undergraduate is human.
B (1) All undergraduates are intelligent.
    (2) This undergraduate is intelligent.
C (1) All undergraduates are deaf.
    (2) This undergraduate is deaf.

We can say that in each pair statement (1) supports statement (2) and, moreover, supports it *conclusively* meaning that if (1) is, or were to be, true then (2) is, or would be, necessarily, true also. In each case a *contradiction* would result from the assertion of (1) and the simultaneous rejection of (2). This is to consider merely the relations between these statements and to consider them in one 'direction' only, the direction, namely, from (1) to (2).

The first members of each pair differ from one another in respect of their truth. If we take 'human' in its widest sense, as merely descriptive and not evaluative, we can say that A(1) is true and that this would be generally accepted. Statement B(1) is more doubtful, depending upon our criteria of intelligence. Some people might say that anyone who gets into a university is intelligent and they would say without hesitation that B(1) is true. Others might disagree. On the other hand, there would doubtless be general agreement that C(1) is false. These differences, however, are irrelevant to the matter in hand. The relations between the statements in each pair can be considered without reference to their truth and falsity and we can say that the supporting relation between (1) and (2) in each pair is the same. It is because of this, and because C(1) is undoubtedly false, that we have to say, for this example that 'C(1) conclusively supports C(2)' means that if C(1) *were* true C(2) *would be* true.

We may generalize the point that is here being made by introducing some elementary symbols so that our three pairs of statements may be represented without any reference to their subject-matter. Let 'X' replace 'undergraduate' in each sentence and 'Y' replace indifferently 'human', 'intelligent' and 'deaf'. Then we can represent all three pairs by the statement skeletons

D (1) All Xs are Ys
    (2) This X is Y.

These skeletons may be taken as representations of the *forms* of the paired statements above. They allow us to consider certain relations between the statements without consideration of their actual truth or falsity.

23

It is obvious that it makes no sense to ask whether statements made with D(1) and D(2) are true or false; as they stand they cannot be used to make statements. The symbols 'X' and 'Y' can now be regarded as variables, that is, as marking empty spaces into which appropriate words can be inserted in order to complete sentences which can be used to make statements. We can say that any statement having the form D(1) supports conclusively a statement of the form D(2) as long as the same word is substituted for X in each appearance and the same word is substituted for Y in each appearance, differences of number being allowed so that 'mice' and 'mouse' count as the same word. The pairs A, B and C conform to this rule.

There is, however, a reservation to be made about this. Many words, in English and other natural languages, are ambiguous. One written shape or spoken sound may have more than one meaning and in considering the supporting of one statement by another we cannot ignore meaning. For example, we cannot take the statement

All dogs are mammals

to support the statement

This dog is a mammal

when in the second statement what is referred to is a firedog or a device used by mechanical engineers. This kind of consideration imposes some limitations on the application of symbols and as we shall see there are other limitations. This does not imply that symbolic expressions are bound to be too misleading to be useful but only that we must use them with caution. For the moment, it will suffice to say that any symbol such as X must here, in the sort of context we are considering, be replaced in the two statements by the same word, allowing for difference in number, used with the same meaning. It might be thought that if a 'word' has two meanings then we have not one word but two, so that this reservation is not necessary. There are, however, difficulties about this and I adopt the convention given as being fairly generally accepted.

Now consider our pairs of statements in, as we might say, 'the opposite direction'. That is, consider whether the second member of each pair supports the first.

A (1) All undergraduates are human.
   (2) This undergraduate is human.

Let us assume that 'undergraduate' is not so defined that an undergraduate *must* be human, so that it is logically possible for a very intelligent monkey to be an undergraduate, and ask whether A(2) supports A(1). If we are talking only about relations between statements we must say that it does to some extent, but only to a very small extent and certainly not conclusively. If one undergraduate is human then this constitutes a small amount of evidence in favour of the statement that all undergraduates are human. If we had what we regarded as sufficient evidence for A(1) then statements like A(2) would form part of that evidence. We should normally say that each of the statements

> These 100 undergraduates are human,
> These 1,000 undergraduates are human,
> These 10,000 undergraduates are human,

supports A(1) to a different extent.

It must also be noted that if we knew that the two statements

> This undergraduate is human,
> This undergraduate is not human,

were true, where 'this', of course, indicates two different individuals, we could still say that the first supported A(1) to exactly the same extent as before, even though the second is enough to refute A(1) completely. That is, we can say that whether we know that A(1) is true or false, A(2) supports it weakly and to the same extent as it does when we do not know whether A(1) is true or false. That is, support is independent of our knowledge.

Now consider again

> C (1) All undergraduates are deaf,
>   (2) This undergraduate is deaf.

Statement C(2) gives some weak support to C(1) although we know C(1) to be false. We know it to be false not because C(2) fails to support it but because we know some other true statement or statements which refute it. As far as comparison is possible, we can say that C(2) supports C(1) to the same extent as A(2) supports A(1). The same applies to B(2) and B(1). We can say this because all the statements are about undergraduates and the proportionality of 'all undergraduates' to 'this undergraduate' figures in each pair.

In general, a statement of the form 'This X is Y' supports a statement of the form 'All Xs are Ys' to some extent, even if only very weakly, as long as our rule for the substitution of X and Y is obeyed. Such support can be conclusive only under one very special condition, namely, where there exist just n Xs (where n is a finite number) and a statement of the form 'This X is Y' is true for each of the n Xs. For example, the statement 'All planets of the sun are spherical' would be conclusively supported by nine statements of the form 'This planet of the sun is spherical' each referring to a different planet, given that there are exactly nine planets.

This condition is never fulfilled when we have just two statements of the forms 'All Xs are Ys' and 'This X is Y', given that there is more than one X. The support of the second statement for the first must therefore always be *inconclusive* under these conditions. We thus have to say different things about the support given by (1) to (2) from what we can say about the support given by (2) to (1) in each pair. We can say that if (1) is true then (2) must be true, and that is conclusive support; we cannot say that if (2) is true then (1) must be true but only that the truth of (2) gives *some* grounds for presuming the truth of (1), and that is inconclusive support. In this latter situation we feel the need to collect further evidence; in the former situation there is, of course, no question of collecting further evidence.

When we have conclusive support we can express the relation by saying 'If (1) is true then (2) *must* be true' or 'If (1) were true then (2) would *necessarily* be true'. These words 'must' and 'necessarily' indicate the logical relation of *following from* and its converse *entailing*. If (1) conclusively supports (2) then (2) *follows* logically from (1) and (1) *entails* (2).

The field in which, *par excellence*, we can expect to find conclusive support of one statement by another is the field of pure mathematics. As a very simple example of this we may take the statements

E (1) 4 is greater than 3,
  (2) 3 is less than 4.

Here, E(1) conclusively supports E(2). Also, in contrast to our earlier examples, E(2) conclusively supports E(1). This is a special case, even in mathematics. It is no more true in mathematics than anywhere else that any statement which conclusively supports another is conclusively supported by that other. We may prove a theorem in elementary geometry starting from certain premisses but we cannot necessarily prove those premisses starting from the theorem taken as given. However, any mathematical proof does require conclusive support of the conclusion by the premisses. We can remove the word 'mathematical' from the last sentence because it is usually held that it is an essential part of the meaning of 'proof' that proving is the providing of conclusive support.

Arguments depend upon supporting relations. We might say that what an argument does, if it is a good one, is to give support to the statement which is its conclusion. I have so far considered supporting relations between only pairs of statements but the arguments we

26

usually use are more complex than this. Most of them depend upon the supporting relation between two or more statements and a conclusion. Continuing to use the simplest kind of example we may go on to consider the relations between three statements.

F (1) All spies are cunning
   (2) James Bond is a spy
   (3) James Bond is cunning.

It is easily seen that (1) and (2) together support (3) conclusively, still in the sense that if (1) and (2) were true and (3) false we should have a contradiction. It is important that, here, we cannot say that (3), alone, supports (1) and (2), however weakly, since there is nothing in (3) which allows us to make any connection with being a spy or with the characteristics of spies. However, (2) and (3) together give some slight support to (1) since it follows from them that there is one spy who is cunning, that is, they make some connection between being a spy and being cunning.

We can go on in this way making longer and longer chains of supporting statements. For example

James Bond is a spy
All spies are human beings
All human beings are mammals
All mammals are vertebrates
James Bond is a vertebrate.

The final statement is conclusively supported by all the others taken together but it is not conclusively supported by any other selection from them.

It should be noted that when we use arguments in the ordinary way, in a political discussion, say, or in working out a conclusion in history or theology, we often do not state the argument in full. We may take a premiss for granted, regarding it as generally accepted, or we may leave the conclusion unstated because it is so obvious. For instance, we might say 'James Bond is a spy, so James Bond is cunning' relying on the general acceptance of 'All spies are cunning' or we might say 'All spies are cunning and James Bond is a spy', because any fool can see what follows.

However, for logical purposes, the missing statements are essential and without them we do not, strictly, have an argument. In analysing an argument someone has used we must include in the argument whatever statements he has *intended* to rely upon, even if he has only taken them for granted. On the other hand, if the statements he has made require other statements, which he did not even have in mind, to make them into an argument, then we must say that he did not really use an argument but was making unsupported statements.

It is possible to make almost any unsound argument into a sound one simply by adding appropriate premises. We should not do this in the course of analysis unless there is reason to believe that the arguer intended to use those premises and took himself to be doing so. If we credit an arguer with premises of which he had not thought we shall find ourselves behaving as if hardly anyone ever uses an unsound argument.

Once we have set out an argument for analysis or criticism we must take into consideration *all* that is set out and *only* what is set out. In particular, we must not take into consideration, in judging that argument, other things we happen to know about the subject-matter in question. Suppose, for example, that we are asked to say whether the following argument is valid or not.

> All mice have two tails
> All cats are mice
> ∴ All cats have two tails.

As long as we are only considering validity, we must not take into account our knowledge, from other sources, that mice do not have two tails and that cats are not mice. These things are simply irrelevant to the relations between these statements upon which validity depends. What we are asked to do is to say whether or not the truth of the first two would guarantee the truth of the third and we must say that it would.

9. THE LOGIC OF NON-STATEMENTS

I have chiefly talked as if logical relations hold only between statements and assertions. I must stress here that this may have given a misleading impression and try to counteract it. Recent work, especially in linguistics and linguistic philosophy, has made it clear that in the past the overwhelming importance attached to statements or propositions as the bearers of logical relations was misplaced. Rational discourse may involve many other activities besides stating and supporting statements by other statements.

This is connected with the fact stressed earlier that sentences may be used to do many different jobs. We may use them to command and exhort, to advise, to warn, to consent, to praise, to criticize, to make contracts, to agree, to persuade and to promise. And so on. The possibilities are enormous and the relations between them and stating or asserting have only just begun to be explored. What does seem clear is that some or all of these activities may involve reasons and reasoning, may figure in rational discourse.

There has appeared in recent years much discussion of the logic of commands, the logic of imperatives and the logic of moral discourse and much more will no doubt appear in future.[12] A comprehensive book on logic should no doubt at least touch on these but such a book would be inordinately large or unbearably superficial. In this book, I shall deal almost entirely with the logic of statements but even this has been affected by the recent work to which I have just referred, so that it is now impossible to say some of the things that were said in books on logic thirty years ago and necessary to say some things that would then have seemed out of place.

Another consequence of this work is that it now appears more difficult to draw sharp lines between stating and other jobs that sentences may be used to do. This accounts for a certain reserve which may be detected in some passages in the book but which may not always be explicitly mentioned or explained.

[12] See J. L. Austin, *How to do things with Words* (Oxford, 1962); R. M. Hare, *The Language of Morals* (Oxford, 1952), *Freedom and Reason* (Oxford, 1963); N. Rescher, *The Logic of Commands* (London, 1966).

CHAPTER II

Some Types of Argument

1. SCHEME OF CLASSIFICATION

The logician's aim to discover principles of valid reasoning carries with it the aim to *generalize* about arguments. Just as the natural scientist hopes to show that large numbers of superficially unconnected events in the world can be connected with one another through laws and theories, so the logician hopes to show that arguments about different subject-matters may be of 'the same type' or have 'the same form' since they conform to the same principle. It is not to be supposed that every argument we use can be brought under just one principle, although logicians once hoped for this, but it may be expected that large numbers of arguments may be brought under just a few principles. This is involved in the very idea of a principle; if we did not think this possible there would be little point in talking of principles and it is doubtful if there would be any such thing as logic. This generalizing aim lies behind most of the conceptions and techniques of logic, as we shall see.

I have already taken the first step in generalizing by pointing to the difference between conclusive and non-conclusive support. This divides all arguments into just two groups, those in which the conclusion is conclusively supported by the premisses and those in which the conclusion is supported by the premisses but not conclusively. I shall call these *conclusive arguments* and *non-conclusive arguments* respectively. Conclusive arguments are also called *deductive arguments*. In the past it was usual to call arguments which were intended to be non-conclusive *inductive arguments* but it is now fairly generally held that, although all conclusive arguments are deductive, not all non-conclusive arguments are inductive. There is a familiar way of defining inductive argument which separates them from certain other kinds of non-conclusive arguments; thus we shall see that the group of arguments classified as non-conclusive contains several broad subgroups of which the group of inductive arguments is only one.

It is important to recognize that these different types of non-conclusive arguments are not merely would-be deductive arguments which fail to reach the standards of deductive validity but are types

30

of arguments in their own right with their own standards of validity. Many of the arguments we normally use, and perhaps most of them outside mathematics and theoretical science, are non-conclusive and, by the very nature of their subject-matter, could never be replaced by conclusive arguments. Just as we can distinguish between allegedly conclusive arguments which are sound and unsound, so we can distinguish between sound and unsound non-conclusive arguments. Non-conclusive arguments are not necessarily aspiring conclusive arguments.

It must be confessed that there is some awkwardness in my terminology, which is brought out at the end of the last paragraph. The word 'conclusive', unlike the word 'non-conclusive', is often used to make an approving judgment of value; if an argument is conclusive then it is conclusive and cannot be unsound. I shall, however, sometimes use the word 'conclusive' as a purely descriptive word having to do with the arguer's intention and then I shall talk of sound and unsound conclusive arguments. An unsound conclusive argument will then be one which was intended to, or is thought to, establish something conclusively but which fails to do so.

I shall mainly be concerned with conclusive arguments although much of what I have to say about language has some bearing also on non-conclusive arguments.

2. CONCLUSIVE ARGUMENTS

We are all familiar with large numbers of conclusive arguments, especially if we have studied mathematics where the best examples are to be found. Consider two simple arguments constructed out of one type of statement mentioned in Section 8 of the last chapter.

(1) $4 > 3$
 $3 > 2$
 $\therefore\ 4 > 2$

(2) $10 > 8$
 $8 > 6$
 $\therefore\ 10 > 6$

(The symbol '$>$' is the familiar mathematical symbol meaning 'is greater than'.) These arguments are alike since in each the last statement is conclusively supported by the first two taken together. They differ in that they involve different numbers but, from our point of view, this difference is merely superficial. There are other important similarities between them. The same relation (indicated by '$>$') is said to hold between the numbers in each statement, there are three

31

numbers each of which appears twice, there is a number common to the first two statements and the last statement relates the other two numbers.

We rely on these similarities when we move from arithmetic to algebra, that is, when we replace each different number by a different letter obtaining

(3) $x > y$
         $y > z$
     $\therefore x > z.$

We have here replaced the *constant* symbols, that is, the specific numbers, in both arguments by *variable* symbols, the letters x, y and z, which now stand for, or can be replaced by *any* numbers whatever. It is in some ways even better to say that x, y and z simply mark empty spaces into which numbers can be inserted. The insertion of numbers is sometimes referred to as 'interpreting' the expressions.

It should be noted that depending upon which numbers replace x, y and z, the resulting statements may be true or false. Any interpretation which results in false statements will be such that the conclusion will not be proved to be true. However, we must bear in mind the distinction between truth and validity discussed in Section 5 of the last chapter; in spite of the possibility of interpretations being false we can say that (3) is a valid inference-pattern, meaning that *if x is greater than y and y is greater than z, then x is greater than z.*

Expressions such as $4 > 3$ can be regarded as statements but the corresponding expressions, containing letters cannot. This is because no expression such as '$x > y$' can be used as it stands to state or assert anything; it can say nothing specific about any number just because, on interpretation, it can say something specific about every number. It gives the *form* of every statement of a certain kind which can be made about numbers, any numbers we choose. It is no more than a pattern of statements.

Now, although we introduced the expression '$x > y$' to stand for any arithmetical expression having a certain form, we can forget its origins and interpret it in other ways. That is, it may be regarded as more general than has so far been suggested. We may interpret the relational symbol '$>$' not only as a relation holding between pure numbers but also as a relation between numbers of things or between sizes of things, if we are prepared to accept different replacements for x, y and z. For example, the expressions of (3) can be interpreted thus,

(4)   Circle A is larger than circle B
         Circle B is larger than circle C
     $\therefore$ Circle A is larger than circle C,

where we take *A*, *B* and *C* to name specific circles, or thus,

(5)   London is larger than Bristol
        Bristol is larger than Bath
∴ London is larger than Bath,

where we take 'larger than' to signify a relation between areas or between populations. These arguments are both clearly valid. If we accept that the form of all of them is represented by

(3) $x > y$
        $y > z$
∴ $x > z$

we can say that their validity rests on the relation '$>$' and the arrangement of the terms represented by x, y and z, and not upon their subject-matter or the particular interpretations given to x, y and z. We can see that the expression represents a valid inference-pattern merely by inspecting its character and the rules for interpreting it, that is, without the need for particular interpretations. Thus there is a certain generality attached to the validity of this inference-pattern.

The symbol '$>$' is strictly only appropriate to the context of pure mathematics. We are merely borrowing it as a convenient device for use in other contexts. We cannot just assume that 'is larger than' conceived as a relation between numbers is identical with 'is larger than' conceived as a relation between, say, sizes, yet there is something common to these relations which forms the basis of the arguments taken as examples. We can write another set of symbolic expressions to represent all these arguments using a new symbol 'R_t' to stand for any relation having the common property of the various uses of 'is larger than' on which these arguments depend, thus

(6) $x \, R_t \, y$
        $y \, R_t \, z$
∴ $x \, R_t \, z.$

(The reason for using the complex symbol 'R_t' will be explained shortly.)

Now, if 'R_t' is thought of as standing for the relation 'larger than', in any usual sense, then 'x', 'y' and 'z' can be replaced by many different sorts of term besides numbers. However, limitations must be placed on the possible replacements in two ways.

(a) 'x', 'y' and 'z' may be replaced only by terms which in the ordinary way it makes sense to regard as related by 'is larger

33

than'; it does not make sense, without some special explanation, to say 'Democracy is larger than oligarchy' so these terms are not candidates for substitution here.

(b) In the expression '$x R_t y$', 'x' and 'y' may be replaced only by terms from the same context. It is not easy to give a precise definition of 'the same context' although most of us can recognize what is to be counted as the same context for such purposes. For example, it does not make sense to say, without some special explanation, '3 is larger than London'; if we substitute a number for 'x' we must substitute a number for 'y' and if we substitute the name of a town for 'x' we must substitute the name of a town, or other geographical entity, for 'y'. We must remember that we are trying to formalize our ways of talking and the rules according to which we talk, rather than to lay down precise rules about how we ought to talk. Our ways of talking provide the standards for logic, at least at this stage, rather than the reverse and the rules governing our ways of talking cannot always be formulated precisely.

Now consider another argument, superficially different from those so far considered.

(7) $$2 + 2 = 4$$
$$4 = 3 + 1$$
$$\therefore 2 + 2 = 3 + 1.$$

We can symbolize this, as before, representing each different term by a different letter, thus,

(8) $$x = y$$
$$y = z$$
$$\therefore x = z.$$

This is identical in pattern with our first set of symbolic expressions (3), except that '$=$' appears wherever '$>$' appeared before. This, together with the fact that (8) is a valid inference-pattern suggests that '$=$' and '$>$' have a common property and if we are now prepared to forget our interpretation of 'R_t' as 'larger than' we can use 'R_t' also to represent the relation '$=$', *in so far as it has this property*. We can then regard (8) as another interpretation of

(6) $$x R_t y$$
$$y R_t z$$
$$\therefore x R_t z.$$

We could go on in this way, finding other relations which have sufficient in common with '$>$' and '$=$' to be representable by the same symbol 'R_t' and such that any argument in the pattern of (6) would be valid. All this is part of the process of generalizing about arguments which I mentioned earlier. We have in fact been making (6) into a more and more general pattern, that is, allowing it to represent more and more particular arguments.

The next thing to notice is that not all the relations we normally make statements about behave in the same way as the R_t relations. In fact, they behave in such a way that they lack just the common property in which we are interested. Consider the pair of statements

(9) John is the father of James
James is the father of Paul.

We cannot conclude from these that John is the father of Paul, although we can reach some conclusion from them, namely, that John is a grandfather of Paul. That is, the conclusion must contain a different relation from that contained in the premisses. This argument cannot, therefore, be represented by (6) although it may be represented by

$$(10) \quad x \, R_t \, y$$
$$y \, R_t \, z$$
$$\therefore \, x \, (R_t)^2 z$$

where $(R_t)^2$ might be said to indicate a double application of R_t. 'Grandfather' here means 'father's father'. $(R_t)^2$ is called the 'relative product' of R_t or the 'square' of R_t.

We may symbolize relations which are comparable to the relation 'father of' by the symbol 'R_i' and we can say, in general, that *no* argument of the form

$$(11) \quad x \, R_i \, y$$
$$y \, R_i \, z$$
$$\therefore \, x \, R_i \, z$$

is valid. However, we can say that even in such a case, some argument of the form

$$(12) \quad x \, R_i \, y$$
$$y \, R_i \, z$$
$$\therefore \, x \, R_o \, z$$

is valid where 'R_o' stands for some relation different from, but derived from 'R_i'. In fact, $R_o = (R_i)^2$.

Again, consider the two statements

(13) A is next to B
B is next to C.

Without further information we do not know whether or not we are justified in concluding that A is next to C. If A, B and C are three spots on paper they may be arranged thus

A B C

when it would not be true that A is next to C, or they may be arranged thus

A

B C

when it would be true that A is next to C as long as it is clear that no other relevant spots are present between A and C. However, given the two premisses (13) and no other information we must say that neither

A is next to C

nor

A is not next to C

follows from them. That is, no conclusion is possible. We may symbolize this sort of relation by 'R_n' and we can say that no argument of the form

(14) $x \, R_n \, y$
        $y \, R_n \, z$
        $\therefore \, x \, R_n \, z$

is valid.

It must be stressed here that '$x \, R_n \, z$' is not incompatible with the two premisses and may very well be true along with them but it does not follow from them. This form, therefore, differs from (11) since in (11) '$x \, R_i \, z$' is incompatible with the premisses. This involves the fact that validity is independent of actual truth and falsity but the general point at issue may be put in another way. In studying conclusive arguments we are concerned with what follows logically from the given premisses. One statement may be compatible with others and yet not follow from them but if it does follow from them it must be compatible with them. Showing that an argument is invalid is not the same as showing that any statements composing it are incompatible with one another but if we show that they are incompatible then we have shown that the argument is invalid in the strongest possible way.

36

I can now give some further account of the symbols 'R_t', 'R_i' and 'R_n'. The symbol 'R' is used for any relation and the subscripts are used to indicate special properties of some relations.

Thus:

> 'R_t' stands for 'transitive relation';
> 'R_i' stands for 'intransitive relation';
> 'R_n' stands for 'non-transitive relation'.

The meaning of these terms should be clear from what has been said about arguments involving them, but in summary we can say that a relation 'R' is transitive if arguments using it having the form

(15) $x \, R \, y$
          $y \, R \, z$
$\therefore \; x \, R \, z$

are valid. If they are not then 'R' is either intransitive or non-transitive. Attempts have been made further to define these properties in ways that are independent of these facts about the validity of inference-patterns[1] using them but a consideration of this would take us too far afield. Initially, however, the notion of transitivity is extracted from some of the arguments which we normally regard as sound and can be regarded as an element of their structure. Given a new relation which, we are told, is transitive, we can conclude that any argument using it and having the form of (15) is valid. A great many of the conclusive arguments we normally use depend upon the transitivity of the relations involved but conclusive arguments can, as has been indicated, be based on intransitive relations although the conclusion cannot contain exactly the same relation as the premisses.[2]

I have so far stressed two main points about logic.

(a) Our interest is in similarities and differences between arguments, that is, in general features of arguments which enable us to classify them into various groups according to their structures.

(b) For the purpose of at least one sort of analysis of conclusive arguments, the nature of the subject-matter or content of particular arguments is largely irrelevant.

---

[1] See, e.g. Bertrand Russell, *Introduction to Mathematical Philosophy* (London, 1919), Chap. II.
[2] For a fuller account of the properties of relations see L. S. Stebbing, *A Modern Elementary Logic* (London, 1943), Chap. V. Further discussion will also be found in Chap. IV below.

I shall now turn to some other kinds of conclusive arguments which differ in various important ways from those discussed so far. Consider, for example, this

(16)   All mammals are vertebrates
          All monkeys are mammals
      ∴ All monkeys are vertebrates

and this

(17)   All voters are adults
          Some liberals are voters
      ∴ Some liberals are adults.

Both appear to be valid conclusive arguments. In the traditional (syllogistic) logic[3] they were both accepted as valid although this presents, and was seen by some to present, certain problems which will concern us later. Compare (16) and (17) with the argument we considered earlier

(1) $3 > 2$
        $4 > 3$
    ∴ $4 > 2.$

(I have here altered the order of the two premisses but not the order of the terms within them or within the conclusion. Such an alteration clearly makes no difference to the validity of the argument.)

We can point to certain superficial resemblances between these three arguments, in the order of the arrangement of the terms. Ignoring the relations involved between the terms, this arrangement can be represented thus

(18) $A - B$
        $C - A$
    ∴ $C - B.$

This pattern alone, as should be obvious, is insufficient to guarantee the validity of any argument and the differences between our three arguments are of considerable importance in this connection. We can approach this by looking more closely at the form of each argument in turn.

---

[3] In the course of this work I shall frequently refer to 'traditional logic', meaning the kind of logic which largely held the field until the beginning of this century and which is a heavily modified version of the logic of Aristotle. Since the modifications were many and various and often the subject of controversy, 'traditional logic' does not refer to a compact system but covers many different systems all having the same central core.

We can represent (16) in more detail by

> (19)   All *A*s are *B*s
>   All *C*s are *A*s
>   ∴ All *C*s are *B*s.

By inspecting this pattern alone we can see, without reference to subject matter, that it is the pattern of a valid inference. That is, if all *A*s are *B*s and all *C*s are *A*s then clearly all *C*s *must be B*s, whatever *A*, *B* and *C* stand for. This is quite general and the pattern might be regarded as a *principle* covering many different specific arguments.

Similarly we can represent (17) in greater detail by

> (20)   All *A*s are *B*s
>   Some *C*s are *A*s
>   ∴ Some *C*s are *B*s

and again, on inspection of the pattern alone, it appears to be valid. That is, if all *A*s are *B*s and some *C*s are *A*s then, on the face of it at least, it must be true that those (i.e. some) *C*s are *B*s. This again is quite general.

We have now added to the pattern (18) the necessary formal conditions for the validity of the original arguments (16) and (17). The only difference between the patterns lies in the occurrence of 'some' in the second premiss and the conclusion of (17), in place of 'all' in the corresponding positions in (16). This difference is of the greatest importance as we can see by considering

> (21)   All voters are adults
>   Some liberals are voters
>   ∴ All liberals are adults

which is identical with (17) except that 'all' appears in place of 'some' in the conclusion. A little consideration will show that this is invalid. It is consistent with the premisses that some liberals be under twenty-one years of age. The premisses give us information about all voters but only about *some* liberals; there is therefore insufficient information given to justify our concluding anything about the ages of *all* liberals. Another way of saying this is to say that the conclusion goes beyond the evidence at our disposal, or what we are *given*, and this is never allowable in a conclusive argument for obvious reasons.

However, if we were now to replace 'some' in the second premiss of (21) by 'all' we should once again have a valid argument, for in place of the pattern

(22)   All *A*s are *B*s
        Some *C*s are *A*s
∴ All *C*s are *B*s

we should have the pattern

(23)   All *A*s are *B*s
        All *C*s are *A*s
∴ All *C*s are *B*s

which is identical with (19). As we have seen, this is a generally valid pattern.

Given the barest skeleton of those arguments represented by (18), what we have seen is that the words 'all' and 'some' are important key words capable of making all the difference between validity and invalidity. This also distinguishes these arguments from the mathematical argument

(1) $3 > 2$
        $4 > 3$
∴ $4 > 2$

which has the form represented by (18) but does not involve the ideas represented by 'all' and 'some'. In using this argument we are not thinking of 4, 3, and 2 as standing for collections such that we can choose to talk of the whole of one of these collections or only part of it. Thus there is no use for such expressions as 'all 4' or 'some 4'. Nevertheless we could represent the arguments (16), (17), and (1), indifferently by the pattern

    $A \ R_t \ B$
    $C \ R_t \ A$
∴ $C \ R_t \ B$

which is a valid pattern. When we do this we must, of course, recognize that the relation R_t is a different relation in (16) from what it is in (1). The important fact is that in each case it has the property of transitivity.

We can make further important alterations in the arguments we have been considering by introducing negatives. If we replace 'all' in the first premiss of (16) by 'no' we get

(24) No mammals are vertebrates
       All monkeys are mammals

which together allow the conclusion

> No monkeys are vertebrates.

Of course, we have changed the first statement from a true one to a false one but we can still say that the argument is valid, that if the two premisses *were* true then the conclusion *would be* true, although two of them are in fact false.

We can similarly replace 'all' by 'no' in the first premiss of (17), obtaining

> (25) No voters are adults
> Some liberals are voters

which together allow the conclusion

> Some liberals are not adults.

Once again, in spite of the falsity of the first premiss we have, according to the traditional logic, a valid argument.

In these two arguments, (24) and (25), we can neglect the subject-matter but we cannot neglect the negative words and yet still see, by inspection, whether we have a valid or an invalid pattern of argument. Symbolizing the subject-indicating words we get as the pattern of (24)

> (26)   No As are Bs
> All Cs are As
> ∴ No Cs are Bs

and as the pattern of (25)

> (27)   No As are Bs
> Some Cs are As
> ∴ Some Cs are not Bs.

Examination of these patterns shows that they are valid patterns but they are different from (19) and (20).

So far, we have four different but valid patterns of inference, namely,

> (19)   All As are Bs
> All Cs are As
> ∴ All Cs are Bs;
> (20)   All As are Bs
> Some Cs are As
> ∴ Some Cs are Bs;

41

    (26)   No *A*s are *B*s
              All *C*s are *A*s
    ∴ No *C*s are *B*s;
    (27)   No *A*s are *B*s
              Some *C*s are *A*s
    ∴ Some *C*s are not *B*s.

These patterns share two important features.

    (a) The two premisses have one term (*A*) in common.
    (b) The common term appears as the first term (the subject) of the first premiss and as the second term (the predicate) in the second premiss. This arrangement can be indicated diagrammatically by *A*

            A.

Given that the term *B* always appears in the first premiss and as the predicate of the conclusion and that *C* always appears in the second premiss and as the subject of the conclusion we can see that in the premisses there are three other possible arrangements of the three terms. We have

      A — B

            \

      C — A

but we could also have

    A — B   *B — A*   *B — A*
     | | /
    A — C   *C — A*   *A — C.*

Given that the same part of the verb *to be* always joins *A* and *B* and *A* and *C*, for each of these possible arrangements some of the resulting patterns of inference are valid and others invalid, depending upon how 'all', 'some', 'no' or 'not' are inserted.

Arguments of these forms are the traditional *syllogisms*. The theory of the syllogism, that is the study of the general conditions of validity of this type of argument, was worked out mainly by Aristotle and was extended by his mediaeval followers. Much of this work still stands, as we shall see.

Before I leave this type of argument there is an important point to be made. I introduced these arguments by means of very simple arguments in everyday English. I then showed that when we are considering merely the validity of the arguments we can ignore the subject-matter, that is, ignore some of the words they contain by replacing them by arbitrary symbols such as *A*, *B* and *C*. However, there are some words in them which we were unable to ignore if we were to pronounce on the validity of the resulting inference patterns. The words in question, so far, are various parts of the verb *to be* and the words 'all', 'some', 'not' and 'no'. These words indicate the relations between the *A*s, *B*s and *C*s of the patterns and these relations in turn determine the relations between the premisses and the conclusion. They are, therefore, words upon which the validity of the original arguments essentially depends. They are sometimes called 'topic-neutral' words, since their properties can be considered without reference to any particular topic or subject-matter, that is, independently of what words are substituted for '*A*', '*B*' and '*C*' in any particular argument.

When I said of an inference pattern that inspection shows it to be valid or invalid, I have relied upon the fact that these topic-neutral words have familiar, everyday uses upon which arguments turn and that any fluent English-speaker has enough knowledge of these properties to enable him to see which inference patterns they allow and which they disallow. It is true that not every fluent English-speaker is conscious of all the relevant properties, but there is a sense in which, since he relies upon them, being fluent, he can be said to know them. Part of the task of the logic textbook or teacher is to bring this hidden knowledge into the light and to develop a sensitivity to the functions and properties of these all-important words. These are among the basic tools for the analysis of arguments.

We might say that the fundamental conceptions of formal logic lie embedded in everyday discourse[4]; one task of formal logic is to abstract and formalize the features of everyday discourse upon which the soundness of arguments depends. Different 'systems' in formal logic depend upon the stressing of different aspects of everyday discourse or upon the different interpretation of its features.

I now wish to mention briefly some other kinds of conclusive arguments which will be discussed in more detail later.

We often argue along these lines

(28)   If such and such is the case then so and so is the case
       Such and such *is* the case
  ∴ So and so is the case.

This is not to say that they are entirely dependent on the conventions of a particular language such as English; we may study logical concepts through any language which is translatable into others and expect our conclusions to be translatable also.

For example,

> (29)   If there is no water in the radiator then the radiator has a leak
>   There is no water in the radiator
> ∴ The radiator has a leak.

We would not always set out a simple argument like this in such detail. We should be more inclined to say, for example, 'There is no water in the radiator *so* the radiator has a leak'. However, for complete clarity and rigour, and especially for purposes of logical analysis, it is necessary to set the argument out in full.

The general form of this argument is this: we have first a *hypothetical* statement, consisting of two categorical statements joined by the words 'if—then', together with a factual statement, which is simply the first component of the hypothetical statement; from these together we draw a conclusion which is the second component of the hypothetical statement.

Considering the argument without reference to its subject-matter, we can represent the categorical statements which are the components of the hypothetical statement by, respectively, 'p' and 'q', when we obtain as the inference pattern

> (30)   If p then q (1)
> p (2)
>   ∴ q.   (3)

The hypothetical statement (1) is compound, asserting a relation between two categorical statements and it is upon this relation that arguments of this form turn. It is the words 'if—then' that indicate this relation, rather than the subject-indicating words, so this is again a general inference pattern which is valid whatever the subject-matter.

In considering syllogistic arguments we symbolized single words, or groups of words which did not make full sentences, treating the arguments as depending upon relations between *terms*, as the traditional logicians treated them. Here, we have used symbols for whole statements, treating the arguments as depending upon relations between statements. As we shall see, some arguments are more satisfactorily treated in one of these ways than in the other.

It is convenient to mention here some other kinds of argument which are conveniently treated as basically involving relations between statements. Consider, for example

 (31) Either John will work hard or he will fail his
     examination
    John will not work hard
 ∴ John will fail his examination.

This is a valid argument which can be represented by the pattern

 (32) Either p or q
    Not p
 ∴ q.

We can see, by inspecting this pattern, that it is valid. Given that one or other of two statements is true, then given further that one of them is false it follows that the other must be true. The key words upon which the argument depends are 'either—or' and 'not'.

 Now consider this argument

 (33) John will not both work hard and fail his examination
    John will work hard
 ∴ John will not fail his examination.

Properly understood, the first statement is compound, since it can be regarded as composed of two statements 'John will work hard' and 'John will fail his examination' joined by means of the words 'not both—and'. This can be brought out by writing it, rather artificially, thus

 (34) Not both (John will work hard and John will fail his
     examination)
    John will work hard
 ∴ John will not fail his examination.

We may now represent it by the pattern

 (35) Not both p and q
    p
 ∴ Not q.

Clearly, given that two statements are not both true and given further that one of them is true, then it follows that the other is false. Here the key words are 'not both' and 'and'. There are, of course, fallacies associated with all the arguments we have just considered; these arise as a result of the misuse of the key words upon which each argument depends.

We have considered a few types of conclusive or deductive arguments and some points which are basic to formal logic which is the study of such arguments. It is not at all clear that non-conclusive arguments can be dealt with in a similar way; that is, it is doubtful that there can be a formal logic of non-conclusive arguments. Certainly, efforts have been, and are being, made to construct such a logic but, for reasons which will emerge, the results appear to have only a very tenuous connection with actual arguments in the contexts in which they are used.

Except in a few, limited fields, most of the arguments that we use are, in fact, non-conclusive and depend upon the weighing of evidence and the assessment of likelihoods. Considerations involving subject-matter are much more important in the assessment of the soundness of such arguments. Their value is much less a formal matter than is the value of conclusive arguments. Nevertheless, the study of conclusive arguments is of considerable importance, for two main reasons.

(a) We do use arguments which are intended to be conclusive, along with others, in every rational discipline and in some fields conclusive arguments figure very largely or even to the exclusion of non-conclusive arguments, for example, in theology, in theoretical physics and in mathematics.

(b) The understanding of non-conclusive arguments depends very largely upon an appreciation of the contrast between conclusive and non-conclusive arguments.

I shall now proceed to some general discussion of non-conclusive arguments.

3. NON-CONCLUSIVE ARGUMENTS

Conclusive arguments *are* conclusive because they do not 'go beyond' the evidence or what is *given*. This point has sometimes been made by saying that their premises *contain* their conclusions and that the function of the argument is to *extract* the conclusion from the premises. This way of putting the matter is often said to be unenlightening because it is metaphorical and, indeed, if we are concerned with the ultimate justification of this type of argument this is a serious criticism. However, we are here mainly concerned to achieve a preliminary and informal grasp of the character of conclusive arguments and their differences from non-conclusive arguments so that some ways of talking may be helpful here even if they would be misleading if our purpose were a more rigorous one.

We may profitably consider again some of our earlier examples. In the argument

> All spies are cunning
> ∴ This spy is cunning

we can say that any particular spy mentioned in the conclusion is covertly mentioned in the premiss. What is asserted in the premiss is, just because it is asserted of *all* spies, asserted of any particular spy including *this* one. Something similar can be said of more complex arguments, such as,

> (16)   All mammals are vertebrates
>   All monkeys are mammals
> ∴ All monkeys are vertebrates.

The conclusion is not directly *stated* in the premisses but we may say that it is indirectly stated. To say *directly* that all mammals are vertebrates and all monkeys are mammals is to say *indirectly* that all monkeys are vertebrates. Indirect stating is stronger than suggestion or innuendo; in one sense it is as strong as direct stating because sometimes in directly stating one thing we cannot avoid indirectly stating something else.

Non-conclusive arguments form a large class which can be subdivided. They all have certain general features in common. They are non-conclusive just because the conclusion 'goes beyond' the evidence or what is given. Continuing the terminology of the last paragraph, the premisses do not indirectly state what the conclusion states. They merely serve to support, to some extent, the conclusion, to make it more likely to be true than it would be without them. For example, the statements

> There are 1,000 gorillas in captivity; 750 of them have been examined and found to be harmless; the rest have not been considered from this point of view

give some, but not conclusive, support to the statement

> All gorillas in captivity are harmless

although it does not state this, either directly or indirectly.

Such arguments, often with the word 'probably', or a cognate word, attached to the conclusion, are widely used and perfectly respectable. A great deal of science and of our thought in most other fields depends upon them. There can, of course, be sound and unsound examples of such arguments; we may attach more weight to one of them than it can bear. The criteria for soundness are, as should be clear from what has gone before, different from those for the soundness of conclusive arguments.

Some logicians regard non-conclusive arguments with suspicion partly, at least, because they are reluctant to recognize them as arguments in their own right with their own criteria of soundness. This results in the inclination to regard non-conclusive arguments as failing to measure up to the standards of conclusive arguments. Other logicians regard this as a mistake since it is to expect these arguments to measure up to a standard which we can see from the context is an inappropriate one. The mistake is understandable because it is much more difficult to define the appropriate standard for non-conclusive arguments than it is to define the appropriate standard for conclusive ones and there is considerable doubt that it can be defined generally for non-conclusive arguments. To understand the mistake is to see that it must be avoided. Clarity about the nature of the arguments we use is, from certain points of view, more desirable than tidiness in our logical systems.

It is convenient to divide non-conclusive arguments into several sub-classes. This is not an entirely uncontroversial division and I shall give some pointers to the advantages of the distinctions I make. I shall use the following headings

> a. Inductive arguments
> b. Arguments from particular to particular
> c. Interpretative arguments.

a. INDUCTIVE ARGUMENTS

Logicians sometimes speak as if all legitimate non-conclusive arguments were inductive and either reject them or defend them in a body. This is possible if one is prepared to define 'inductive' in the widest possible way. As my scheme of classification indicates, I shall not do this.

Those who regard inductive arguments as important are inclined to think that their importance lies mainly in their function in the natural sciences; those who reject inductive arguments attempt to give an account of the sciences which does not depend on the use of inductive arguments.[5] Historically, most philosophers of science have probably taken the former view but in recent years it has become a matter of controversy, largely through the work of Sir Karl Popper.

The standard kind of example of inductive arguments is that in

[5] See, e.g. K. R. Popper, *The Logic of Scientific Discovery* (London, 1959).

which a general statement is taken to be supported by a statement, or set of statements, of lesser generality or narrower scope. Consider

> All the spies I have any information about are (or were)
> cunning
> ∴ All spies are cunning.

(It should be noted that, if I were being as cautious as possible, I should say for the conclusion '*Probably* all spies are cunning'. However, it is implicit in the recognition of non-conclusive arguments as a separate class that the conclusions of all of them must, strictly, have some such word attached to them. In this section this will be taken as understood.)

In this argument we may assume that the premiss is always narrower, less general, than the conclusion since I can never be sure that there are not past, present or future spies about which I have no information and who are therefore not covered by the premiss; but no restriction is placed upon the conclusion. 'All spies', taken literally, mentions *all* spies, past, present and future. Thus my conclusion is not, and cannot be, supported up to the hilt and the extent to which it is supported depends upon the width of my experience of, and information about, spies. Thus, the extent to which we regard this as a sound argument depends upon something other than the mere forms of the statements, namely, their subject-matter or the extent of our knowledge of the subject-matter.

It is true that, in a rudimentary way, this argument can be formalized. Traditionally the premiss was represented as

> *Some* spies are cunning (and none are known not to be)

to make it clear that the extent of the evidence is narrower than it could be. The conclusion

> All spies are cunning

includes all the possible evidence as well as all the actual evidence. We may, then, formalize the argument thus

> Some Ss are C (and none are known not to be C)
> ∴ All Ss are C.

However, this formalization is of little value except to expose some of the problems. We found that the formalization of conclusive arguments did not remove the possibility of assessing the soundness of the arguments in question; indeed, in a sense it was positively helpful because it enabled us to ignore questions of actual truth and falsity which were irrelevant to judgments of validity. However, all

49

we can say about the present inference pattern is that, as long as 'S' and 'C' each stands for the same term in each appearance, some support is given to the conclusion by the premiss. Apart from this, all it does is to exhibit the form of any inductive argument, good or bad. It is characteristic of non-conclusive, in contrast to conclusive, arguments that they are not just sound or unsound but are more or less sound than one another. What we need to know in order to assess their soundness is something about the extent of the evidence in the premiss. The word 'some' obscures this since it may be used whether the extent of the evidence is very large or very small. Moreover, it is important to know the extent of the evidence in relation to the extent of the conclusion. Worse even than this, the amount of evidence which we would accept as reliable or significant is likely to vary with different subject-matters.

Let us consider a modified version of our example. Suppose that there happen to be just 1,000 spies living at this moment and that we somehow know this. The support which we could give to the statement

All living spies are cunning

would depend upon the number of spies about whom we could legitimately include information in our premiss or evidential statement, that is, upon the number of spies about whom we had the relevant information. Consider three possibilities, such that each of the following statements mentions *all* our evidence.

(1) 5 living spies are cunning;
(2) 100 living spies are cunning;
(3) 900 living spies are cunning.

As we move from (1) to (3) we move from less to more evidential value or strength of support. Clearly the support given by (1) is very weak, that given by (2) stronger and that given by (3) considerably stronger, since the proportion of the total about which we have evidence is $\frac{1}{200}$ in (1), $\frac{1}{10}$ in (2) and $\frac{9}{10}$ in (3). We should feel relatively safe in generalizing from (3) but we should not, of course, be entirely safe with any evidence about fewer spies than the total of 1,000. The general conclusion would be shown to be false if only one living spy were shown not to be cunning.

All these considerations are, of course, left out of account if we formalize the premiss indifferently by 'Some Ss are C'; this obscures important differences between our possible premisses. In place of 'some' we might, in the favourable circumstances of our example, write for (1), (2) and (3), respectively,

(1) $\frac{1}{200}$ of the Ss are C
(2) $\frac{1}{10}$ of the Ss are C
(3) $\frac{9}{10}$ of the Ss are C,

but we are seldom faced with this possibility.

In most real situations, we are unable even to say, 'Most Ss are C' since even this depends upon our knowing the total number of Ss. I chose, to begin with, an example of a generalization of which we could conceivably know the scope. We can at least say that there is a finite number of living spies, even if it is difficult to know for certain how large that number is. In practice, when we use inductive arguments we are seldom in a position even to know this much about the subjects of our generalizations. We may generalize about metals or stars or vertebrates and clearly we shall never be in a position to know how many samples of each of these there are. It follows that we shall never be able, for such generalizations, to replace 'some' by a fraction or a percentage. This is a severe impediment to the assessment of the soundness of inductive arguments; it appears, so far, that the most we can say is that, given a specific subject-matter and two evidential statements for two different generalizations, if one of the evidential statements is of greater extent than the other, e.g. covers more instances, then it gives more support to the appropriate generalization.

The condition relating to subject-matter in the last statement is necessary because it is difficult or impossible to compare the soundness of inductive arguments about different subject-matters, especially when we are not dealing with a known, finite number of instances. This is at least partly because different materials differ considerably in homogeneity and this must enter into our estimation of the soundness of our generalizations. If we are dealing with samples of pure silver we are prepared to generalize about them after examining very few samples compared with the number we require if we are generalizing about mice or vertebrates or even cells. It is not merely that our methods of dealing with biological subjects are less precise and that we must repeat our observations to rule out what the scientist calls 'experimental error' but also that the materials with which we are dealing themselves vary much more from sample to sample than do inorganic substances such as pure silver.

The most quoted example of an inductive argument whose conclusion was eventually refuted by new evidence is the argument from the fact that all the swans known to Europeans were white to the conclusion that all swans whatever were white. Enormous numbers of swans had been observed and no exceptions had been found so it seemed perfectly safe to generalize. Still the conclusion went beyond the evidence since it was extended to cover swans as yet unseen and unborn. However, the exploration of Australia revealed the existence of black swans so the generalization was upset, as indeed it would have been by the discovery of only one black swan.

This example brings out an important point about inductive arguments which also applies to some other non-conclusive arguments. There is a sense in which the discovery of black swans showed, not that the previous argument was unsound, but only that the conclusion was false. Those who used this argument had a great deal of evidence for and no evidence against their generalization; they could hardly be criticized for supposing that they had sufficient evidence to risk the generalization or for supposing that the risk was not very great. *On the basis of the only premiss available*, the conclusion was a reasonable one. There was no basis whatever for the conclusion 'some swans are not white'. The discovery of black swans showed that the premiss was no longer acceptable and not that on that premiss the argument was bad. A new premiss was needed and that supported a different conclusion. A different argument was needed but only because the original premiss was no longer available. One way of putting this to emphasize the contrast with conclusive, or deductive, arguments is this: if we accept the premisses of a sound deductive argument and reject the conclusion we produce a contradiction but we may accept the premisses of a sound inductive argument and reject the conclusion without contradiction because further evidence is always possible and it may conflict with the evidence we now have. It may be unreasonable to do this but it does not produce a contradiction. The premisses of inductive arguments always involve such reservations as 'so far'.

Care is needed in adopting the traditional method of symbolizing inductive arguments of the sort I have been considering. Such statements as

> All spies of whom we have any knowledge are cunning

has sometimes been represented, for logical purposes by such statements as

> Some spies are cunning

and symbolized by

> Some Ss are C.

This is misleading because the original statement makes it clear that we have never come across any spy who is not cunning whereas the second statement and the symbolized version obscure this. 'Some spies are cunning' is consistent with 'Some spies are not cunning'; but 'Some spies are cunning' is consistent with 'All spies are cunning' whereas 'Some spies are not cunning' is not. Thus, we could not justifiably infer 'All spies are cunning' from 'Some spies are cunning' unless, at least, we had no knowledge of spies who were not cunning. We can remove the difficulty by saying that whenever we represent an inductive argument by

> Some As are B
> ∴ All As are B

we assume that the premiss represents *all* the evidence available. However, this can also be represented as another premiss, for the argument should strictly be represented as

> Some As are B and no As are known not to be B
> ∴ All As are B.

As a formalization of an inductive argument this is relatively satisfactory but we are still, of course, left with the difficulty that the word 'some' successfully obscures the extent of the evidence which is available and with the related difficulty that 'A' and 'B' obscure the nature of the subject-matter, which is relevant to judging the satisfactoriness of the extent of the evidence.

The examples so far considered are fairly trivial but there is an important respect in which they resemble many more complex and non-trivial arguments. When we accept a general statement on the basis of evidence which is less complete than it could be we covertly make predictions. If, for example, we say that all spies are cunning, since no restriction is placed upon the 'all', the statement applies to spies which cannot be observed now, including unborn spies. About these, we are covertly making a prediction which may or may not be fulfilled. Conversely, whenever we make a prediction we are going beyond the evidence we actually have. This is just another way of saying that our evidence for most general statements and for all predictive statements cannot be, or be known to be, complete. This applies to any general statement, however complex, which is more than a complete summary of the available evidence. This is important in relation to the general statements which are regarded as laws by the scientist and to the predictions he makes.

We may sum up this discussion by making four points of contrast between conclusive and non-conclusive arguments.

(1) Conclusive arguments can often be formalized in such a way as to make clear what their soundness or unsoundness depends upon. Non-conclusive arguments can be formalized but when we formalize them we eliminate features which are relevant to the assessment of their soundness or unsoundness.

(2) An acceptable conclusive argument is such that if the premisses are true the conclusion cannot be false; an acceptable non-conclusive argument is such that the premisses may be true and yet the conclusion false.

(3) The conclusions of conclusive arguments are not predictions which may turn out to be true or false except in so far as the premisses are predictions which may turn out to be true or false; the conclusions of non-conclusive arguments *which are inductive* always tacitly contain predictions which may turn out to be true or false. This is so if we are prepared to regard any extrapolation from the evidence as a prediction.

(4) The refutation of a non-conclusive argument may be conclusive. If we have inferred that all swans are white then the discovery of even one black swan implies that this conclusion can never more be entertained.

There are inductive arguments which differ in some respects from those we have been considering and which are sometimes classified separately. However, it appears that their logic is similar enough for them all to be regarded as inductive.

All inductive arguments in a sense depend upon arguing from samples. Most of them depend upon samples from populations whose extent is unknown, and possibly infinite, but we are sometimes in the position of having to deal with populations of known finite extent. For example, a chemist might be asked to determine the proportion of iron in a consignment of iron ore and he would do this by analysing samples which constituted measurable fractions of the whole consignment. Given certain precautions about mixing and sampling at random he would then assume that the percentage of iron in the samples is a measure of the percentage throughout the consignment. We may call such arguments 'sampling arguments'. They are arguments from the properties of a known fraction of the whole to the properties of the whole and they involve generalization just as any other inductive argument does.

However, arguments of this sort have important features in which they differ from inductive arguments involving unknown and possibly infinite populations. The analysis of several samples may indicate the extent to which the whole population varies in constitution. Using this information and the relation of the size of the sample to

54

the size of the whole population it is possible to estimate the 'fairness' of the sample and to decide how many samples should be taken in order that the argument from the sample to the total should be as free from error as possible. The subject of statistics is partly concerned with such calculations of fairness and probable error. The logic of these arguments is, however, clearly inductive since they are arguments from 'some' to 'all' but the 'all' is limited and its extent at least roughly known and it is possible to give a reasonably precise estimate of the weight of 'some'.

Similar arguments are used by actuaries on behalf of insurance companies and may be called 'frequency arguments'. In connection with life insurance, companies need to know what is the likelihood of a person of a given age and in a given state of health dying within some specified term of years. The estimation of the premium which can economically be charged depends upon this. Actuaries examine the death rates among various classes of people over periods in the recent past and assume that death rates among these classes will be similar in the near future. Suppose that it is found that out of 10,000 men in good health at 30 years of age, barring wars and other large-scale upheavals, 1,000 died before they were 60, then it may be said that the likelihood of a man who is now 30 dying before he is 60 is 1 in 10 or $\frac{1}{10}$. Premiums would be charged accordingly. The probability figure is in effect a forecast or a prediction about all men of a certain class made on the basis of the examination of some men of that class. This argument is, again, an argument to a finite population since insurance companies are interested, at any given time, in people aged 30 or 40 or 50 and the evidence upon which they base their estimates is taken from periods of years in the immediate past similar in size to the limited future periods which concern them at that time. Because of this limitation and because fairly precise estimates of frequencies of death among various well-defined classes can be made these arguments are less unreliable than those we first considered in this section.

I have treated inductive arguments as arguments essentially involving generalization, i.e. moving from one statement about a given subject-matter to a more general statement about the same subject-matter. More precisely, I have treated them as arguments from statements asserting that some instances of a certain kind of thing possess some property to statements asserting that all instances of that kind of thing do, or will, possess that property, with greater or lesser probability.

Induction has been defined in other ways, usually more vague. I shall mention three other possibilities.

55

(i) 'Induction is arguing from the known to the unknown.'

In the first place, this is unhelpful because there is certainly a sense in which we sometimes do not know the conclusion of a deductive argument until we have been through the argument, especially if that argument is at all complex.[6] We cannot immediately see all that follows from conjunctions of statements. This statement thus fails to distinguish inductive arguments from deductive arguments. It is also unhelpful because it tells us nothing whatever about the form of the arguments which it covers and it in fact covers, apart from both deductive arguments and generalizing arguments, certain arguments which do not proceed from less general to more general statements about the possession of some property by a whole class of things. Finer distinctions can be made than it allows us to make. Furthermore it uses psychological grounds for making a distinction which may be made on logical grounds, which in this context would be preferable.

(ii) 'Induction is arguing from the past and the present to the future.'

This is too narrow since it excludes certain arguments which we would wish to call inductive because they are sufficiently similar to those it includes. For example, since dodos are extinct, it is unlikely that any argument about them concerns future dodos; yet we may argue from records of the properties of some past dodos to the properties of all past dodos and the argument has the same generalizing form as an argument from the properties of some existing giraffes to the properties of all giraffes existing during the next 100 years. It might be objected that any conclusion about all past dodos would cover any future dodos, in case there should be any. An example which escapes this objection would be one from partial statistics about deaths in England in the late eighteenth century to the average expectancy of life in, say, 1800.

(iii) 'Induction is arguing to a conclusion which goes beyond the evidence.'

There are some arguments which 'go beyond the evidence' which are, however, so unlike generalizing arguments that it would be misleading to classify them under the same heading. There may be an important difference between an argument whose conclusion is the same as its premiss except in generality and an argument in which the

---

[6] For an interesting historical example of this see John Aubrey, *Brief Lives*, ed. Anthony Powell (London, 1949), 'Thomas Hobbes', p. 242.

premiss and the conclusion do not differ in generality but in which there is some difference in content between the premiss and the conclusion. These are different ways of 'going beyond the evidence' which it is useful to distinguish. There are arguments from particular to particular and there are some philosophical arguments which, as we shall see, are non-conclusive arguments and do go beyond the evidence but do not involve generalization.

The word 'induction' has been used, in the past, even more widely than I have so far suggested. For example, philosophers have talked about 'perfect' or 'summary' induction, in which the conclusion is just a summary of all the possible evidence, and about 'intuitive' induction, in which we see the truth of a general axiom from one instance of it.[7] These are mentioned only for the purpose of pointing out that they are different from the kind of induction here considered. It must also be noted, especially by those familiar with mathematical terminology, that the process called 'mathematical induction' is not inductive but deductive, in the senses of those words used in this book.

I have so far used 'induction' to cover only what some philosophers have called 'enumerative induction'. The point of that title is to distinguish this from 'eliminative induction'. This is the process of establishing a general statement or hypothesis by eliminating rival general statements or hypotheses. For example, we might seek to establish that one product of the reaction of zinc and hydrochloric acid is hydrogen by testing the gas given off and eliminating the hypotheses that it was carbon dioxide or oxygen or nitrogen, without directly testing for hydrogen. I have not classified this as a special kind of induction because such arguments are really in two parts, one of which is deductive and the other inductive, in my sense that it depends on enumeration. When we eliminate the statement

> Zinc and hydrochloric acid react to produce nitrogen

by showing that a sample of the gas given off is not nitrogen we are refuting the general statement conclusively. That is, the argument from

> This gas is not nitrogen

to the *falsity* of

> Zinc and hydrochloric acid react to produce nitrogen

[7] See L. Susan Stebbing, *A Modern Introduction to Logic* (London, 1943) and W. E. Johnson, *Logic* (Cambridge, 1921–22).

is a deductive argument. This is the *eliminative* part of the argument.

On the other hand, each instance which conflicts with the general statement

> Zinc and hydrochloric acid react to produce a gas other than hydrogen

supports, though not conclusively, another general statement, namely,

> Zinc and hydrochloric acid react to produce hydrogen.

This is the *enumerative*, or properly inductive, part of the argument.

It may be contended at this point that the eliminative argument is inductive because we can never be sure that our experimental results are correct; since we may always be mistaken about them, they cannot be used to establish something conclusively. This last statement may be true but the argument is a *non sequitur*. The alleged uncertainty of experimental results applies, if at all, to both the enumerative and the eliminative arguments but there is a difference between these arguments which is independent of this. The statement

> This product of the reaction of zinc and hydrochloric acid is not nitrogen

whether it is true or false, has a certain relation to the statement

> Zinc and hydrochloric acid react to produce nitrogen

and a different relation to the statement

> Zinc and hydrochloric acid react to produce hydrogen.

These relations can be expressed by saying that if the first statement were true then the second could not be but the third could be and is more likely to be than if we had no such statement as the first. That is, the first relation is deductive and the second is inductive.[8]

b. ARGUMENTS FROM PARTICULAR TO PARTICULAR

Sometimes, especially in history and in the sciences, we argue from one unique state of affairs to another without going through any process of generalization as an intermediate step. For example, if the orbit of a planet shows unexpected irregularities at certain points we may conclude that there is a hitherto unknown body which attracts the original planet at those points sufficiently to cause an observable irregularity. The planet Neptune was in fact discovered in just this way.

[8] For an excellent discussion of induction see S. F. Barker, *Induction and Hypothesis* (Ithaca, N.Y., 1957), esp. Chaps. III and IV.

Positions of the planet Uranus had been observed and recorded over a number of years. In 1820 an attempt was made to plot the orbit of Uranus from these records and it was found to be impossible. If only the recent figures were considered a relatively good representation of an orbit could be obtained but then it was found on further observation that Uranus was not in the expected position. It was suggested that this was due to disturbance by an as yet unknown body. Two theoretical astronomers, J. C. Adams, an Englishman, and U. J. J. Leverrier, a Frenchman, independently worked out the position in which the postulated body could be expected to be found. These results were communicated to observatories in 1845 and the planet Neptune was discovered very close to the calculated position.[9]

It is, of course, true that general statements would be used if the argument were set out in full but these would be statements of accepted laws and not conclusions, either intermediate or final. The argument itself does not move from a narrower to a wider statement of the same form; it moves from a statement about one particular state of affairs to a statement about another particular state of affairs. The argument is, however, non-conclusive, since the same effect might be accounted for by the presence of two or more hitherto unknown planets. It is not inductive, in the sense here adopted, and neither does it move from past and present to future except incidentally. It does, indeed, 'go beyond the evidence' but in a different way from a generalizing argument.

Many arguments, including historical ones, which are concerned to exhibit the causes of specific events, are like this in that, although their conclusions are not general, they are non-conclusive because other explanations are consistent with the available evidence.

C. INTERPRETATIVE ARGUMENTS

Philosophical arguments form a large and diffuse group within which many differences are to be found and no attempt can be made here to sort out their varieties. Many philosophical arguments, however, may be said to be non-conclusive and non-inductive and yet not to fit into any of the other classes of non-conclusive arguments so far mentioned. This is because many of them may be regarded as *interpretative* and in accepting them one is deciding that some particular interpretation is more appropriate than others. Very often this depends upon a decision about what we mean when we talk in certain ways and this may be, to some extent, a matter of controversy which cannot be settled conclusively.

[9] See art. 'Neptune' by S. Newcomb in *Encyclopaedia Britannica*, 11th edition (Cambridge, 1911).

For example, scientists have been able to give an account of lightning in terms of the movement of electric charges and this account, from the scientific point of view, is a complete account. Some philosophers have concluded from this that lightning is *nothing but* the movement of electric charges or that lightning *is really* the movement of electric charges.[10] That this is a non-conclusive argument is shown by the fact that other philosophers, not conspicuously lacking in intelligence or scientific knowledge, do not accept this interpretation of the scientific findings. It may be appropriate to say this sort of thing in a purely scientific context but is it appropriate to all contexts? It *may explain* other things we say about lightning but does it exhaust what we *mean* when we say these things? If not, are there other good reasons for accepting the view? The arguments used in this connection attempt to arrive at the meanings of various things we say by considering the relations between all the things we say in the relevant contexts. This is not a matter of generalizing in the inductive manner or of assessing probabilities but rather a matter of exploring the relations between the meanings of the things we say in relation to the contexts in which we say them. The opinions of intelligent speakers of the language may be relevant to this activity.

Consider another example. A subject which has concerned philosophers for many centuries is the analysis of knowing and believing. What is it to know something and how is this to be contrasted with believing something? What are the conditions under which we are entitled to say that we know something? A small part of one kind of argument may be put in the following way. We can correctly say

> I *believe* that a train leaves for London at 10.15 but I may be wrong,

but we cannot correctly say

> I *know* that a train leaves for London at 10.15 but I may be wrong.

This last statement appears both to make a claim and reject it, that is, it appears to involve an inconsistency. Whereas the first statement seems merely cautious, the second seems confused. This confusion is the basis of the old joke 'Mr Smith knows a great deal that isn't so'. Thus, it is argued, knowing and believing differ in that knowing a statement *s* entails the truth of *s* whereas believing *s* does not. So

---

[10] See, e.g., J. J. C. Smart, *Philosophy and Scientific Realism* (London, 1963), esp. Chap. V.

one of the conditions that must be satisfied in order that anyone should be justified in saying 'I know that *s*' is that *s* must be true. This is said to be part of the meaning of 'know'.

However, this is not conclusive since there may be other facts of language, other perfectly correct ways of speaking, which conflict with it and which would lead others to reject this conclusion; there may even be reasons for saying that we are not justified in arguing in this way from the facts of language or from the facts of one particular language. These considerations, in their turn, would form the basis of further arguments which would also be non-conclusive.

Interpretative arguments are to be found in other fields, notably in the Law. When a court ascribes responsibility for an action or decides that there was negligence this is not the conclusion of a deductive or an inductive argument. Neither is it a clear statement of fact. It is an interpretation of the facts and it may be controversial.[11]

I shall not continue with the enumeration of types of argument since my aim is not to produce a complete and watertight classification but merely to indicate some of the most important types and some of the reasons which lead us to classify arguments differently. No doubt numerous headings and sub-headings could be added if we considered arguments in history, anthropology, the biological sciences and other fields but this is not necessary for the present purpose.

[11] For examples, see H. L. A. Hart, 'The Ascription of Responsibility and Rights', *Proceedings of the Aristotelian Society*, Vol. VIII (London, 1948–49).

CHAPTER III

Language and its Formalization

1. GENERAL

The remaining chapters of this book will largely concern deductive arguments. What I aim to show is the way in which the satisfactoriness or unsatisfactoriness of would-be deductive arguments depends upon certain features of language; when logicians formalize arguments they are building upon some features of language and neglecting others. This is what makes it possible to say that two arguments about radically different subject-matters are of the same type or have the same logical form. I wish to stress, also, that when we set out to formalize we are often faced with choices about how this should be done and that different choices may lead to different classifications of arguments and even different judgments about their soundness. We may draw the lines separating types of argument in different ways depending upon which features of particular arguments we decide to emphasize.

In any language there are correct and incorrect uses; there are ways in which we may, and ways in which we may not, combine words and there are situations in which a given admissible combination is appropriate and other situations in which it is inappropriate. This is to say that languages are rule-governed and that language-using is a rule-governed activity. An incorrect use involves the breaking of some rule; a minimal condition for a correct use is that it breaks no rules. As soon as this is said, however, difficulties arise because the rules for natural languages are never all explicitly stated; rather, they are implicitly followed by those familiar with the language in question and have to be extracted from their linguistic behaviour. Some of these rules are not easy to state explicitly and shortly and one cannot hope to produce a list of short rules comparable to the rules of a game. This is partly because languages have *rules of meaning* which are of a different type from any of the rules of games.

Languages have two main kinds of rule: rules of structure or formation and rules of meaning.

(i) Rules of structure or formation, sometimes called 'syntactical' rules, are those which govern the ways in which words may be combined to make sentences. When we learn the grammar and syntax of a language we are learning these rules even if they are not always explicitly set out as rules. If we break them we fail to produce proper sentences; strictly speaking we get, instead, meaningless strings of words. For example, in English, 'We are going to London' is a sentence but 'We is going to London' is not.[1]

(ii) Rules of meaning, sometimes called 'semantical' rules, are those which govern the appropriateness of the use of syntactically allowable combinations of words in different linguistic or non-linguistic contexts. There are various kinds of inappropriateness. In contexts in which English is spoken the perfectly good sentence 'Pigs fly' is usually inappropriate because it is false. If someone is asked 'How many cows are there in that field?' and replies 'Yesterday', this is inappropriate in a different way. In the first case we might say that anyone who said 'Pigs fly' was mistaken about the facts but this would not be our immediate reaction to the second case. In either case, it might be that the person saying these things did not understand the meanings of certain words and combinations of words, that his utterances broke some semantical rules; someone might think 'Pigs fly' true because he did not understand its meaning. It is difficult to state semantical rules because of their complexity. When we learn a language they are not stated for us; we learn gradually the sorts of things we may and may not say in different contexts. The complexity is a function of the flexibility of natural languages, of the fact that meanings are dependent on context and of the fact that we use language in such an enormous variety of contexts. Dictionaries do not tell us very much about this, as anyone knows who has tried to understand a foreign language with only the help of a dictionary.

As I have said (see Chap. I, Section 2) sentences are just strings of words obeying syntactical rules and they may be used in different ways, depending upon the aims of the user and the context. The same sentence may, for example, be used to state something or command that something be done and the same sentence in these two uses will have different meanings. A similar thing can be said about words: the same written shape may mean different things when combined with different words or when the resultant combinations are used in

[1] The qualification 'strictly speaking' is necessary because, of course, ungrammatical sentences can often be understood and so cannot be regarded as entirely meaningless. See, Paul Ziff, *Semantic Analysis* (Ithaca, N.Y., 1960).

63

different contexts. Meaning is a function of the uses to which words may be put.[2]

It might be said that there is a third kind of rule which should be discussed here, namely, rules of inference or transformation. I do not here distinguish these as constituting a separate type because I am inclined to think that the rules which are sometimes called 'logical laws', such as the law of contradiction, are implicit in our conception of a language and that more specific rules of inference used in arguments in everyday discourse are derivative from the types of rules already mentioned.[3] My approach in this book is intended partly to exhibit this last point.

I have said that the validity of deductive arguments used in every-day discourse depends mainly on the correct use of certain key words. In the partial symbolization of statements and arguments which I have already used these are, on the whole, the words which remained when the subject-indicating terms were replaced by arbitrary symbols. In fact, modern logic has developed in such a way that the ideas indicated by these key words are also symbolized. This makes it necessary to distinguish among symbols between *constants* and *variables*. This distinction is already familiar to most of us from elementary algebra.

In the algebraic expression

$$x > y$$

'*x*' and '*y*' can be regarded as merely marking empty spaces in which *any* numbers may be written. (It is not relevant, at the moment, that some numbers will give us true statements and others false statements; we are not prevented by any rule of algebra from making false statements.) Thus, '*x*' and '*y*' may be called 'variables' because they allow the substitution of any numbers. However, '>' stands for a specific relation which holds between many pairs of numbers and does not hold between other pairs of numbers. If it is regarded as marking an empty space it must be regarded as marking a space which may be filled only by the words 'is greater than' or some synonymous expression. Whatever numbers are substituted for '*x*' and '*y*', this relation does not change and that is why some of the

[2] For discussions of these points see: P. F. Strawson, *An Introduction to Logical Theory* (London, 1952); J. L. Austin, *How to Do Things with Words* (Oxford, 1962); Gilbert Ryle, 'The Theory of Meaning', *British Philosophy in the Mid-Century*, ed. C. A. Mace (London, 1957); P. F. Strawson, 'On Referring', *Mind*, Vol. LIX, p. 320; both reprinted in C. E. Caton, *Philosophy and Ordinary Language* (Urbana, Illinois, 1963).

[3] This is not to say that rules of inference do not form a separate type in 'artificial' logical systems which are constructed in an abstract way and not closely tied to inferences in everyday discourse.

resulting statements will be true and others false. It is therefore called a 'constant'.

Various systems of symbolic logic are possible and have been constructed. If we begin constructing a system of logic from arguments in everyday discourse these possibilities depend upon the fact that the key words are complex in their use and meaning. They have various 'properties' or 'ingredients in their meanings', which is to say that each may be used in different ways in different contexts, and when we come to symbolize them we may decide to stress one use rather than others. One of the aims of symbolizing arguments is to remove imprecision and ambiguity; if, for example, a key word has different uses we must, for logical purposes, keep them distinct, so we may standardize one use and ignore the others or we may introduce different symbols for different uses.

Various types of relation have been regarded as important bases for inference and a system of logic may be designed to explore one or other of these. Historically, the fundamentally important relations have been thought to be relations between *terms*, relations between *classes*, relations between *predicates* and relations between *statements*, or, as some prefer to say, sentences or propositions. Corresponding to these are the traditional syllogistic logic and the more modern branches or systems of logic usually called *the class calculus, the predicate calculus* and *the propositional calculus.*

In the next few sections I shall examine some of the logically important features of our everyday uses of certain key words, with a view to showing how the stressing of different features may lead to these various systems of logic. It will not be possible here to deal fully with the technical matter of the development of these systems and it is not necessary since this has been adequately treated in a great many other books which have this as their central aim. My aim is rather to give some account of the basis in everyday discourse of these different systems and so to indicate their character and point in relation to arguments we actually use.

The so-called traditional logic, developed by Aristotle and his followers in mediaeval times, was one such system which still has its interest and value. It stressed the form of argument called *the syllogism.* Its main weakness lay in its lack of generality, although generality was just what its proponents hoped to achieve and claimed to have achieved. Some of them mistakenly thought that all deductive arguments could be regarded as syllogistic in form. Modern logic was developed largely with the aim of achieving greater generality and rigour but also with the aim of avoiding some of the problems and ambiguities of the traditional logic. I shall try to show, though not in a strictly historical way, how some modern conceptions have been developed as a result of criticisms of this system.

A typical syllogism is

> All mammals are vertebrates
> All cats are mammals
> ∴ All cats are vertebrates

and one of the traditional ways of symbolizing it is

> All Ms are P
> All Ss are M
> ∴ All Ss are P,

where 'S' and 'P' are used respectively for the subject and predicate terms of the conclusion, wherever they appear, and 'M' stands for the term which appears in both premises but not in the conclusion and which is called 'the middle term'.

A syllogism of a different type is

> All spies are cunning
> Some women are spies
> ∴ Some women are cunning

which may be symbolized

> All Ms are P
> Some Ss are M
> ∴ Some Ss are P.

There are many varieties of syllogism and it is not to the purpose to examine the possibilities here.[4] I wish to point only to some of its fundamental features. It is essential to it that there be just three statements, each having a subject term and a predicate term joined by some part of the verb 'to be'. Each statement must begin with 'all' or 'some' or, in some syllogisms containing negative statements, with 'no', which may be regarded as a negative form of 'all'. It is a controversial question whether a statement in a syllogism may begin with a proper name, such as 'Socrates', or with an expression such as 'The man in the garden'. The words 'all', 'some', 'no' and 'not' and the parts of the verb 'to be' are among the words which I have been referring to as key words and which I now propose to examine along with some others, such as 'and', 'or', and 'if', which are important in other forms of argument.

---

[4] Accounts of these may be found in many elementary textbooks. See, e.g., L. S. Stebbing (revised Mundle), *Modern Elementary Logic* (London, 1952).

It is convenient to introduce here the notions of *necessary conditions* and *sufficient conditions*, which will be used later. A necessary condition of something is a condition without which that something cannot occur or be the case; a sufficient condition of something is a condition which ensures that that something occurs or is the case. We shall be concerned mainly with necessary and sufficient conditions for the truth of statements. If *A* and *B* are two statements, then *A* is a necessary condition of *B* if *B* cannot be true unless *A* is true; this may be expressed by 'If *B* then *A*'. *A* is a sufficient condition of *B* if the truth of *A* ensures the truth of *B*; this may be expressed by 'If *A* then *B*'.

2. KEY WORDS

a. THE VERB 'TO BE'

It is important to note, first of all, that there is a timeless or 'tenseless' use of the verb 'to be' and that it is this use which figures in the syllogism. We often use the present tense form of the verb when we do not intend to make any specific reference to the present time; time may be just irrelevant or, in so far as it is relevant, we are referring to all times and no particular time. For example, if we say that 'Murder is wrong' or 'Men are mortal' the present tense is taken as avoiding the temporal suggestion of 'Murder was wrong'. It is only the present tense form which has this temporally neutral use.

Logicians tend to be interested in this use since they are interested in relations which *always* hold between certain terms. In the syllogism it is standard. This does not mean that we can ignore arguments where temporal relations do play an essential part but it does mean that they must be dealt with separately.

Present tense forms of the verb 'to be' are used in at least three different ways which it is important to distinguish since a failure to do so may radically affect our verdicts on the validity of arguments. For example, the three statements

> There *are* unicorns
> Water *is* H_2O
> This book *is* red

contain three different uses of the verb. The first concerns *existence*, the second concerns *identity* and the third concerns *predication* or *attribution*. I shall consider these uses in turn.

(i) The 'is' of Existence

When we say 'There are unicorns' or 'There is a two-headed man in the circus' we may be asserting that something exists. We normally

67

do this only when there is some doubt about the existence of the thing in question. It is true that philosophers sometimes assert, in very special circumstances, the existence of such things as tables and chairs but we are not here concerned with these special circumstances. Usually when a part of the verb 'to be' is used to assert existence it may be replaced, with some risk of artificiality, by 'exist' or 'exists'; we may say 'There exist unicorns' or 'Unicorns exist' instead of 'There are unicorns'.

It must be noted, here, that it is essential to know what kind of question we are answering, implicitly or explicitly, if we are to understand the statement which purports to answer it. For example, we sometimes use the expression 'There is . . .' not to introduce an assertion of existence but to introduce a statement which points something out or indicates where something is. We may use almost, or exactly, the same form of words to answer quite different questions and so to make quite different statements. For example, the words 'There is a book about the Queen of Sheba' might be used to answer the question 'Is there a book about the Queen of Sheba in this bookcase?' or the question 'Is there (such a thing as) a book about the Queen of Sheba?' The reply to the first question, especially if accompanied by a gesture, could be taken as indicating the book in its place in the bookcase and not to be translatable into 'There exists a book about the Queen of Sheba'. In speech, we usually make this use clear by stressing 'there'. In the reply to the second question the sense is retained if 'exists' replaces 'is' and in speech we should make this use clear by stressing 'is'. These uses must not be confused; the use of 'there is' to point something out is not the same as the use of 'there is' to assert the existence of something. It is this latter use that we are considering here.

This use of the verb 'to be' can always be made more explicit by avoiding the use of 'there' or by using other words which indicate that existence is in question. Instead of saying 'There are unicorns' we can say 'There exist unicorns' or 'Unicorns exist' or, again at the risk of some artificiality, 'Unicorns are'. (Compare 'God is'.) If we try to do this with the indicating use of, say, 'There is a two-headed man' we arrive at something like 'A two-headed man is over there' or, more naturally, 'There is a two-headed man over there' or 'That is a two-headed man'.

Consider the two questions 'Is there (such a thing as) a two-headed man?' and 'Where is the two-headed man?' The statement 'There is *the* two-headed man' would be appropriate as an answer to the second question but not quite appropriate as an answer to the first. The more appropriate answer to this would be 'There is *a* two-headed man'. The use of the indefinite and definite articles, 'a' and 'the' respectively, help to indicate, though not, of course, conclusively, that we are using the 'is' of existence and the indicating sense of 'there is' respectively. A lesson to be learnt from this is that small differences in linguistic construction may indicate, and should at least lead us to suspect, important differences in meaning.

(ii) *The 'is' of Identity*

When we say such things as 'Water is H_2O' or 'A bachelor is an unmarried man' we are not usually asserting that water or bachelors exist. We may be assuming this or taking it for granted or presupposing it but to do any of these things is not to assert it. We are saying that water is the same as, or is identical with, H_2O, properly understood. We would mean the same by 'H_2O is water' or 'Water is the same as H_2O'. Such statements may also be put as statements about the meaning or the reference of certain words or other symbols involved in them. For example, we could say that 'Water is H_2O' can be translated into 'The word "water" means the same as the symbol "H_2O" ' or 'The word "water" is used to refer to the same substance as the symbol "H_2O" '. This is a controversial matter; for one reason, it can be argued that the first of these translations is misleading in a way that the second is not. We can say that 'water' gives no information about the composition of the substance in question whereas the symbol 'H_2O' does, if it is properly understood. There is, therefore, some ground for saying that 'water' and 'H_2O' do not *mean* the same although they are used to refer to the same substance.

However, one thing that is not controversial is that, if we are using the 'is' of identity in any expression of the form '*A* is *B*', we do not change the meaning of the expression as a whole if we change it to '*B* is *A*'. In this respect the 'is' of identity functions in a similar way to the sign of equality in arithmetic.

This is the 'is' used in explicit definitions. If we regard 'Bachelors are unmarried men' as a definition of 'bachelors' then we do not change its meaning if we write 'Unmarried men are bachelors'. We indicate this when we write definitions in the form 'A man is a bachelor *if and only if* he is unmarried'. This is to be contrasted with such statements as 'Bachelors are lucky men' since, even if this is true it does not follow that all lucky men are bachelors. To say 'Lucky men are bachelors' would be to say something different from 'Bachelors are lucky men'. It must be noted that although definitions may be put in the form '*a* if and only if *b*', a statement of this form is not necessarily a definition.

A somewhat unusual use of 'is' can be found in the statement 'God is love'. Compare this with 'God is benevolent'. We can say 'Jones is benevolent' but it would be odd to say 'Jones is love'. That is, 'God is love' looks like a piece of bad grammar unless we regard the 'is' as that of identity, so that it makes sense to say 'Love is God'. Our difficulties with this are perhaps largely theological rather than logical. There is some difficulty in saying that in such statements as 'John is in love with Mary' we are using 'love' in the same sense as that in which we are using it in 'God is love' and the problem is that of saying what are the differences in meaning between these two uses of 'love'; this is largely the theological problem of saying what is meant by 'love' in the statement about God.

(iii) *The 'is' of Predication or Attribution*

The statement 'This book is red' may be regarded as a property-statement, which is intended to attribute the property of redness to the object indicated. If we wish to stress the linguistic aspect we may say that it is intended to attach the predicate 'red' to the subject 'this book'. What we mean to assert by it is not the existence of books or redness, although we may take this for granted, and not the identity of an object and a property but rather that a certain object has a particular property.

We could, in fact, recast our statement without change of meaning to read 'This book has the property of being red'. We do not usually do this with such statements as 'There are unicorns' or 'Water is H_2O'. I say that we do not usually do this because some philosophers are inclined to say that this can be done and that what is meant by 'There are unicorns' can be put 'At least one space-time region is characterized by the properties we associate with unicorns' and that what is meant by 'Water is H_2O' can be put 'Anything characterized by the properties we associate with water is also characterized by the properties we associate with H_2O'. This is not to eliminate important differences between statements of identity and statements of predication, as a close inspection of the translation shows, but it is to raise further matters beyond differences of meaning which we normally associate with everyday uses of parts of the verb 'to be'. For the present, I am content to make certain distinctions in our everyday uses.

Another controversial matter may be mentioned here. The question whether 'existence' can be regarded as a predicate has figured importantly in the history of philosophy. Some philosophers have talked as if, for example, 'There are apples' asserts that we can apply to apples, besides a number of predicates such as 'red', 'smooth' and 'sweet', the predicate 'exists'; as if existence were another property which apples have along with sweetness or sourness, redness or greenness, and so on. This has been particularly important in connection with the statement 'God exists' and arguments in its support. Much has been written about this but it will suffice to say here that if we say, for example, that sugar is sweet, white, crystalline, and so on, we are usually *presupposing* the existence of sugar. There is thus no need to add 'and exists' at the end of the list of properties.[5]

Other kinds of statement which, at least on the face of it, use the 'is' of predication are the kinds of statement which figure in the syllogism, for example, universal statements such as 'All men are mortal', particular statements such as 'Some men are intelligent' and statements with proper names as subjects such as 'John is lazy'. There are, however, complications about these which I shall expose later.

It is important to make distinctions between different uses of 'is' because confusion of them may make radical differences to the inferences we are prepared to make and may lead us into making invalid inferences. The fact is that we may have different arguments which appear to be of the same form unless we distinguish between different uses of 'is' in them. This may lead us to classify an invalid argument as valid.

For example, the argument

> Water is H_2O
> Water is a solvent for sugar
> $\therefore$ H_2O is a solvent for sugar

and the argument

> Smith is a pleasant fellow
> Smith is a man who is always late for appointments
> $\therefore$ A pleasant fellow is a man who is always late for appointments,

appear to have the same form which can be represented by

> x is A
> x is B
> $\therefore$ A is B.

In fact we should normally say that the first argument is valid and the second invalid. This is because the 'is' in the first premiss of the

---

[5] Important papers on this point are to be found in Alvin Plantinga (ed.), *The Ontological Argument* (New York, 1965).

first argument is the 'is' of identity whereas that in the first premiss of the second argument is the 'is' of predication. This difference is obscured by the symbolic representation of the two arguments.

We could, perhaps, regard the second argument as valid by putting a somewhat unusual interpretation on the conclusion, regarding it as meaning '*One* pleasant fellow is a man who is always late for appointments'. This would be to regard the arguments as different in form and this difference would also be obscured by the symbolic representation given.

In the traditional logic, the verb 'to be' was taken as an essential link between the terms of allowable statements and was called *the copula*. The distinctions between different senses of 'is', in this context, were either not made or not given sufficient importance. Statements which could figure in the syllogism had to be in, or translatable into, one of four standard forms, labelled '*A*', '*E*', '*I*' and '*O*'.[6] Examples of these forms, together with expressions which exhibit the forms independently of any subject-matter, are

A	All cats are black	All Ss are P
E	No cats are black	No Ss are P
I	Some cats are black	Some Ss are P
O	Some cats are not black	Some Ss are not P.

It was hoped by some logicians that all deductive arguments could be shown to be of the syllogistic type, which meant that the statements composing them had to be expressed in one or other of these standard forms. The 'is' was, at least implicitly, taken in the predicational sense, as is indicated by the convention of using '*S*' and '*P*', standing for 'subject' and 'predicate', as symbols for the terms.

This project involved logicians in some strange mental gymnastics and led them sometimes to distort language, and the arguments under consideration, in order to show that they were, in spite of appearances, syllogistic. For example, the statement-form '*a* is greater than *b*' was taken by some as predicating 'greater than *b*' of *a*, as if being greater than *b* were a property of *a* just as redness is a property of some roses. There was also the danger of treating all uses of the verb 'to be' as the predicational use and so treating invalid arguments as valid.

In the partial symbolization of the four types of statement just given such differences were obscured. Sometimes a further step in

---

[6] These letters come from the first two vowels in 'affirmo' (I affirm) and the two vowels of 'nego' (I deny).

72

formalization was taken, when the types of statement were represented in the following way.

A	SaP
E	SeP
I	SiP
O	SoP

Here the letters '*a*', '*e*', '*i*' and '*o*' indicated only differences in the types of statement which did not depend upon the interpretation of the verb 'to be'. Thus, '*a*' merely indicates that the statement begins 'All *S*', and is affirmative in contrast to statements beginning 'No *S*' or 'Some *S*' indicated by '*e*' or '*i*' and '*o*' respectively. The letters '*a*' and '*i*' indicate *affirmative* statements and the letters '*e*' and '*o*' *negative* statements.

In modern logic, different uses of the verb 'to be' are indicated explicitly in the symbolization but discussion of this must be postponed until after the words 'all' and 'some' have been discussed.

b. 'ALL' AND 'SOME': UNIVERSAL, PARTICULAR AND SINGULAR STATEMENTS

(i) '*All*' and '*Some*' in Everyday Discourse and in Logic

In the ordinary way, if we say 'All cats are mammals' we are talking about every cat whatever or, to put it in a slightly artificial way, we are talking about the whole of this kind or class of things. No exceptions are allowed. In logic, such statements are called *universal statements*. On the other hand, if we say 'Some cats are black' we are quite obviously not making an assertion about every cat; we are making an assertion about only part of this kind or class of things. In logic, such statements are called *particular statements*.

These terms, 'universal' and 'particular' are used in logic as technical terms. It is important to note that the term 'particular' is used in a way which may at first seem strange because it involves an interpretation of certain statements which perhaps differs from what we would expect on the basis of everyday discourse. We interpret statements of the form 'Some *A*s are *B*' as referring to any *A*s fewer than all and more than none. That is, if we know that just one *A* is *B* we can represent this by the particular form 'Some *A*s are *B*'.

The reason for this can be put in the following way. Two statements of the form 'No *A*s are *B*' and 'All *A*s are *B*' cannot both be true at the same time, if we are talking of the same *A* and *B*. The existence of one or several *A*s which are *B* is enough to render 'No

*A*s are *B*' false and the existence of one or several *A*s that are not *B* is enough to render 'All *A*s are *B*' false. As far as these relations, which are of great importance for inference, are concerned we do not need to distinguish the situation in which one *A* is *B*, or is not *B*, from the situations in which several *A*s are *B*, or are not *B*. These relations discriminate just four types of statement forms

> All *A*s are *B*,
> No *A*s are *B*,
> Some *A*s are *B*,
> Some *A*s are not *B*.

We therefore give to 'some' in particular statements a minimum interpretation so that it means 'at least one'. This is different from our usual interpretation, where 'some' appears to indicate plurality, but it is a suitable interpretation for certain logical purposes.

Another notion of traditional logic which has been regarded as important from time to time is that of the *distribution* of terms. In statements of the form 'All *S*s are *P*' the word 'all' is said, under one interpretation, to indicate that the term *S* is distributed, which is to say that it is used to cover everything to which *S* may be applied; in statements of the form 'Some *S*s are *P*' the word 'some' is said to indicate that *S* is *undistributed*, which is to say that it is used to cover only some of the things to which *S* may be applied. We shall have occasion to return to this notion.

There is another possible ambiguity which should be mentioned here. In everyday discourse we may use a sentence of the form 'Some *S*s are *P*' in two ways.

(a) We may use it in such a way that its truth excludes the truth of 'All *S*s are *P*', that is, it has the implication that 'Some *S*s are not *P*' is also true.

(b) We may use it in such a way that its truth does not exclude the truth of 'All *S*s are *P*', that is, it does not have the implication that 'Some *S*s are not *P*' is true, or that it is false.

As an example of (a) consider this: someone says that although he has seen many cats he has never seen a white cat. We might reply 'Well, *some* cats are white'. Emphasizing 'some' makes it clear that we are not suggesting that all cats may be white and the context makes it clear that we are accepting that 'some cats are not white'.

As an example of (b) consider this: none of us, in a certain group, has ever seen a wombat and we are wondering what colour wombats are. We go to the zoology department where we know that they have half-a-dozen wombats. We find that they are brown. For all we know, this may be the colour of all wombats but the most we are entitled to say, on the evidence we have, is 'Some wombats are brown'. Clearly we do not wish to exclude the possibility that 'All wombats are brown' is true.

In logic we are concerned with relations between kinds of statements which we represent by such expressions as 'Some Ss are P'. If we consider these apart from any particular context, as most formal logicians think we can, we have to allow that the expression 'Some Ss are P' when it is simply written on a blackboard does not distinguish between these two uses if it is entirely unqualified. We must avoid ambiguities which might arise from this. We could do so by writing

Some (but not all) Ss are P

and

Some (and possibly all) Ss are P

to distinguish the two cases, but this is cumbersome. Instead we 'standardize' the second use and interpret 'Some Ss are P' always in that sense, so that it is compatible with 'All Ss are P'.

If we are analysing an argument in everyday English in which 'some' is used in the first way, to mean 'some but not all', then we need both the expression 'Some Ss are P' and the expression 'Some Ss are not P' to capture the full meaning of this.

A similar convention must, of course, be adopted for 'Some Ss are not P'; unqualified, it is always taken to be compatible with 'No Ss are P'.

According to this set of conventions for universal and particular statements we can say

(a) 'Some Ss are P' is compatible with both 'All Ss are P' and 'Some Ss are not P', although the last two forms are, of course, incompatible with one another;

(b) 'Some Ss are not P' is compatible with both 'No Ss are P' and 'Some Ss are P', although the last two forms are, of course, incompatible with one another.

In everyday discourse we often take one statement to suggest another, where suggesting is a weaker notion than asserting or implying. In logic, it is important to keep these notions clear and separate. In the ordinary way, I may say 'Some cats are white' in different tones of voice and with different emphases, so as to suggest, or not to suggest, that some cats are not white. It is difficult to take note of tones of voice and emphases in formal logic so certain conventions are necessary. On the whole, we are normally held accountable only for what we assert or for what is *implied* by what we assert but, less frequently, for what we suggest in the course of asserting.

When I say 'Some cats are white' I can be said to be *asserting* that some cats are white; what I say can be said to *imply* that not all cats are black but I cannot be said, if we are being strict, to have asserted that; I may also have spoken in such a way as to *suggest* that some cats are not white, but it cannot be said that I asserted that or that what I said implied it.

In formal logic, we try to consider the relations between statements or types of statement independently of any particular context of utterance; suggestions made by way of tones of voice belong rather to the context than to the statements themselves. However, if an actual argument which we examine depends necessarily upon a suggestion made in making an assertion we have two courses open to us in analysing the argument in formal logic. We can either take notice only of what was asserted, ignoring what was suggested, and this may result in a distortion of the argument which was intended. On the other hand, we can take notice of the suggestion, but then we must treat it as an assertion rather than a mere suggestion.

For example, suppose I say 'Some cats are white' and use this as one premiss of an argument. Suppose also that I say this in such a way as to suggest that I accept also 'Some cats are not white' and suppose further that my conclusion followed only from 'Some cats are white' along with this suggestion. Then in a formal analysis, in order to show the argument to be valid and to do justice to my argumentative intentions, I have to treat both 'Some cats are white' and 'Some cats are not white' as premisses, that is, as assertions. It would not be enough to treat only 'Some cats are white' as a premiss since this does not *imply* 'Some cats are not white', although it was used, on that occasion, in such a way as to suggest it.

This is just one example of the sort of problem which may arise in analysing an actual argument in terms of formal logic or in applying the principles of formal logic to actual arguments. In this situation we inevitably meet with considerations which are not purely formal and which depend not merely upon the actual words uttered but also upon their interpretation, which in turn depends upon various contextual features, including even tone of voice or individual peculiarities of English style. We shall meet this kind of problem in various connections.

We shall see later that there are also problems of quite a different sort connected with the traditional treatment of universal and particular statements. In the meantime, we can note that, according to this treatment, statements of the form 'Some Ss are P' follow from statements of the form 'All Ss are P', where 'S' and 'P' stand respectively for the same terms in both, but the second does not follow from the first. A similar relation holds between statements of the form 'No Ss are P' and 'Some Ss are not P'. On the other hand, neither of two statements of the form 'Some Ss are P' and 'Some Ss are not P' follows from the other.

(ii) *Singular Statements*

Statements having proper names as subjects, and some related statements, have from time to time given logicians considerable trouble. For the traditional logician it was, at first sight, difficult to fit them into the classification of statements which can figure in syllogisms. However, it appeared that such statements could be used in syllogisms so it was essential to fit them into the A, E, I, O classification.

Perhaps the most famous example of a syllogism is

> All men are mortal
> Socrates is a man
> ∴ Socrates is mortal.

How are the statements 'Socrates is a man' and 'Socrates is mortal' to be classified? They are both clearly affirmative but are they universal or particular (A or I)? The clue to answering this question lies in the supposition that 'Socrates' is intended and taken as naming a unique individual and not one of a number of individuals bearing this name. When this is stated it seems clear that, for logical purposes, these statements may be taken as universal. Just as a statement beginning 'All cats . . .' can be regarded as being about every animal that is correctly called a cat, so 'Socrates is a man' can be regarded as being about every individual that bears that name, it being assumed that there is only one. We are not, as in a particular statement beginning 'Some cats . . .' saying something about only some (or one) of a number of things correctly called by that name, since we have excluded that possibility. One peculiar consequence of this convention is that there is no particular statement corresponding to the universal statement 'Socrates is a man'.

Many men are called 'Paul'. We could say 'All Pauls are male' and this would be a universal statement. We could also say 'Some Pauls are adults' and this would be a particular statement. (If these statements seem too artificial they could be changed to 'All people called "Paul" are male' and 'Some people called "Paul" are adults'.)

If we take it that there is only one Socrates, or only one person that can be meant if that name is used without qualification, then 'Socrates is a man' is, in its logical properties, more like a universal statement than a particular statement. It is, at any rate, sufficiently like a universal statement to be treated in this way for the purposes of the syllogism.

Such statements are called *singular statements*. It is important to note, however, that singular statements need not have proper names as their subjects; they may also have descriptive expressions which specify unique individuals. For example, the statements

The present Queen of England is married

and

The horse in my garden is hungry

are singular statements, uniqueness being ensured by the italicized expression, especially the definite article. The same may be said of statements beginning with demonstratives such as

This book is red

where 'this' along with some kind of indicating device, such as a gesture, secures uniqueness. As long as the whole of the italicized portion of each sentence is taken as its subject, as being what the statement is about, these statements may be treated as universal for the purposes of syllogistic theory.

It must be pointed out, however, that caution is needed in arguing from such statements. We cannot argue from, for example, 'The horse in my garden is vicious' to a statement about all horses, even though both statements are universal. To do this is to treat the horse in my garden as one horse among the rest and not as a unique individual, namely, *the* horse in my garden, and this is to treat the original statement as particular rather than as singular or universal.

A more modern interpretation of these traditional forms of statement treats them as relating *classes* of things, named by their subjects and predicates. This will be discussed further but here it will help to point the connection between universal and singular statements. According to this interpretation, a statement beginning 'All cats . . .' is about the whole of the class of cats whereas a statement beginning 'Some cats . . .' is about only part of that class. Then we can say that a singular statement is about the whole of a class but a rather peculiar one which has, *and can have*, only one member. This is not to say that no one besides the celebrated Socrates can have that name but only that if this happens we can no longer regard a statement beginning 'Socrates . . .', with no uniqueness-indicator attached, as a singular statement. Thus, 'Socrates is a man' is about the whole of the class mentioned in the subject but the class contains only one individual. As the popular phrase has it, Socrates 'is in a class by himself'.

(iii) *Existential Import*

In everyday discourse when we say such things as 'All monkeys are playful' and 'Some monkeys are vicious' we usually take ourselves to be talking about animals which actually exist. To use a technical term of logic, we take these statements to have *existential import*. This is how Aristotle interpreted such statements for logical purposes and some of the allowable inferences in his logic depended upon this interpretation. Later logicians have cast doubts on the correctness, or the usefulness, of this interpretation and have regarded it as essential to distinguish between universal and particular statements in this respect.

Consider, first, universal statements. When I say 'All monkeys are playful' what I *mean to assert* is not that there are monkeys but rather that a particular relation holds between a certain kind of thing and a certain property, between monkeys and playfulness. This is the information I intend to convey. I am not *asserting* that monkeys exist although I may be *assuming* that they do. Putting it in another way, my statement may be regarded as excluding a certain possibility, namely, the possibility that there are monkeys that are *not* playful. In asserting merely that certain possibilities do not occur I am not asserting the existence of anything. Moreover, I need not even be assuming the existence of anything.[7]

When we assert something while assuming something, the assumption and the assertion may be separated, and saying what the statement *means* involves mention only of what is asserted and not of what is assumed. The assumption is not part of the meaning of the statement; my statement means the same and I assert the same whether or not I assume the existence of what is mentioned in the subject. Thus, although we may usually use statements of the form 'All *S*s are *P*' or 'No *S*s are *P*' in contexts in which we assume the existence of *S*s this is not a necessary condition of the meaningfulness of such statements.

Some examples will help to make the point. I can perfectly well say, and be understood if I do, 'All men over ten feet tall are giants'

---

[7] P. F. Strawson in *An Introduction to Logical Theory* (London, 1952), uses the more precise notion of *presupposition* to deal with some of these problems (p. 175 ff.). See also I. M. Copi, *Introduction to Logic* (New York, 1964), p. 154 ff.

even though we do not suppose that there *are* any men over ten feet tall. What I can be taken to mean is that if we were to come across any men over ten feet tall we should properly call them giants. The sense of this statement depends upon the meaning we already attach to the word 'giant'. However, I can also invent a new word which happens at present to have no application, define it so that I know how to apply it in future if the need arises and state all or part of its definition in a universal statement. Suppose that butterflies appear to be evolving in such a way that I think it possible that one day there will be a new kind of butterfly which lives in the tropics, has blue spots on yellow wings and can swim under water. For convenience, I need a name for this, so I invent the name 'snorvel'. Then, in the course of explaining what this word means, I can say

All snorvels are amphibious.

This is now perfectly understandable even if nobody believes that there are, at present, any snorvels. Even if these creatures never were discovered, or thought to exist, the statement would still be meaningful; I have given the word 'snorvel' a meaning just by defining it. The statement can be regarded as laying down conditions for the application of the word, should an application ever become possible; it can be regarded as excluding the application of the name 'snorvel' to anything that is not amphibious.

Similar things can be said about universal negative statements. For example, I can say

No snorvels are mammals

and this can be taken as excluding the application of the name to anything that is a mammal or as excluding the existence of any mammalian snorvel.

Anything we assume in making a statement may be considered, for the present purpose, as part of the context in which the statement is made. When we represent a statement by one of the partially symbolized forms, for example, 'All Ss are P', we are abstracting from such contexts and considering those properties of statements which are independent of them. When we represent a statement by 'All Ss are P', with no qualification, there is no means of telling whether existence is being assumed or not. We must adopt some convention which will avoid ambiguity over this. We therefore interpret 'All Ss are P' in such a way as to make the minimum assumption consistent with its being meaningful. We therefore interpret 'All Ss are P' and 'No Ss are P' always as representing statements making no existential claims or, as we may also say, having no existential import. The hope is that, in this way, we capture the element of meaning of these statements which is common to all their utterances, whether or not existential assumptions are involved.

According to the account being presented, particular statements are to be contrasted with universal statements. Statements of the forms 'Some *S*s are *P*' and 'Some *S*s are not *P*' are said only to make sense if *S*s exist, which amounts to saying that part of the assertion made by statements of these forms is that *S*s exist. The whole point of saying 'Some professors are absent-minded' is to distinguish absent-minded professors from others and this makes sense only if there *are* some professors among whom we can distinguish some from others. In order for there to be some point in, and justification for, making statements beginning 'Some *S*s . . .' there must be *evidence* about *S*s and evidence about them depends upon their existing.

My definition of 'snorvels' allowed me to make statements beginning 'All snorvels . . .' just because, being a definition, it specified properties which must be possessed by anything that is to be called a snorvel. It gives no basis for making any statement beginning 'Some snorvels . . .' which is not also a basis for making the corresponding universal statement; it thus ensures that there is no *point* in making any particular statements about snorvels. From the definition we know of no way in which snorvels differ among themselves but only ways in which they must resemble one another. It remains to be seen from an examination of actual snorvels, if any turn up, whether there are 'accidental' properties in which they differ from one another. It may turn out that some are white under their wings and some are black, but we cannot know that unless there are snorvels to examine.

It might be supposed that we can at least say

Some snorvels are male

on the grounds that we can have evidence for this in advance from other species of animals. We could say it on the ground that

All animal species are divided into male and female

but we know this to be false because some animals are hermaphrodites. Even if we knew this to be true of all known animals we would have no grounds, from our definition, for supposing that snorvels will not turn out to be hermaphrodites. We cannot choose between these possibilities now since our definition leaves them open.

If this account is accepted, it can be said that a universal and a

81

particular statement having the same subject and the same predicate do not differ merely in respect of generality but differ also in that the universal statement does not make an existential claim whereas the particular statement does make an existential claim. The distinction can be made, rather more formally, in at least two other ways.

The first way is to say that universal statements merely exclude certain possibilities while particular statements assert certain actualities. Thus

> All cats are mammals

means the same as

> Nothing is both a cat and not a mammal

while

> Some cats are black

means the same as

> There is at least one thing that is a cat and black.

In general, assuming that S and P respectively stand for the same terms throughout,

> All Ss are P

means the same as

> Nothing is both an S and not P

and

> No Ss are P

means the same as

> Nothing is both an S and P

while

> Some Ss are P

means the same as

> There is at least one thing that is an S and P

and

> Some Ss are not P

means the same as

> There is at least one thing that is an S and not P.

82

These 'translations' make it clear that it is only the particular statements which make existential claims.

The second way of distinguishing is by saying that universal
statements can be translated into hypothetical statements without
change of meaning but particular statements cannot. Thus

>All cats are mammals

means the same as

>If anything is a cat then it is a mammal

or

>If *there are* any cats then they are mammals

but no such translation can be found to catch the exact meaning of
'Some cats are black' or 'Some cats are not black'. In general,
assuming that S and P respectively stand for the same terms throughout,

>All Ss are P

means the same as

>If anything is an S then it is P

and

>No Ss are P

means the same as

>If anything is an S then it is not P.

Thus we can translate universal statements into statements which are
clearly about *possible* existents but we cannot so translate particular
statements.

These arguments are taken to show that universal statements can
be meaningful and, in a sense, true, without being about actual
existents whereas particular statements cannot be.

It must be stressed that the distinction between what is assumed
and what is stated was not explicitly made by early logicians and that
the theory of syllogistic reasoning depends in part upon assuming
that there is no difference, in respect of existential import, between
universal and particular statements, and that there are no problems
attached to the inferring of particular statements from universal
statements. Attention was drawn to the distinction by problems which
arose in connection with the *immediate inferences* of traditional
logic. (See Chap. IV, Section 2.)

One consequence of the alleged difference in existential claims between universals and particulars is that we cannot infer a particular statement of the form 'Some Ss are P' from a universal statement of the form 'All Ss are P' without the addition of some existential statement to the universal statement. The same holds for the inference of 'Some Ss are not P' from 'No Ss are P'. If 'All Ss are P' makes no existential claim but 'Some Ss are P' does make an existential claim then to infer the latter from the former is to 'go beyond the evidence'. The evidence was not evidence about the existence of anything. It is not permissible to infer the existence of something from a statement which does not assert the existence of anything. If the only information we have about snorvels is my definition of them, we have no ground for the statement that 'Some snorvels are amphibious butterflies' since this covertly claims that snorvels exist. In general, we cannot infer the existence of something from a definition. Some traditional 'proofs' of the existence of God fell into this error.[8]

Traditionally, it was held that if a statement of the form 'All Ss are P' is false then a statement of the form 'Some Ss are not P' must be true. If we take statements of both forms to *assert* the existence of Ss we cannot hold this, since both might be false. For example, if there are no Martians then the falsity of

All Martians are male

does not imply the truth of

Some Martians are not male.

The traditional view may be saved by holding that statements of both forms *presuppose*, rather than asserting, the existence of Ss. If existence is merely a presupposition of these statements then it is a condition of both their truth and falsity but is not asserted by them. Thus, on this view, if there are no Martians, neither of our statements is true *or* false. (See footnote 7 on page 79.)

(iv) *Quantifiers*

A relatively modern device for dealing with this difference between universal and particular statements is the use of symbols called *quantifiers*.

If we take 'All Ss are P' to indicate no existential import then we cannot represent 'All professors are absent-minded' by this form *if* we wish to include a presupposition of the existence of professors.

[8] See, e.g. Descartes, *Discourse on Method* in *The Philosophical Works of Descartes*, trans. E. S. Haldane and G. R. T. Ross (Cambridge, 1911).

We should have to represent it by some more complex form such as

There are Ss and all of them are P

or

There are Ss and all Ss are P.

Strictly, these do not represent just what is asserted; they represent what is asserted together with what is presupposed on some occasion but which need not always be presupposed. Usually, for purposes of formal logic, we are interested only in what is asserted, just because what is presupposed need not always be presupposed. We are interested in generality. We therefore use 'All Ss are P' to represent the form of what is asserted by universal affirmative statements.

We may symbolize this, and make it clearer just what we are symbolizing, thus

(x) (If x is S then x is P).

Ignoring presuppositions of existence our example,

All professors are absent-minded

would then be represented by

(x) (If x is a professor then x is absent-minded)

which may be read

For any x, if x is a professor then x is absent-minded

which is a more precise way of saying

If anything is a professor then that thing is absent-minded.

The symbol '(x)' is called the *universal quantifier* and it may be read 'for all x' or 'for any x'. Its use in the way illustrated makes it clear that no existential claims are being made, or considered, in such symbolic representations of universal statements. Other examples, in which it is especially important that this be made clear are

(x) (If x is a unicorn then x is white)
(x) (If x is a man over ten feet tall then x is a giant)
(x) (If x is a snorvel then x is an amphibious butterfly).

In general, for the limited purposes of formal logic,

All Ss are P

means the same as

(x) (If x is S then x is P)

and

> No Ss are P

means the same as

> (x) (If x is S then x is not P).

In particular statements, existential claims are not presuppositions but part of what is asserted; these claims must therefore be embodied in any symbolic representation.

> Some wombats are brown

must be taken to mean

> There are wombats at least one of which is brown.

We may symbolize this, making plain the existential claim, thus,

> $(\exists x)$ (x is a wombat and x is brown)

which may be read

> There is at least one x such that x is a wombat and x is brown.

In general, according to the interpretation under discussion

> Some Ss are P

means the same as

> $(\exists x)(x$ is S and x is $P)$

and

> Some Ss are not P

means the same as

> $(\exists x)(x$ is S and x is not $P)$.

The symbol '$(\exists x)$' is called the *existential quantifier* or the *particular quantifier*. The two quantifiers, (x) and $(\exists x)$, are so-called because they indicate whether a statement is universal or particular and in the terminology of the traditional logic these were referred to as the *quantity* of a statement.

The contrast between universal and particular statements is further brought out by the fact that in the new forms the particular statement contains 'and', suggesting an association between S and P which may be accidental, while the universal statement contains 'If ... then ...', suggesting a non-accidental association between S and P.

The four types of statement of the traditional logic may now be represented thus

All Ss are P	by (x)(If x is S then x is P)
No Ss are P	by (x)(If x is S then x is not P)
Some Ss are P	by (∃x)(x is S and x is P)
Some Ss are not P	by (∃x)(x is S and x is not P).

Now we see that if we wish to represent 'All professors are absent-minded' in such a way as to include a presupposition of existence we must use both quantifiers and represent it by the expression

(x)(If x is a professor then x is absent-minded) and (∃x) (x is a professor)

which is to be read 'For all x if x is a professor then x is absent-minded and there is at least one x such that x is a professor'.

The difficulty about this way of representing the four traditional types of statement is that, as I have already mentioned, if we accept them then certain operations of the traditional logic are inadmissible. I have mentioned that the inferring of a particular statement from a single universal statement is inadmissible but there are other cases. For example, one form of syllogism traditionally regarded as valid was

All cats are mammals	A
All mammals are vertebrates	A
∴ Some vertebrates are cats.	I

We must regard this as invalid if we accept the equivalences given above. On the other hand, the traditionally valid syllogism

All mammals are vertebrates	A
Some sea-going animals are mammals	I
∴ Some sea-going animals are vertebrates	I

remains valid. This is because in this syllogism, in contrast to the first, the existence of both sea-going animals and mammals is asserted in the second premiss.

Referring back to an earlier discussion (see Chap. III, Section 2a) we may say that particular statements, according to the new interpretation, involve both the predicative and the existential use of the verb 'to be', while universal statements involve only the predicative use. This underlies the difference in respect of validity between our two syllogisms.

This discussion can now be seen as bringing out the fact that both traditional and modern interpretations of 'All' and 'Some' statements *are* interpretations which depend upon the abstracting from the uses of everyday discourse in different ways or on the focussing of attention on different features of our everyday uses of 'All' and 'Some'. This means that neither interpretation captures the exact meaning, or all the uses, of these words. That is, the 'All' and 'Some' of traditional logic are as much technical terms as the '(x)' and '$(\exists x)$' of modern logic. This is easily missed because the same words 'All' and 'Some' are used as quantifiers in syllogistic theory.

This is perhaps best brought out by a consideration of what has been said about particular statements and the use of the word 'Some'. The traditional theory of the syllogism takes both universal and particular statements as making existential claims. The need to distinguish between universal and particular statements in this respect springs partly from the pressure of everyday uses and partly from problems which arise within logic. (See Chap. IV, Section 2.) An examination of everyday uses suggests that for universal statements existence is a presupposition rather than a claim of the statement itself and that particular statements differ in having an existential claim built into them.

One argument for this depends upon the view that statements of the form 'Some Ss are P' in everyday discourse have point only if the Ss mentioned are contrasted with others and that such contrasts are possible, or have point, only if there are Ss. This makes the existence of several Ss, i.e. more than one, a requirement for the appropriateness of the statements in question.

However, as I have said, the 'Some' in the 'Some Ss are P' of traditional logic is taken to mean *one or more* and this is emphasized if we regard this form as equivalent to

$$(\exists x)(x \text{ is } S \text{ and } x \text{ is } P)$$

and read this as

There is at least one x such that x is S and x is P.

This appears to be in conflict with the argument for distinguishing between universals and particulars in respect of existential import, on which the properties of '(x)' and '$(\exists x)$' partly depend, until we notice that the 'All' and 'Some' of traditional logic are technical terms. We could say that the argument from everyday discourse, among other things, leads us to draw the distinction but that it is convenient, for logical purposes, to draw the distinction in a different way from that implicit in everyday discourse.

We may say that 'Some Ss are P' is used to represent what is common to 'An S is P', 'Most Ss are P', 'Many Ss are p', 'A few

Ss are P' or indeed any such expression which is narrower in scope than 'All Ss are P', that is, which mentions fewer than all the Ss. It was indeed the practice of traditional accounts of the syllogism to represent all these by 'Some Ss are P'. For certain purposes, we can so use the modern quantifiers. If we are only concerned with what might be called 'All or some' arguments, with the relations between universal statements and *any* statements of narrower scope, we are concerned only with the contrast between 'For all x . . .' and 'There is *at least one x* . . .'.

We may make the point in another way. Particular statements may be regarded as just those which arise from the denial of universal statements. For example, if we say 'It is not the case that *all cats are black*', that is, if we deny the italicized universal statement, the denial is equivalent to the assertion that at least one cat is some other colour than black. This, however, brings us to a new subject, *denial and negation*, introduced by the key words 'not' and 'no' and related words. The point is explained more fully in the next section.

In the meantime, it is important to say something in the present section about uses of the word 'only'. There are, of course, familiar possibilities of ambiguity concerning the word, which may be removed by careful placing of it or by careful punctuation or, in speech, by careful inflection. I am not concerned about these ambiguities here. What I am concerned about is the relation between 'only' and 'all'.

Sentences like 'Only adults are voters' cannot figure, just as they stand, in syllogistic arguments; they must be transformed into sentences of one of the four traditional forms which have the same meanings as the originals, that is, which can be used to make precisely the same statements.

'Only adults are voters' means that among the voters there are to be found only adults; it does not mean that every adult is a voter but that every voter is an adult. In Great Britain, for example, it is true that only adults are voters but it is also true that those serving a prison sentence, even if they are adults, are not allowed to vote. Thus, in Great Britain, it is true that

> Only adults are voters

but false that

> All adults are voters.

It is also true that

> All voters are adults.

Therefore, 'Only adults are voters' cannot mean the same as 'All adults are voters' or the first could not be true without the second also being true; it does mean the same as 'All voters are adults'.

Another example which brings this out, perhaps even more clearly, concerns the disease *myxomatosis* which is a disease confined to rabbits and which was, until recently, fatal to them. It is true that

>   Only rabbits catch myxomatosis

but false that

>   All rabbits catch myxomatosis.

The first sentence means the same as 'All animals that catch myxomatosis are rabbits'.

In general, we may say that

>   Only Ss are P

is equivalent to

>   All Ps are S

but *not* to

>   All Ss are P.

c. COMPOUND STATEMENTS

(i) *General Considerations*

I have so far dealt mainly with what may be called 'simple' statements. These may, for our present purposes, be regarded as statements, which make a single assertion and which cannot be broken up into parts all of which are statements or merely linking words. The four types of categorical statement of the traditional logic are of this sort. We can regard the statements 'All spies are cunning', 'Some spies are not prosperous' and '007 is a spy' as each making a single assertion or stating one fact.

Simple statements may be joined together or 'compounded' in various ways, making what I propose to call 'compound' statements. A simple statement may also be denied as a whole: the denial of 'All Ss are P', for example, may be represented by 'Not (All Ss are P)' and it is important to note that the denial may not be equivalent to the original statement with 'not' inserted somewhere in it. Since this way of denying a statement may be regarded as an operation performed on a simple statement it is conveniently treated in this section along with compound statements.

The branch of modern logic known as *propositional calculus* is largely concerned with relations between (a) simple statements and their denials and compounds and between (b) compound statements and their denials and other compound statements. It is important to consider some of the everyday uses of words which are used in operating on, or compounding, simple statements. These uses underlie the particular conventions of various logical systems. The most important of the words in question are 'and', 'either ... or', 'not both', 'not' and 'if ... then'.

(ii) *Conjunction: 'and'*

Conjunction is a technical term of logic applied to the joining of simple statements by 'and'.

The simplest everyday use of 'and' is in the making of lists, where the order in which the items are listed is unimportant. If someone asks 'Who was at your party?' you may reply, 'John and Mary and Frank and Susan ...' where the order in which the names are listed makes no difference to the meaning of, or what is asserted by, the reply. The order may make some difference to what is suggested about your preferences or your judgments of importance but we are concerned here only with what is asserted and not with what is suggested.

The reply can be regarded as an abbreviation of a compound statement of the form '(John was at my party) and (Mary was at my party) and (Frank was at my party) and (Susan was at my party) ...' and still, of course, the order in which the component simple statements are put makes no difference to the meaning of the whole.

This is a very common use of 'and' which does not figure only in compound statements whose components give the same sort of information. For example, if someone asks 'What happened at your party?' you may reply '(There was dancing) and (John sang folk songs) and (Mary quarrelled with Susan) and ...' where, again, unless there is some intention of listing the occurrences in chronological order, the order is unimportant.

If we adopt the device of representing simple statements by small letters p, q, r ... we may represent a conjunction of two statements by

p and q

where it is understood that what is being asserted is that (p and q) as a whole is true. In the use I am at present considering, where the order of the components makes no difference to the meaning or the truth of the compound, we can say that

p and q

means the same as

> q and p.

The rule governing the truth of such compounds is clear and simple. The whole statement (p and q) is true if and only if p, considered separately, is true and q, considered separately, is true. This, of course, also determines the truth of (q and p). It follows that both (p and q) and (q and p) are false if any one of the following conditions holds

> (a) p is true and q is false;
> (b) p is false and q is true;
> (c) p is false and q is false.

These rules give what is called the *truth conditions* of (p and q) for this use of 'and'. I call this use, where the order of the components p and q is irrelevant to the meaning and truth of the whole, the *symmetrical* use of 'and'.

(It may be wondered why we are so concerned about truth conditions. There are two reasons. In the first place, they help us to differentiate between different meanings: if two statements are not true or false under the same conditions, then they must differ in meaning because, clearly, they must assert different things. In the second place, this will form the basis for one method of testing the validity of arguments, as we shall see in Chap. IV, Section 8.)

There are, however, other uses. There are, first of all, uses which superficially look very like this but which, on closer inspection, can be seen to be very different. Consider

> John and Mary were married yesterday.

This would not usually be taken to mean the same as

> (John was married yesterday) and (Mary was married yesterday)

since this latter statement would not be taken to mean that John was married to Mary, which is the normal use of the former statement. Of course, the two statements *could* be used to mean the same and would be so understood in certain contexts, for example, if John and Mary were known to be brother and sister, but this would be unusual.

This is not just a consequence of the 'and' appearing in the subject of the sentence since the same can be said about

> The vicar married John and Mary yesterday.

In these examples, we have the relatively rare situation in which it is difficult to regard 'and' as joining statements. In fact, what is said could perhaps be more clearly said by

> John was married to Mary yesterday

and

> The vicar married John to Mary yesterday.

Next consider the statement

> (John took off his shoes) and (dived into the river)

which, if we are being strict, means

> (John took off his shoes) and (he (John) dived into the river).

We may reverse the order of the component simple statements and still get an understandable, or meaningful, statement

> (John dived into the river) and (he took off his shoes)

since this still describes a possible state of affairs. However, it does not describe the same state of affairs as the original statement. The two statements would normally be taken to mean different things. We would normally regard the original statement as involving a temporal order in which the actions were done and the new statement as involving a *different* temporal order. This is due to the subject-matter of the simple statements and special relations which hold between their meanings and between the events they describe.

This would have been clearer if we had said, instead of the original statement,

> John took off his shoes *and then* he dived into the river.

In this particular use, 'and' may be replaced by 'and then' which clearly indicates the importance of temporal order and the order of the simple statements in the original compound one. It makes it quite clear that we cannot reverse the order of the simple statements and retain the original meaning. In this use, therefore

> p and q

does not mean the same as

> q and p.

Thus, (p and q) may be true and (q and p) false. In fact, if we are talking of one particular occasion (p and q) and (q and p) can never both be true unless we are using 'and' differently in the two statements.

We may, of course, explicitly indicate a temporal order, by using 'and then' or some other device, but we frequently do not. If no such device is used the compound (*p* and *q*) is true if and only if *p*, separately, is true, *q*, separately, is true and the order of *p* and *q* in the compound corresponds to the temporal order of the events described.

It follows that here we have four conditions under any one of which (*p* and *q*) is false, namely,

(a) *p* is true and *q* is false;
(b) *p* is false and *q* is true;
(c) *p* is false and *q* is false;
(d) *p* and *q* are not in the correct order.

I call this use of 'and' an *asymmetrical* use.

It must be noted that the replaceability of 'and' by 'and then' is not an infallible test for the importance of temporal order. We sometimes say, in answer to a request for a mere list, something like

John was at my party and Susan and then . . . Paul

where 'and then' is merely a means of playing for time while we try to remember who should go into the list. If it means anything, it means 'and also'.

The use of 'and' involving temporal order is not the only asymmetrical use. There is at least one other important use. Consider,

John dropped the baton and (John) lost the race

and

John lost the race and (John) dropped the baton.

Here, again, both compound statements are meaningful but they do not mean the same. In the first one there is, no doubt, a temporal order involved but there is also involved a causal relation. We would normally take it to mean that John lost the race *because* he dropped the baton. This implication of a causal relation is absent from the second statement and the suggestion of a temporal order is exceedingly weak or even absent. The causal element can be captured by replacing 'and' by 'and so', as we would be prepared to do in this use, so that the first statement becomes

John dropped the baton and so lost the race.

In this use

p and *q*

does not mean the same as

> q and p

so this is another asymmetrical use of 'and'.

The truth conditions here are even more complex than those of the first asymmetrical use. In the first place, of course, (p and q) and (q and p) may both be *true* but only if we understand 'and' differently in the two statements. As with the first asymmetrical use, certain words may be introduced to make explicit the assertion of a causal relation. If we do not make this explicit then (p and q), in this use, is true if and only if p, separately, is true and q, separately, is true and the order of p and q in the compound corresponds to the temporal order of the events described and also p is the cause of q. We have five conditions under any one of which (p and q) is false, namely,

(a) p is true and q is false;
(b) p is false and q is true;
(c) p is false and q is false;
(d) p and q are not in the correct order in the compound;
(e) p was not the cause of q even though p and q are both true and in the correct temporal order.

In logic, it is important for certain purposes to study the properties of 'and' in general or to have a conception of 'and' which is independent of any particular context or subject-matter. Any two statements may be joined by 'and' to make a meaningful compound, although in some cases its meaning may be only minimally different from that of the meanings of the two statements taken separately. If we represent a conjunction in the partially symbolized form (p and q) we leave open the possibility of ambiguities in the compound statement owing to the different uses of 'and' which I have explained. One of the aims of logic is to eliminate any possibility of ambiguity so we adopt the device of inventing a new symbol to replace 'and' in its most central use, for the purposes of logic. The most usual symbol is '·', so that we symbolize a conjunction of p and q by

> $p \cdot q$.

This new symbol must be precisely defined to avoid the ambiguities of 'and'. How is this to be done? If we consider the various uses of 'and' with which I have dealt we see that their truth conditions have what we might regard as a common element. The minimum condition (or the *necessary* condition) for the truth of (p and q), however 'and' is being used, is that p be true and q be true. This is not a *sufficient* condition for the truth of (p and q) if 'and' is used asymmetrically, when further conditions must also be satisfied, but it is nevertheless a minimum or necessary condition. Moreover, in any of these uses, there are three conditions any one of which is sufficient for the falsity of (p and q), namely,

(a) p is false and q is true;
(b) p is true and q is false;
(c) p is false and q is false.

These common conditions for all the uses considered are, in fact, just the truth conditions for the symmetrical use of 'and'. We use these as the truth conditions for '·'. That is, for the present logical purposes we standardize the symmetrical use of 'and', which also has some, but not all, the properties of other uses. Whatever we now discover about '·' should also be true of the symmetrical use of 'and' and may also tell us something, but not everything, about other uses. According to this convention

$$p \cdot q$$

is always equivalent to

$$q \cdot p.$$

This is called *the conjunctive function*. We have selected a particular use of 'and' from among several everyday uses and taken it as the standard use for the propositional calculus.

It follows that, in this system, using '·' alone we will not be able to represent all the properties of 'and' used asymmetrically although we will be able to deal with those properties it has in common with the symmetrical use. If we wished to represent asymmetrical uses fully we should have to introduce other symbols. This is unnecessary for some purposes, notably that of exploring the logic of mathematical reasoning, but it does present difficulties if we attempt to analyse certain everyday inferences in terms of this system.

It is convenient to set out the truth conditions defining constants such as '·' in *truth tables*. A truth table is a device for exhibiting the truth conditions for expressions and so forms a means of defining them but it may be used, as we shall see later, for testing the validity of arguments or, more strictly, argument-forms expressed in symbols.

An expression of the form ($p \cdot q$) is true if and only if p is true and q is true. In constructing a truth table for this we must set out all the possible combinations of truth values of p and q together with the resulting values of ($p \cdot q$). Thus, p may be true or false and q may, independently, be true or false. There are thus four possible combinations of values of p and q and they may be represented by

	p	q
(1)	T	T
(2)	T	F
(3)	F	T
(4)	F	F

It is advisable to write the values in this order whenever we are dealing with only two variables. In talking about truth tables it is convenient to refer to vertical *columns* and horizontal *rows*. Each row represents fixed values of p and q for that row, however far it is extended. Thus, in row (1) we consider that happens when p and q are both true, in row (3) we consider what happens when p is false and q is true, and so on.

Now we may extend the truth table to represent the consequent value of $(p \cdot q)$ for each row. This is simply an application to each possibility of the truth conditions for '·' already discussed. We obtain

	p	q	$p \cdot q$
(1)	T	T	T
(2)	T	F	F
(3)	F	T	F
(4)	F	F	F

The new column shows the value of the whole expression for each possible combination of values for p and q; or, as we may also put it, it shows under what conditions the relation indicated by '·' holds or fails to hold. Thus, row (1) tells us that when p and q are both true, $(p \cdot q)$ is also true; rows (2)–(4) tell us that under every other possible condition $(p \cdot q)$ is false.

The truth table may also be written more shortly, thus

p	$\cdot$	q
T	T	T
T	F	F
F	F	T
F	F	F

where the centre column contains the values for the whole expression under the conditions specified in the outer columns.

There is another convention which is sometimes useful. We may write '1' instead of 'T' and '0' instead of 'F' so that the last truth table becomes

p	$\cdot$	q
1	1	1
1	0	0
0	0	1
0	0	0

This form of truth table has the advantage that it can be represented by a number. Given the standard arrangement of 1s and 0s under p and q, the conjunctive truth table can be represented by 1,000. This is unique: no other truth table for a single connective has this value. This numerical representation has important applications in computer science.

(iii) *Disjunction and Alternation: 'either . . . or'*

Disjunction and *alternation* are technical terms for two different uses of 'either . . . or'. It is important to note that there is not complete uniformity in logicians' uses of these terms although there is agreement about the distinction they are intended to mark.[9]

The words 'either . . or', and the word 'or' can always be regarded as joining statements even if we do not always set these statements out in full. For example, if we say 'Tulips are either red or yellow or white' this can be expanded to 'Tulips are red or tulips are yellow or tulips are white'.

In everyday discourse we use 'either . . . or' in two ways which it is important to distinguish since they allow different inferences. Consider the following two situations.

(a) The hostess at a children's party is distributing presents. She says 'Johnny may have either the toy car or the toy train' and would normally mean, and be taken to mean that he may have one or the other but not both.

(b) Two schoolmasters are trying to decide why Johnny has such low marks. One says 'He is either stupid or lazy'. This allows for Johnny's being both; we would not say that the schoolmaster's statement was false if this were so. It would account for Johnny's low marks just as well as, or even better than, his being one but not the other.

The first use, where 'either p or q' means 'one of the other but not both', is called the *exclusive* use of 'either . . . or' because it excludes

9 See, e.g. L. S. Stebbing, *A Modern Introduction to Logic* (third edition, London, 1942) p. 70 and p. 186 fn.

the case in which both are true. A statement of the form 'p or q', where the 'or' is used exclusively, is, according to our terminology, an *alternative* statement. It is true under either of two conditions, namely,

(a) p is false and q is true;
(b) p is true and q is false;

and it is false under either of the two remaining conditions, namely,

(c) p is true and q is true;
(d) p is false and q is false.

The second use, where 'Either p or q' means 'one or the other or both', is called the *inclusive* use of 'either . . . or' because it allows one of the cases excluded by the exclusive use. A statement of the form 'p or q', where the 'or' is used inclusively, is, according to our terminology, a *disjunctive* statement. It is true under any one of three conditions, namely,

(a) p is false and q is true;
(b) p is true and q is false;
(c) p is true and q is true;

and it is false under only one condition, namely,

(d) p is false and q is false.

If we were to symbolize any statement containing 'or' simply by 'p or q' we should leave open the possibility of ambiguity since we should be ignoring any context or subject-matter which could make it clear whether the 'or' was being used exclusively or inclusively. Once again, we adopt a convention which removes the possible ambiguity. The expression 'p or q', unqualified, is always taken for logical purposes as disjunctive, that is, as using the inclusive 'or'. If we then wish to symbolize an alternative statement, using the exclusive 'or', we have to make it explicit that we are excluding the case in which both p and q are true, as well as the case in which both p and q are false. The simplest way of doing so is to write 'p or q and not both p and q' for the exclusive use.

Although it does not strictly matter what convention we adopt, this one is perhaps clearer than taking the exclusive use as basic and the inclusive use as derivative. If we used 'p or q', unqualified, to represent the exclusive use of 'or' then we should have to represent the inclusive use by '(p or q) or (p and q)'. However, according to that convention 'p or q' would mean 'one or the other but not both' and the expression for the inclusive use would have to be read 'one or the other but not both or both'. This has the awkward appearance of taking away with one hand what we are giving with the other.

Another reason is that since the truth conditions for the inclusive use are wider than the truth conditions for the exclusive use, the truth of an exclusive statement implies the truth of an inclusive statement, whereas the truth of an inclusive statement does not imply the truth of an exclusive statement. Thus we can regard ourselves as placing a limitation on the inclusive use to produce the exclusive use.

There is a special case of the exclusive use where the two component statements *cannot* both be true because they are mutually exclusive for logical reasons. An example is 'John was first or second in the race'. Here, because of what we know about ordinal numbers and about races, we know that 'John was first in the race' and 'John was second in the race' cannot both be true. This, however, is a comparatively rare kind of alternative statement and for this reason it will not do to base our distinction between disjunctions and alternations on such examples. Moreover, the character of this statement depends upon a property of the terms related by 'or' rather than on a property of 'or' itself.

We may make the distinction between the inclusive and exclusive uses of 'or' even clearer by using different conventional symbols, governed by different rules, for the two uses. For the inclusive use I shall use '$\vee$' and for the exclusive use '$\wedge$'. Thus the simplest disjunctive statements will be represented by

$$p \vee q$$

and the simplest alternative statements by

$$p \wedge q.$$

Truth tables may be constructed for these in the way outlined in the last section using the truth conditions stated above. We thus obtain

p	$\vee$	q		p	$\wedge$	q
T	T	T		T	F	T
T	T	F		T	T	F
F	T	T		F	T	T
F	F	F		F	F	F

We have seen, however, that the inclusive use may be taken as basic and the exclusive use defined in terms of it. This can be represented symbolically thus

$$(p \wedge q) =_{df} (p \vee q) \cdot \sim (p \cdot q).$$

100

I have here introduced two unfamiliar symbols. The symbol '$=_{df}$' is used in stating definitions and may be read 'is defined as' and the symbol '$\sim$' simply stands for the negation of the bracketed expression following it and may be read 'not' or, in conjunction with the contents of the bracket, 'not both p and q'. This means that we need not regard the truth table for '$p \wedge q$' as one of our basic truth tables since we can arrive at it by using the truth tables for '$\vee$', '$\cdot$' and '$\sim$'. The full significance of the defining expression will be discussed later.

The difference between the inclusive and exclusive uses of 'or' is important because they allow different inferences. Whether 'either ... or' is used inclusively or exclusively the following inference is valid.

> Either John is stupid or John is lazy
> John is not stupid
> ∴ John is lazy.

However, there is another form of inference which is valid on the exclusive use but invalid on the inclusive use. For example,

> Either John is stupid or John is lazy
> John is stupid
> ∴ John is not lazy.

It is clear that this is valid if 'either ... or' is exclusive because the exclusive use allows the truth of only one statement and not both. Because the inclusive use allows the truth of both, on that use the argument is invalid. This will be discussed further in a later section.

(iv) *Denial: 'not' and 'no'*

(a) *The Denial of Simple Statements*

We have seen that simple statements may be affirmative or negative. Of the four traditional types of statement two are affirmative (A and I) and two are negative (E and O). For example,

(1) All spies are neurotic   (A)
(2) Some spies are diplomats   (I)
(3) No spies are trustworthy   (E)
(4) Some spies are not male.   (O)

The first two are affirmative; the second two are negative, as indicated by 'no' and 'not', respectively. It is worth noting that it is not advisable to write universal negative statements in the form

> All spies are not trustworthy

since this would usually be taken to mean

> Some spies are trustworthy and some are not

rather than

> No spies are trustworthy.

Moreover, since it *might* be taken in either way it must be regarded as ambiguous.

Any simple statement, whether affirmative or negative, may be denied. We deny a statement when somebody makes it and we reply 'No' or 'That's not true' or 'That's false'. This is equivalent to inserting a negative particle somewhere in the sentence used, or to removing one, but considerable care must be exercised in doing this if we are to avoid saying more or less than was intended or justified by the denial. This is best approached by representing the denial of an original statement by the expression 'Not (. . .)' where the original statement appears inside the brackets.

For example, if we deny

> All spies are neurotic

this is the same as asserting

> Not (All spies are neurotic).

Now this denial will be true even if there is just one spy who is not neurotic since that is enough to make the original statement false. Putting this the other way round, given that it is true that

> Not (All spies are neurotic)

the most we can infer is

> Some spies are not neurotic.

We cannot infer, from the denial alone, that

> No spies are neurotic.

If we deny

> Some spies are diplomats

this is the same as asserting

> Not (Some spies are diplomats)

and this denial is true if, and only if, there is not even one spy who is a diplomat, so we can infer from its truth

> No spies are diplomats.

When we deny a negative statement we cannot always simply remove the negative particle from the original statement or simply replace 'No' by 'All'. For example, if we deny

> No spies are trustworthy

this is the same as asserting

> Not (no spies are trustworthy)

which is true even if only one spy is trustworthy. Thus the most we can infer from the truth of the denial is

> Some spies are trustworthy.

We cannot infer, from the denial alone

> All spies are trustworthy.

Finally, if we deny

> Some spies are not male

this is the same as asserting

> Not (some spies are not male),

and this is true if, and only if, not even one spy is not male. Thus, from its truth we can infer

> All spies are male.

We may tabulate these results in a more general way

The denial of $\left\{\begin{array}{l}\text{All } S\text{s are } P \\ \text{Some } S\text{s are } P \\ \text{No } S\text{s are } P \\ \text{Some } S\text{s are} \\ \quad \text{not } P\end{array}\right\}$ is equivalent to the assertion of $\left\{\begin{array}{l}\text{Some } S\text{s are} \\ \quad \text{not } P \\ \text{No } S\text{s are } P \\ \text{Some } S\text{s are } P \\ \text{All } S\text{s are } P\end{array}\right.$

The relationship between each statement in the left-hand column and the corresponding statement in the right-hand column is called *contradiction*. The pairs of statements are said to be *contradictories* and to be in *contradictory opposition*.

Of course, if I deny a statement of the form 'All Ss are P' I may do so on the grounds that, as I happen to know, 'No Ss are P'. I may, for example, deny 'All cats are reptiles' on the grounds that no cats are reptiles, because I know that cats are mammals and mammals are never reptiles. Similarly, I may deny 'No Ss P' on the grounds that, as I happen to know, 'All Ss are P'. However, it is of the greatest importance to recognize that there is a difference between the grounds on which a statement may be denied and what may be inferred from that denial alone. We may say that the most that may be inferred from the denial alone is the *minimum* grounds for the denial.

Given that I know that

> Not (all spies are male)

is true, and that I have no further relevant information, I am entitled to infer

> Some spies are not male

but *not*

> No spies are male.

The truth of this last statement would, of course, give me grounds for denying 'All spies are male'; the point I am making is that it gives more than adequate grounds for denying it. That is why I cannot infer it from the denial alone. The relationship between 'All spies are male' and 'No spies are male' is called *contrariety* and the two statements are said to be *contraries* and to be *in contrary opposition*.

The relations between statements of different types but having the same subject and predicate are traditionally summarized in a diagram called *the square of opposition* which is conveniently dealt with at this point because it largely concerns the denial of simple statements. In expounding this I shall neglect difficulties arising from the more modern distinction between universal and particular statements from the point of view of differences in existential import.

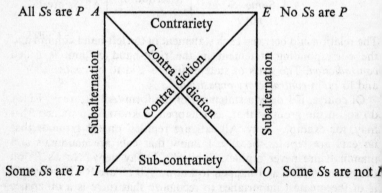

The corners of the square represent types of statement and the diagonals and sides represent relations between them, given that S and P stand respectively for the same two terms throughout. A more complex diagram is sometimes used[10] but this will suffice for our purpose.

I shall explain the four kinds of relation involved in turn.

Contradiction

As I have already explained if an A statement is false then the corresponding O statement is true, and if an O statement is false then the corresponding A statement is true. However, as the denial of either is *equivalent* to the other, we can also say that if either is true then the other must be false. Exactly parallel things can be said of E and I statements: if either is false then the other is true and if either is true then the other is false.

Contradiction is the 'strongest' type of opposition since only when two statements are contradictories can we say both that from the truth of either the falsity of the other follows and that from the falsity of either the truth of the other follows.

Contrariety

If two statements are in contrary opposition then from the falsity of one of them it does not follow that the other is true but from the truth of one of them it follows that the other is false. Contrariety exists only between A and E statements. We can thus say of two statements in contrary opposition that if either is true then the other must be false but if either is false then the other may be true or false, that is, it is *undetermined*.

These facts about contradiction and contrariety follow from the discussion of the denials of simple statements earlier in this section.

Subcontrariety

This is the relation that holds between I and O statements having the same subject and the same predicate. As would be expected from its name, it is analogous to, but not the same as, the relation of contrariety.

In view of the meaning given to 'some' (see Section b(i) of this Chapter), if it is true that

> Some spies are liars   (I)

it may or may not be true that

> Some spies are not liars   (O)

10 See, e.g. L. S. Stebbing, *Op. cit.*, p. 59.

although it is, of course, false that

> No spies are liars.

On the other hand, if it is false that

> Some spies are liars

it must be true that, at least,

> Some spies are not liars.

It will, of course, also be true that

> No spies are liars.

Similarly, if an *O* statement is true, the subcontrary *I* statement may be either true or false but if the *O* statement is false the corresponding *I* statement must be true.

Thus, of two subcontrary statements, if either is true then the other is undetermined whereas if either is false then the other must be true. The contrast with contrariety is this: in dealing with contraries we may infer from the truth of one of them but not from its falsity; in dealing with subcontraries we may infer from the falsity of one of them but not from its truth.

Subalternation

This relation holds between *A* and *I* statements and between *E* and *O* statements, having the same subject and the same predicate. The principles of it are involved in what has gone before.

If it is true that

> All spies are hypochondriacs   (*A*)

then it is also true that

> Some spies are hypochondriacs   (*I*)

but if the first statement is false then the truth or falsity of the second is left open, that is, it is undetermined. However, if it is false that

> Some spies are hypochondriacs

then it is also false that

> All spies are hypochondriacs,

but if the second statement is false then the truth or falsity of the first is left undetermined. If not even some spies are hypochondriacs then it cannot be that all are. Similarly, the truth of an *E* statement implies the truth of the corresponding *O* statement and the falsity of

106

the *O* statement implies the falsity of the *E* statement. The falsity of the *E* statement and the truth of the *O* statement both leave the corresponding statement undetermined. In this account, differences in existential import between universal and particular statements are still being ignored.

In general, if two statements are subalterns then from the truth of the universal one we can infer the truth of the particular one and from the falsity of the particular one we can infer the falsity of the universal one but no other inferences are possible.

The various implications which are implicit in the square of opposition may be summarized in the following table.

Given	Implied				
	A	*E*	*I*	*O*	
A true		F	T	F	
A false		U	U	T	T = true
E true	F		F	T	F = false
E false	U		T	U	U = undetermined
I true	U	F		U	
I false	F	T		T	
O true	F	U	U		
O false	T	F	T		

Although I have explained these relations in terms of the four traditional types of statement, it is possible to generalize their definitions so that they apply to any types of statement whatever. For any two statements *p* and *q* we define these relations in the following way.

Contradiction: *p* and *q* are contradictories if and only if the truth of either implies the falsity of the other and the falsity of either implies the truth of the other.

Contrariety: *p* and *q* are contraries if and only if the truth of either implies the falsity of the other and the falsity of either leaves the truth or falsity of the other undetermined.

Subcontrariety: *p* and *q* are subcontraries if and only if the falsity of either implies the truth of the other and the truth of either leaves the truth or falsity of the other undetermined.

Subalternation: *p* and *q* are subalterns if and only if the truth of *p* implies the truth of *q*, and the falsity of *q* implies the falsity of *p* while the falsity of *p* and the truth of *q* each leave the truth or falsity of the other undetermined.

It is most important not to confuse contradiction and contrariety since these clearly allow different inferences. Contradiction is the stronger relation in the sense that it involves more implications, and therefore allows more inferences, than contrariety. Although we can infer from the falsity of a statement something about a contradictory statement, we cannot infer anything about a contrary statement. If I know it to be false that John votes Labour, I cannot infer that it is true, or that it is false, that he votes Conservative, since there are other possibilities. The statements 'John votes Labour' and 'John votes Conservative' are contraries and not contradictories.

I have dealt with contradiction and contrariety as relations between statements but there are analogous or, perhaps better, derivative relations between terms. For example, if 'red' applies to a given uniform patch of colour then 'non-red' cannot apply and if 'non-red' applies then 'red' cannot. On the other hand, if 'red' does not apply then 'non-red' must and if 'non-red' does not then 'red' must. Thus the terms 'red' and 'non-red' are in a relation comparable to contradiction. This may be regarded as derivative from contradiction between statements since it depends upon the fact that

> *a* is red

and

> *a* is non-red

are contradictory statements, given that *a* stands for the same object in each case.

Now consider the relation between 'red' and 'blue'. If 'red' applies to a given uniform patch of colour then clearly 'blue' cannot apply and if 'blue' applies then 'red' cannot. However, if 'red' does not apply then it does not follow that 'blue' does apply or does not apply and if 'blue' does not apply, similarly, nothing follows about 'red' applying or not applying. The terms 'red' and 'blue' are in a relation comparable to contrariety. Once again, it may be regarded as derivative from contrariety between statements, since it depends upon the fact that

> *a* is red

and

> *a* is blue

are contrary statements, given that *a* stands for the same object in each case.

If we wish to refer to terms, or predicates, as contradictory or contrary we can make the distinction through the idea of a *universe of discourse.* If we are talking about the colours of things then the universe of discourse is the total context of coloured things, all those things to which colour-words apply. In general, the universe of discourse is the largest context essential to what we are talking about. We can say that contradictory terms exhaust the universe of discourse while contrary terms do not. 'Red' and 'non-red' exhaust the universe of discourse because every coloured thing is either red or non-red; 'red' and 'blue' do not exhaust the universe of discourse because not every coloured thing is either red or blue. This may be represented by the following diagrams. The rectangle represents the universe of discourse, coloured things.

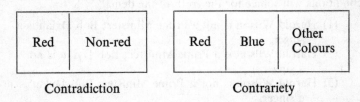

| Red | Non-red |

Contradiction

| Red | Blue | Other Colours |

Contrariety

The connection may be put in another way. Contraries, whether terms or statements, leave open further possibilities whereas contradictories do not. Between red and blue there are many other possibilities, such as yellow, green and purple, which, however, are all included in non-red. Between 'All *S*s are *P*' and 'No *S*s are *P*', there is the possibility 'Some *S*s are *P* and some *S*s are not *P*'.

We may now return to the notion of denial itself. As I have indicated, a widely used symbol for denial is '∼'. Given a simple statement *p* then its denial is represented by ∼*p*. These are, of course, contradictories. The truth table for the *contradictory function* is the simplest of all the truth tables and embodies the features of contradiction just discussed. It is

p	$\sim p$
T	F
F	T

(b) *The Denial of Compound Statements*

I have so far dealt only with the denial of simple statements; the denial of compound statements is rather more complex and will now be discussed under the appropriate headings.

(1) *Conjunctive Statements*

Consider the following statement

> Harold Wilson is a Prime Minister and Bob Dylan is a
> singer.

To deny this is to assert

> Not (Harold Wilson is a Prime Minister and Bob Dylan
> is a singer).

This denial is, of course, true under any condition under which the original statement is false. That is, any one of the following three conditions will suffice for the truth of the denial.

(1) Harold Wilson is not a Prime Minister; Bob Dylan is a
    singer.
(2) Harold Wilson is a Prime Minister; Bob Dylan is not
    a singer.
(3) Harold Wilson is not a Prime Minister; Bob Dylan is not
    a singer.

Thus, if we represent our denial by

$$\sim (p \cdot q)$$

then we can represent our three truth conditions for this by

(a) $\sim p \cdot q$
(b) $p \cdot \sim q$
(c) $\sim p \cdot \sim q$

Since any one of these conditions is sufficient to make the denial true we can say that they are alternatives, and join them by 'or' or '$\lor$'. Thus the truth conditions for

$$\sim (p \cdot q)$$

are the same as the truth conditions for

$$(\sim p \cdot q) \lor (p \cdot \sim q) \lor (\sim p \cdot \sim q).$$

We may now introduce the symbol '$\equiv$' which may be read 'is equivalent to' or 'has the same truth conditions as' or 'has a truth table with the same final column as'. I shall sometimes abbreviate this last expression to 'has the same truth table as'. Thus we may write

$$\sim (p \cdot q) \equiv \{(\sim p \cdot q) \lor (p \cdot \sim q) \lor (\sim p \cdot \sim q)\}.$$

It may be wondered whether it is correct to use '$\lor$' rather than '$\land$' to join these conditions since no more than one of them may be fulfilled in any given case. However, although '$\vee$' allows cases in which any pair of the conditions or all three are fulfilled, this is excluded by the nature of the conditions themselves. No error will arise from using '$\vee$' rather than '$\wedge$'. Indeed, we can build on the use of '$\vee$' to simplify the equivalence since the falsity of p or the falsity of q or the falsity of both suffices to make $\sim (p \cdot q)$ true we can write

$$\sim (p \cdot q) \equiv (\sim p \vee \sim q)$$

since the inclusive 'or' allows all three conditions.

The denial of conjunctions follows the same pattern, however many component statements there are. Thus

$$\sim (p \cdot q \cdot r) \equiv (\sim p \vee \sim q \vee \sim r),$$
$$\sim (p \cdot q \cdot r \cdot s) \equiv (\sim p \vee \sim q \vee \sim r \vee \sim s)$$

and so on. These equivalences amount to instructions for 'taking the negation sign inside the bracket' where what is already inside the bracket is a purely conjunctive statement.

As I have just pointed out, the symbol '$\equiv$', in the context of formal logic, may be read 'has the same truth conditions as'. Thus, two expressions correctly joined by it will have truth tables with the same final column. We may construct truth tables for $\sim (p \cdot q)$ and $(\sim p \vee \sim q)$ to show that '$\equiv$' is correctly used in the expression

$$\sim (p \cdot q) \equiv (\sim p \vee \sim q).$$

The truth table for $(p \cdot q)$ is, as we have seen,

p	$\cdot$	q
T	T	T
T	F	F
F	F	T
F	F	F
	*	

By applying to the centre column the truth table for '$\sim$' we see that the truth table for $\sim (p \cdot q)$ is

$\sim$	$(p$	$\cdot$	$q)$
F	T	T	T
T	T	F	F
T	F	F	T
T	F	F	F
*			

111

The values of '$\sim$' are the opposite of the values under '$\cdot$' and represent the values for the whole expression, marked by *.

The truth table for $(\sim p \lor \sim q)$ is derived from the truth tables for '$\sim$' and '$\lor$'. We simply use these tables mechanically in that order. For example, here '$\lor$' joins '$\sim p$' and '$\sim q$' so when in the first row we have 'F' under both we read off from the table for '$\lor$' on p. 100 the value 'F', from the last row, as the value for '$\lor$' here. We thus obtain the following truth table, where the order of the steps is indicated by the numbers under the columns.

$$
\begin{array}{ccccc}
\sim & p & \lor & \sim & q \\
F & T & F & F & T \\
F & T & T & T & F \\
T & F & T & F & T \\
T & F & T & T & F \\
(3) & (1) & (5) & (4) & (2) \\
 & & * & &
\end{array}
$$

Column (5) is arrived at simply by using the truth table for '$\lor$' on columns (3) and (4). We see that the final column in this table is identical with that of the truth table for $\sim (p \cdot q)$. The equivalence therefore holds.

(2) Disjunctive Statements

When we deny

        John is stupid or John is lazy

we are asserting

        Not (John is stupid or John is lazy)

and what this means depends on whether the 'or' in the original statement was inclusive or exclusive. In the inclusive use, as we saw, $(p \lor q)$ is true under any one of the following conditions

    (a) p is true and q is false;
    (b) p is false and q is true;
    (c) p is true and q is true.

The denial $\sim (p \lor q)$ will be true only when $(p \lor q)$ is false, that is, under the only other possible condition, namely,

    (d) p is false and q is false.

That is,

$$\sim (p \lor q) \equiv (\sim p \cdot \sim q).$$

112

This may be checked by constructing the truth tables for the two expressions said to be equivalent in the way already explained. They are

~	(p	∨	q)		~	p	·	~	q
F	T	T	T		F	T	F	F	T
F	T	T	F		F	T	F	T	F
F	F	T	T		T	F	F	F	T
T	F	F	F		T	F	T	T	F
*					*				

The final columns are identical so the equivalence holds.

(3) *Alternative Statements*

In the exclusive use of 'or', as we saw, an alternative statement such as $(p \wedge q)$ is true under one of the following two conditions, only.

(a) p is true and q is false;
(b) p is false and q is true.

The denial, $\sim (p \wedge q)$, will be true only when $(p \wedge q)$ is false, that is, under either of the remaining conditions

(c) p is true and q is true;
(d) p is false and q is false.

That is

$$\sim (p \wedge q) \equiv \{(p \cdot q) \vee (\sim p \cdot \sim q)\}.$$

This may be checked by constructing the truth tables for the two expressions said to be equivalent. They are

~	(p	∧	q)		(p	·	q)	∨	(~	p	·	~	q)
T	T	F	T		T	T	T	T	F	T	F	F	T
F	T	T	F		T	F	F	F	F	T	F	T	F
F	F	T	T		F	F	T	F	T	F	F	F	T
T	F	F	F		F	F	F	T	T	F	T	T	F
*						*							

The denial of compound statements may now be summarized.

(1) Conjunctive $\sim (p \cdot q) \equiv \{(\sim p \cdot q) \vee (p \cdot \sim q) \vee$
$(\sim p \cdot \sim q)\}$
$\equiv (\sim p \vee \sim q)$

(2) Disjunctive $\sim (p \vee q) \equiv (\sim p \cdot \sim q)$

(3) Alternative $\sim (p \wedge q) \equiv \{(p \cdot q) \vee (\sim p \cdot \sim q)\}.$

As I have explained, the symbols '·', '∼', '∨' and '∧' are to be regarded as standing for only certain features of the everyday uses of 'and', 'not' and 'or'. These symbols have standardized and partly conventional characteristics which are defined by their truth tables. Their advantage is that they allow the precision and clarity required in logic, but it must constantly be remembered that they cannot be simply identified with the everyday uses of 'and', 'not' and 'or'. They may in fact be regarded as analogous to these words and this limitation must be borne in mind whenever an expression in words is represented by an expression in the logical symbolism, or vice versa. Some important problems arise from the application of the conceptions of formal logic to the arguments of everyday discourse, as we shall see from time to time.

(v) *Implication:* '*if . . . then*'

An important class of compound statements comprises those formed by joining simple statements with 'If . . . then'. These may be called 'implication statements'. I shall begin by discussing some everyday uses of 'If . . . then' but it must be stressed that there is much more to be said on this subject than can be, or need be, said for our present purpose.

Consider such statements as

(1) If John is English then John is European;
(2) If it is raining then the pavements are wet;
(3) If this gas is heated then it will expand;

that is, statements of the general form

If *p* then *q*.

The first thing to note is that, for the present purpose, differences of tense may be ignored, although there are contexts in which such differences are of great importance. Here, we may regard these examples as all involving the timeless or omnitemporal present tense since we are not concerned about date or temporal succession but only about certain logical relations between the component statements which may be considered independently of date or temporal succession.

In general, the form 'If *p* then *q*' can be read 'If *p* is true then *q* is true', that is, as indicating that the truth of *q* follows from the truth of *p*. There are certain other relations, consequential on this, which we must consider.

Statements of this form are called *hypothetical* statements but it is worth mentioning that this is not necessarily the same as calling

114

them *hypotheses*. A hypothesis is a statement which is considered or entertained rather than asserted or accepted and it need not be put in the hypothetical form. If I say 'I believe that all bees sting' I can be regarded as entertaining the hypothesis 'All bees sting'. On the other hand, not every statement in hypothetical form is a hypothesis. In the course of a proof I may say 'If $2 + 2 = 4$ then $176 + 22 = 198$' without being in any way uncertain about either statement or the relation between them; I should be equally prepared to say '$2 + 2 = 4$; therefore $176 + 22 = 198$'.

In a statement of the form 'If p then q', the first statement, p, is called the *antecedent* or the *protasis*, and the second statement, q, is called the *consequent* or the *apodosis*. These terms are restricted to the components of hypothetical statements and should not be used of the components of other types of compound statements.

I shall consider particularly statement (1), 'If John is English then John is European', but what I say of this could also be said of statements (2) and (3). This statements tells us what is the case, or what follows, if John *is* English, namely, that John is (or must be) European; it does not tell us what is the case, or what follows, if John is not English. If John is not English several possibilities are left open; putting these as concisely as possible, he may or may not be European for all we are told in the given statement. Similarly, (1) does not give us any information about what follows if he *is* European; he may or may not be, for all we are told, English. Since more than one possibility is left open we have no right to infer to one rather than another of them.

However, the hypothetical does allow us to say what follows if John is not European. The force of the statement is that in order to be English he must be European; so if he is not European than he cannot be English. Thus, the hypothetical tells us, directly, something that follows from John's being English and, by implication, something that follows from his not being European but nothing about what follows from the other two possible state of affairs.

These points are conveniently illustrated by a diagrammatic representation invented by the Swiss mathematician Leonhard Euler (1707–83) and known as 'Euler's circles'. These are merely spatial analogies for logical conceptions and must not be taken too literally. They should not be used as a method of proof. We represent each term of a simple statement by a circle and the relations between the terms of the statement by the spatial relations between the circles, that is, by the inclusion, exclusion and overlapping of the circles. If our statement contains a proper name as one of its terms it is convenient to use a point for that term.

115

Now consider

If John is English then John is European.

We begin by representing the antecedent

John is English

by

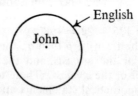

The point representing John must be put inside the circle because John is said to be English rather than not English. Now the truth of the hypothetical is independent of the fact that we happened to mention John rather than any other Englishman. The sense of the statement is

If anyone is English then he is European

or

If x is English then x is European

whatever person x stands for. The hypothetical statement may be regarded as depending on the statement

All Englishmen are Europeans.

Thus, we may draw the circle for Europeans as, at least, coincident with the circle for the English or as entirely containing it. John has already been placed within the 'English' circle, so we obtain

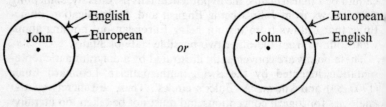

In drawing these diagrams we must rely only upon what we are told in the given statement; we must not take into consideration other things we happen to know about Englishmen and Europeans. The diagram is intended to represent only the given statement. It does not justify our accepting the first diagram rather than the second, since this would be to accept 'If John is European then John is English' as

116

well as 'If John is English then John is European'. This is not a consequence of accepting the second diagram. It is safer to accept the least assumption consistent with the original statement, that is, to accept the second diagram. This at least allows the possibility, left open by the original statement, that some Europeans are not English. We accept this *not* because we already know that it is true but because the original statement allows this as a possibility. The first diagram rules it out.

Consider now the diagram without the point representing John.

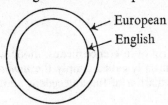

European

English

This allows us to illustrate the various inferences allowed by the original hypothetical statement.

(1) As I have already indicated, if John *is* English then his representative point goes inside the English circle, so it must also be inside the European circle, indicating that John *is* European.

(2) If John is *not* European then his point goes outside the European circle so it must also be outside the English circle; so he is not English.

(3) If John is European then we have not enough information to allow us to decide whether the point goes inside both circles or between them so no inference is possible.

(4) If John is not English then, similarly, we have not enough information to allow us to decide whether the point goes outside both circles or between them so, again, no inference is possible.

These considerations concern everyday uses of 'If ... then' and determine whether arguments involving compound statements of this sort are valid or invalid. Clearly there are two valid and two invalid forms. In the traditional logic the two valid forms were given names and set out in the following way.

(1) *Modus ponendo ponens*

This is the first of our valid forms. To continue our example, it is valid to argue

    If John is English then John is European
    John is English
∴ John is European.

The first premiss is a hypothetical statement, the second is a categorical statement and the conclusion is a categorical statement. The general form of this is

$$\text{If } p \text{ then } q$$
$$p$$
$$\therefore \quad q$$

or

$$p \text{ implies } q$$
$$p$$
$$\therefore q.$$

The name of this form of inference means 'mode which by affirming, affirms'. It is now usually called simply the *modus ponens* form. Its rule is that the affirmation of the antecedent allows the affirmation of the consequent.

(2) *Modus tollendo tollens*

This is the second of our valid forms. It is valid to argue

If John is English then John is European
John is not European
∴ John is not English.

The general form of this is

$$\text{If } p \text{ then } q$$
$$\text{Not } q$$
$$\therefore \text{ Not } p$$

or

$$p \text{ implies } q$$
$$\text{Not } q$$
$$\therefore \text{ Not } p.$$

The name of this form of inference means 'mode which by denying, denies'. It is now usually called simply the *modus tollens* form. Its rule is that the denial of the consequent allows the denial of the antecedent.

The other two forms which are apparently possible are invalid. We cannot validly argue

If John is English then John is European
John is European
∴ John is English.

This involves what is called *the fallacy of affirming the consequent*. Neither can we validly argue

> If John is English then John is European
> John is not English
> ∴ John is not European.

This involves what is called *the fallacy of denying the antecedent*.
In general, the two forms

> If *p* then *q*
> *q*
> ∴ *p*

and

> If *p* then *q*
> Not *p*
> ∴ Not *q*

are invalid.

Of the three hypothetical statements taken as examples on p. 114 I have used only the first because the points at issue are most clearly illustrated with its help. It is worth considering briefly the second example 'If it is raining then the streets are wet' in connection with the two invalid forms. They are

> If it is raining then the streets are wet
> The streets are wet
> ∴ It is raining

and

> If it is raining then the streets are wet
> It is not raining
> ∴ The streets are not wet.

Although these may look plausible at first sight and although we sometimes do say such things, they cannot stand as valid deductive arguments. This is because the streets might be wet from some other cause and these arguments treat rain as the only possible cause. This is not justified by the premisses. The hypothetical statement

> If it is raining then the streets are wet

is perfectly compatible with other hypothetical statements such as

> If the river is flooding then the streets are wet

and

> If a water main has burst then the streets are wet.

119

It follows that we cannot infer anything deductively from the statement 'The streets are wet' or from the denial of any of the antecedents.

This has an important consequence in the sciences. Suppose that we are considering a theory, T_1, which has certain deductive consequences C. We can then say 'If T_1 then C'. We attempt to confirm the theory by observation or experiment by showing that C squares with the facts. If it does we regard this as partially confirming our theory; if it does not we regard this as refuting our theory. The logic of refutation may then be said to be straightforwardly deductive, having the form of *modus tollens*, that is,

> If T_1 then C
> Not C
> $\therefore$ Not T_1.

However, the logic of confirmation presents difficulties, some of which arise from the fact that we appear to be arguing

> If T_1 then C
> C
> $\therefore$ T_1

which is, *by deductive standards*, invalid since it commits the fallacy of affirming the consequent. This has been, and still is, the subject of lively discussion.[11] Here I wish merely to make one point. What this logical consideration shows is that the confirming of a theory leaves open the possibility that, on the evidence we have, some different theory is equally acceptable. This follows from the compatibility of different hypothetical statements having the same statement as consequent. If we apply this to theories and their logical consequences, we see that

> If T_1 then C

is, as a whole, compatible with

> If T_2 then C

where T_1 and T_2 are themselves rival theories which have the same consequences C. This is the logical point underlying the well-known fact that there are great difficulties in deciding between rival theories covering the same observable phenomena.

There are certain connections that can be made between everyday uses of hypothetical statements and everyday uses of conjunctive and disjunctive statements. Consider the example

> If John will work then he will pass.

[11] See K. R. Popper, *The Logic of Scientific Discovery* (London, 1959).

Our discussion of hypotheticals has shown that this leaves open the possibility that John will pass without working. If we concentrate only on the inferences that can be made with the help of this statement we can say that, in this respect, it is translatable into the disjunctive statement

Either John will not work or he will pass,

where 'either . . . or' is used inclusively. We have seen (p. 101) that valid inferences using this form are

Either John will not work or he will pass
John will work
∴ John will pass

and

Either John will not work or he will pass
John will not pass
∴ John will not work

but that it is invalid to argue

Either John will not work or he will pass
John will not work
∴ John will not pass

or

Either John will not work or he will pass
John will pass
∴ John will work.

These parallel the inferences that can be made using the hypothetical. Thus it is valid to argue

If John will work then he will pass
John will work
∴ John will pass

and

If John will work then he will pass
John will not pass
∴ John will not work

but invalid to argue

If John will work then he will pass
John will not work
∴ John will not pass

121

or

> If John will work then he will pass
> John will pass
> ∴ John will work.

Apart from the first premiss in each case, the pairs of valid arguments are identical and so are the pairs of invalid arguments. If these are all the inferences possible using the respective first premisses we may say that, in respect of the inferences that can be drawn, the hypothetical statement

> If John will work then he will pass

is translatable into, or equivalent to, the disjunctive statement

> Either John will not work or he will pass.

In a similar way it can be shown that the conjunctive statement

> Not (John will work and John will not pass)

allows precisely the same inferences as the original hypothetical statement

> If John will work then he will pass,

so we can say that, in this respect, these two statements are also equivalent or translatable into one another.

In general we may say that, in respect of the inferences they allow, a statement of the form

> If p then q

or

> p implies q

is equivalent to a statement of the form

> Either not p or q

and to a statement of the form

> Not (p and not q).

It should be noted that I have said that statements in these forms are equivalent to or translatable into one another *in a certain respect*, namely, in respect of the inferences in which they can figure. This may not entitle us to say that the two statements in everyday discourse

> If John will work then he will pass

and

> Either John will not work or he will pass

have precisely the same meanings. This is in fact a matter over which there is some controversy and we need not reach a conclusion about it here. It is sufficient for our purpose that they will serve as premisses for the same inferences, at least those inferences of the type we are considering.[12]

We already have symbols analogous to 'either ... or', 'and' and 'not', each defined by its truth table. It is convenient to introduce a symbol analogous to 'implies' and to construct a truth table for it since it is one of the most important relations for inference. We use the symbol '$\supset$', which may be called the *hook* or *horseshoe*, and whose properties are relatable to 'if ... then' or 'implies' as these are used in everyday discourse. Thus we may write

$$p \supset q$$

to represent

> If p then q

or

> p implies q

as long as we are cautious in our interpretation of 'represent' here. I shall return to this matter shortly.

Problems immediately present themselves concerning the way in which we can construct a truth table for '$\supset$'. If we merely consider everyday uses of hypothetical statements it is not easy to see how truth values are to be assigned to such expressions as '$p \supset q$' on the basis solely of the truth values of p and q. We clearly require that the truth table for '$\supset$' be consistent with those for '$\cdot$', '$\vee$' and '$\sim$' and that the relations between them be clear. The equivalences which we have just discussed provide a means of deriving the truth table for '$\supset$' from truth tables which we have already accepted.

The equivalence between

> If p then q

and

> Either not p or q

---

[12] One reason for not taking the two statements to mean the same is that it is sensible to say

> Either London is not in England or Paris is in France

but not obviously sensible to say

> If London is in England then Paris is in France.

This is because 'if ... then' suggests a closer connection between the components than does 'either ... or'.

may now be represented in the symbolism of the propositional calculus by

$$(p \supset q) \equiv (\sim p \lor q)$$

and that between

>If p then q

and

>Not (p and not q)

may be represented by

$$(p \supset q) \equiv \sim (p \cdot \sim q).$$

We have now set up certain analogies between key words of every-day discourse and some symbols of the propositional calculus. It will be convenient to summarize these.

Everyday Discourse	Propositional Calculus
Not p	$\sim p$
p or q (inclusive)	$p \lor q$
p or q (exclusive)	$(p \lor q) \cdot \sim (p \cdot q)$
p and q	$p \cdot q$
Not-p or q	$\sim p \lor q$
Not (p and not q)	$\sim (p \cdot \sim q)$
If p then q	$p \supset q.$

We also have another analogy which I have been using without dwelling upon the fact that it is an analogy. I have been using the expressions 'has the same meaning as', 'is equivalent to' and '$\equiv$' more or less interchangeably without any defence of that procedure. It is reasonable to say when two statements have the same meaning in everyday discourse that they are equivalent to one another. For example, we may say that a statement of the form

>p or q

has the same meaning as, or is equivalent to, a statement of the form

>q or p.

However, I pointed out that we may regard a statement of the form

>If p then q

as being equivalent, *in a certain respect*, to a statement of the form

Either not *p* or *q*

although we might not want to say that they mean the same.

The symbol '$\equiv$' is strictly a symbol of the propositional calculus. It means, as I explained, 'has the same truth table as'. It is doubtful that we ever use 'means the same as' or 'is equivalent to' in that way in everyday discourse. The symbol '$\equiv$' may be regarded as analogous to these expressions and as resembling the restricted notion of 'is equivalent to in a certain respect' more closely than it resembles 'means the same as'.

Now we may return to our two equivalences

$$(p \supset q) \equiv (\sim p \vee q)$$

and

$$(p \supset q) \equiv \sim (p \cdot \sim q).$$

Given that '$\equiv$' may be interpreted as 'has the same truth table as', these equivalences give us two ways of building the truth table for '$\supset$', one using the truth tables for '$\sim$' and '$\vee$' and the other using the truth tables for '$\sim$' and '$\cdot$'. As we might expect, the two methods result in the same truth table.

The truth table for $(\sim p \vee q)$ is

$\sim$	p	$\vee$	q
F	T	T	T
F	T	F	F
T	F	T	T
T	F	T	F
(3)	(1)	(4)	(2)
		*	

Therefore, the truth table for $(p \supset q)$ is

p	$\supset$	q
T	T	T
T	F	F
F	T	T
F	T	F
	*	

We arrive at the first simply by mechanical construction from the basic truth tables for '$\sim$' and '$\vee$'; we arrive at the second simply by taking columns (1), (2) and (4) from the first.

Similarly, the truth table for $\sim (p \cdot \sim q)$ is

$\sim$	$(p$	$\cdot$	$\sim$	$q)$
T	T	F	F	T
F	T	T	T	F
T	F	F	F	T
T	F	F	T	F
(5)	(1)	(4)	(3)	(2)
*				

Therefore, the truth table for $(p \supset q)$ is

p	$\supset$	q
T	T	T
T	F	F
F	T	T
F	T	F
	*	

which is arrived at by using columns (1), (2) and (5) in the first truth table.

The relation indicated by '$\supset$' is called *material implication* to distinguish it from other types of implication and to make it clear that '$\supset$' is a technical term of logic. It depends only upon the truth values of the statements which it joins. It is a relation which holds between *any* two statements under any one of the following conditions.

(1) Both statements are true.
(2) The first statement is false and the second true.
(3) Both statements are false.

These conditions are simply 'read-off' from the truth table.

An examination of these conditions brings to light some features which, at first sight, may seem puzzling. It follows from the definition of '$\supset$' that any two true statements materially imply one another and that any false statement materially implies any statement, whether true or false. The one condition in which material implication does not hold is that the first statement is true and the second false.

It is instructive to compare these characteristics of material implication with the characteristics of ordinary implication represented by 'If ... then'. We should not, in the ordinary way, regard it as sensible to say 'If p then q' or 'p implies q' merely because p and q are both true statements; even less would we regard it as sensible

126

to say these things just because p is false, whether q is true or not. On the other hand, we do, in the ordinary way, regard it as correct to say that p does not imply q, on the ground that p is true and q false. This is where the analogy between material implication and other sorts of implication mainly lies. We can say that the failure of material implication to hold between p and q is a *sufficient* condition for saying that the relation expressed by 'If p then q' does not hold. We cannot say, however, that the fact that p materially implies q is a sufficient condition for the holding of the relation expressed by 'If p then q'.

For example, the hypothetical statement

> If he will work then he will pass

would be taken to be false if it were true that he had worked and failed to pass. On the other hand, the statement

> If it is raining then London is in England

would not be taken to be true just because the components happen both to be true or just because the first one happened to be false. We may say that the truth of

$$p \supset q$$

is a necessary condition for the truth of

> If p then q

but not a sufficient condition. It follows that the falsity of

$$p \supset q$$

is a sufficient condition for the falsity of

> If p then q

but not a necessary condition.

These considerations show that great care must be exercised in using the symbols of the propositional calculus to represent everyday hypothetical statements; we must be quite clear what we are doing if we use them in this way. We must not regard all that can be said about '$p \supset q$' as being all that can be said about 'If p then q'. Suppose that we attempt to apply the truth conditions of the former to the latter. We have the following possibilities.

(1) Since $(p \supset q)$ is true whenever p and q are both true, we can write

> Paris is in France $\supset$ Ireland is a republic

127

because both statements happen to be true. If we now simply replace '⊃' by 'If . . . then' we obtain

If Paris is in France then Ireland is a republic

which is not the sort of thing we should normally regard it as sensible to say. This is because there is not the sort of connection between the two components which we usually expect when 'If . . . then' is used.

(2) Since $(p \supset q)$ is true whenever p is false and q is true we can write

President Johnson is the Pope ⊃ Ireland is a republic

because the first statement is false and the second true. But it would be odd, indeed, to write

If President Johnson is the Pope then Ireland is a republic.

(3) Since $(p \supset q)$ is true whenever p is false and q is false we can write

President Johnson is the Pope ⊃ $2 + 2 = 5$

since both statements are false.

Again, it would be very odd to regard

If President Johnson is the Pope then $2 + 2 = 5$

as a literally true statement.

In the ordinary way, these hypothetical statements would not be thought to be proper things to say. We cannot, therefore, regard the expressions using material implication as exactly translatable into ordinary hypothetical statements or the symbol '⊃' as exactly representing the 'If . . . then' or the 'implies' of everyday discourse. Statements to the effect that a false statement implies any statement, whether true or false, and that a true statement is implied by any statement, whether true or false, have been regarded as embodying a paradox, sometimes called *a paradox of material implication*.[13] This, however, is highly misleading and depends upon the attempted identification of 'materially implies' with the more usual sense of 'implies' expressed by 'If . . . then'. There is nothing paradoxical about these statements if we understand the word 'implies' in them to mean 'materially implies' and recognize that this is defined solely by the truth table for '⊃' and so is not the same concept as that expressed by 'If . . . then'. The allegedly paradoxical statements are false if we do not understand them in this way and unparadoxical if we do.

---

[13] There are other paradoxes of material implication. One device that is alleged to eliminate them is that of always reading $(p \supset q)$ as $(\sim p \lor q)$.

Thus, material implication is a less complex relation than the implication expressed by 'If ... then' and is not identical with it. This is not to say that there is no connection between the two concepts. The connection has already been explained but another way of putting it is to say that material implication is the 'weakest' form of implication and can be regarded as giving minimum conditions for any implication. When we use statements of the form 'If p then q' in everyday discourse we require the satisfaction of certain conditions over and above the exclusion of the joint truth of p and falsity of q. One of these conditions is that there be a connection of meaning between p and q. What makes the statement

If London is in England then $2 + 2 = 4$

unacceptable is that we do not see the sort of connection between the two components that we are led to expect by the use of 'If ... then'. On the other hand, the statement

If John works hard then he will pass

is acceptable because we think that studying has some relevance to the passing of examinations.

We are not inclined to say that the statement

If London is in England then $2 + 2 = 4$

is true but neither are we inclined to say that it is false; we are more inclined to say that it is just inappropriate. Although the two components are true, they have been linked in an inappropriate way because some of the conditions for using this particular linkage are not satisfied. It might be perfectly appropriate to link them, for certain purposes, in some other way, for example, by 'and'.

The traditional names, 'antecedent' and 'consequent' for p and q, respectively, in 'If p then q' indicate a general condition for the appropriateness of the hypothetical form. It is not enough for p and q to be true; the truth of q must be a *consequence* of the truth of p. The consequence may be logical, or causal, or of some other sort. This is connected with an important difference between 'If p then q' and '$p \supset q$'. As Bertrand Russell has pointed out[14] 'p implies q' is useful for deduction only if it can be known to be true independently of the truth values of p and q. One cannot deduce q from p using the implication relation if in order to know that 'p implies q' we first have to know whether q is true or false. Because of the way in which '$p \supset q$' is defined, we can never know it to hold independently of the

[14] See P. A. Schilpp, *The Philosophy of Bertrand Russell* (Evanston, Illinois, 1946), p. 696.

truth values of p and q. This is a characteristic which it does not share with 'If p then q'.

We may regard the idea of material implication as being derived from ordinary implication by abstracting from ordinary implication just some of its features and using these in defining material implication. We have seen that an essential feature of implication is that it does not hold when we have 'p implies q' and p is true but q false; if we regard this as the only condition under which it does not hold then we have a *truth-functional* interpretation of implication, which is what we call 'material implication'. This allows us to define material implication by a truth table, which seems a plausible way of defining the other logical constants such as '$\sim$', '$\cdot$' and '$\vee$'. If it is necessary to distinguish various kinds of implication it is hoped that we can show that material implication involves only conditions common to all of them and so is the weakest relation 'contained in' the other sorts of implication. If we add further conditions we move away from material implication towards stronger relations.

I have been using the expression 'ordinary implication' freely without ever defining it with the precision with which material implication is defined. One difficulty which faces logicians is that it is very difficult to define ordinary implication, or the various forms of it if there is more than one, in a precise enough way to enable it to figure in a formal system.[15] I have contented myself with the assertion that there is a stronger form of implication represented by 'If . . . then' and pointing to some of the reasons for saying this. In the present context there is no need to do more than this.

It is convenient to deal now with the symbol '$\equiv$' in a rather more formal way than I have so far used. The relation represented by the symbol is usually called *material equivalence* and may be derived from material implication.

When we define a term, in mathematics or the sciences, we frequently use the expression 'if and only if'. For example, in Euclidean geometry we may define 'triangle' thus

> A figure is a triangle *if and only if* it is plane and bounded by three straight lines

which may be represented by

> p if and only if q.

---

[15] See C. I. Lewis, *A Survey of Symbolic Logic* (Berkeley, Calif., 1918, reprinted N.Y., 1960).

The expression 'if and only if' can be regarded as a shorthand expression indicating that the whole statement can be divided into two different hypothetical statements, namely,

(1) If a figure is a triangle then it is plane and bounded by three straight lines

and

(2) If a figure is plane and bounded by three straight lines then it is a triangle.

These may be represented by

(1) If p then q (i.e. p only if q)

and

(2) If q then p (i.e. p, if q).

Thus the expression

p if and only if q

may be regarded as equivalent to the conjunction of these two expressions, that is,

If p then q and if q then p.

The analogy for this in the symbolism of the propositional calculus is

$$(p \supset q) \cdot (q \supset p)$$

which is sometimes called the *bi-conditional*. It may be abbreviated to $(p \equiv q)$ and read 'p is materially equivalent to q'. When '$\equiv$' joins two simple statements we may regard it as meaning that they have the same truth values; when it joins compound statements we may regard it, as we earlier did, as meaning that they have the same truth tables.

Using the truth tables for '$\cdot$' and '$\supset$' we may construct the truth table for $(p \equiv q)$ by taking $(p \supset q) \cdot (q \supset p)$ as its definition and constructing the truth table for that. We obtain

p	q	$(p \supset q)$	$\cdot$	$(q \supset p)$
T	T	T	T	T
T	F	F	F	T
F	T	T	F	F
F	F	T	T	T
(1)	(2)	(3)	(5)	(4)
			*	

131

Thus the truth table for $(p \equiv q)$ is

p	$\equiv$	q
T	T	T
T	F	F
F	F	T
F	T	F
	*	

which we obtain by using columns (1), (2) and (5) from the first truth table. We see that the relation of material equivalence holds when the truth values for p and q are the same but not otherwise.

Once again, we have an analogy between the symbol '$\equiv$' and certain expressions of everyday discourse, such as 'if and only if' and 'means the same as'. We may say that

> 'x is a bachelor' means the same as 'x is unmarried'

or

> x is a bachelor if and only if x is unmarried.

The analogy for these in the propositional calculus is

> x is a bachelor $\equiv$ x is unmarried.

However, we do not have exact translatability since the statement

> London is in England $\equiv$ Paris is in France

is true, simply because both components are true, but it does not follow that

> 'London is in England' means the same as 'Paris is in France'.

As a consequence of the derivation of material equivalence from material implication, to say that two expressions are materially equivalent is to say something only about their truth values and is not to say anything about their meaning.

It might be wondered what is the point or value of inventing these weak and trivial-sounding relations and how they can help us to deal with the arguments we normally use in the various fields in which we use deductive inferences. One of the first concerns of those who developed the various calculi of formal logic and truth-functional relations was with the logic of mathematics. One of their aims was to exhibit the logical foundations of mathematics, to show that mathematical truths could be derived from purely logical principles.[16]

---

[16] For example, A. N. Whitehead and Bertrand Russell in *Principia Mathematica* (Cambridge, 1910–13).

In fact, a great deal can be done in the analysis of mathematical arguments using the sorts of relations which I have been discussing. If the attempt to derive pure mathematics from logic has not been entirely successful it has nevertheless revealed a great deal about its structure and procedures.

How much can be done with this kind of logic in other directions is a controversial matter. However, its techniques can assist us, to some extent, in testing the validity of deductive arguments in any field. This is so because the truth-functional relations can be regarded as involving the necessary conditions for relations used in any everyday deductive inference. Suppose that we have a complex deductive inference which can be represented as having the form

$$\{(p \text{ and } q) \text{ or } (r \text{ and } s)\} \text{ and } (p \text{ and } r), \text{ therefore } (q \text{ or } s).$$

It would be difficult to decide simply by inspection of the original argument, or even of this skeletal representation of it, whether it was valid or not. However, we may represent it by

$$[\{(p \cdot q) \lor (r \cdot s)\} \cdot (p \cdot r)] \supset (q \lor s)$$

and then test it by constructing its truth table, using the basic truth tables for the connectives, or by using a method based upon its truth table. The method of doing this will be explained in Chap. IV, Section 8. If, by this means, we find that the relation '$\supset$' does not hold then we can conclude that the original argument was invalid, unless there is some other way of expressing it symbolically which gives a different result. This is not quite uncontroversial but is fairly generally accepted and it would seem to follow from the account I have given.

Some logicians, disturbed by the weakness of the truth-functional relations here outlined and the difficulty of using them to formalize, exactly, many of the arguments of everyday discourse, have attempted to develop formal systems using stronger relations, especially in place of material implication. This has led to the development of systems of *modal logic*, systems in which such ideas as possibility and necessity can be represented. The success of such a project would enable us to make sense, in an abstract calculus, of the relation 'follows necessarily from', which we cannot do if material implication is the only kind of implication at our disposal.[17]

One notion that has been put up against this is that of *strict implication*. We have seen that *p* materially implies *q* if it happens not

[17] See A. N. Prior, *Formal Logic* (2nd Edn., Oxford, 1962); G. H. von Wright, *An Essay in Modal Logic* (Amsterdam, 1951).

to be the case that p is true and q false; C. I. Lewis held that p strictly implies q only if it *could not* be the case that p is true and q false.[18] Unfortunately this idea presents problems of its own but logicians have for long been actively engaged in the attempt to construct satisfactory systems of modal logic.

A logic which interprets relations only in terms of the truth values of the related statements is called an *extensional* logic; a logic which takes into account the meanings of the related statements in explaining relations is called an *intensional* logic. Systems of modal logic are intensional. A detailed discussion of intensional logic cannot be undertaken here but reference may be made to some of the works mentioned.

[18] C. I. Lewis and C. H. Langford, *Symbolic Logic* (2nd Edition, New York, 1951); C. I. Lewis, *A Survey of Symbolic Logic* (Berkeley, Calif., 1918, N. Y., 1960). W. and M. Kneale, *The Development of Logic* (Oxford, 1962).

CHAPTER IV

Some Principles of Inference

1. INTRODUCTORY

I have from time to time mentioned various inferences we make and have related them to the everyday uses of certain key words. In the course of this I have touched on some concepts of logic which are used in the analysis of inference. I now wish to discuss, rather more systematically, various kinds of inferences as they have been classified and analysed in both the traditional logic and modern logic. In Chap. II, I made the broad distinction between conclusive and non-conclusive inferences and I shall now be considering distinctions which can be made within the group of conclusive, or deductive, inferences.

Deductive inferences were traditionally divided into *immediate inferences* and *mediate inferences*. Immediate inferences are those in which a conclusion is drawn from just one premiss whereas mediate inferences are those in which a conclusion is drawn from two or more premisses. The syllogism and the hypothetical arguments, of which we have considered some examples, are both forms of mediate inferences. I shall discuss immediate and mediate inferences in turn, beginning with traditional treatments of each and then proceeding to consider more modern developments in these treatments.

2. IMMEDIATE INFERENCES

According to the description just given, the square of opposition, discussed in the previous chapter, can be regarded as illustrating relationships which underlie some immediate inferences. We saw that if we are given as true a statement of the form

> All Ss are P

we can infer from it the falsity of a statement of the form

> Some Ss are not P.

The square of opposition indicates that the relation underlying this inference is that of contradiction. In discussing the square we took it

135

as obvious that some inferences from single statements could just be seen to be acceptable while others could just be seen not to be, on the basis of the meanings of certain of the words involved.

The aim of the traditional theory of immediate inferences was to specify a set of operations by which it would be possible to move from any single statement in the appropriate form to every statement which could be inferred from it alone. The starting point was that certain inferences are intuitively obvious, which means that understanding the language involves seeing that the inferences can be made. The theory was an attempt to build up all the possible inferences from as few basic inferences as possible. Using the four traditional types of statement, four kinds of immediate inferences were distinguished, two of them basic and two derived from these.

At first sight, these inferences may seem trivial and of little practical interest. It is worth remembering, however, that one of the aims of logic is to exhibit the principles underlying our everyday inferences and that this is a purely theoretical aim which is not relevantly criticized on grounds of practical utility or the lack of it. Moreover, involved in this project is the aim of building up the most complex inferences from, if possible, absolutely clear and uncontroversial beginnings; it is an unfortunate truth that nothing is absolutely clear and uncontroversial that is not utterly trivial. The more fundamental notions of logic are therefore very likely to appear trivial to the uninitiated. We may comfort ourselves with the reflection that our achievement will be the more impressive if we are able to deal with all the complexities of actual inferences using only trivial concepts and entirely uncontroversial steps.

Apart from this, a study of the traditional immediate inferences is valuable because it reveals some important logical problems and, historically, it helped to lead to the introduction of some new logical conceptions.

One way of dealing with the traditional immediate and mediate inferences is through the idea of the distribution of terms, a comparatively late introduction into traditional logic. It is first necessary to extend the application of this idea, which was mentioned in Chap. III, Section b(i). There the idea was applied only to the subjects of the traditional types of statement, but just as the subject term may be distributed, as in universal statements, or undistributed, as in particular statements, so the predicate term may be distributed or undistributed.

The least controversial way of introducing the distribution of terms is by means of a mere formal convention which it is convenient to accept, even though it is difficult to state, in an unexceptionable way, the *rationale* for this convention. Its acceptance enables us to analyse those arguments which are properly regarded as traditional syllogisms so that we can distinguish valid from invalid ones. The convention is: the subject-terms of universal statements and the predicate-terms of negative statements are distributed, while the subject-terms of particular statements and the predicate-terms of affirmative statements are undistributed. We may summarize this in the following way.

Type of Statement	Subject	Predicate	Symbolized
A	distributed	undistributed	$\overset{D}{S}\ a\ \overset{U}{P}$
E	distributed	distributed	$\overset{D}{S}\ e\ \overset{D}{P}$
I	undistributed	undistributed	$\overset{U}{S}\ i\ \overset{U}{P}$
O	undistributed	distributed	$\overset{U}{S}\ o\ \overset{D}{P}$

Thus each type of statement is unique in respect of distribution and this can form a basis for making the distinction into types. Mediaeval logicians had a mnemonic for these distributions, namely, the word $ASEBINOP$. The vowels correspond to the types of statement and the consonants indicate which terms are distributed so it is to be read: A statements have their *s*ubjects distributed, E statements have *b*oth subjects and predicate distributed, I statements have *n*either distributed and O statements have their *p*redicates distributed.

I shall attempt to give some account of the reasons underlying the notion of distribution and what it means but it must be remembered that this is a controversial matter and it is difficult to give more than a rough idea of what is involved.[1]

I shall say that a term in a traditional subject-predicate statement is *distributed* when that statement is about all those things to which the term could be applied, otherwise it is *undistributed*.

Thus 'All cats are mammals' is about every animal that can properly be called a cat so the term 'cats' is distributed. This is what is indicated by the word 'all'. Similarly, in 'No cats are reptiles' the term 'cats' is distributed, which is part of what is indicated by the word 'no'.

On the other hand, 'Some cats are white' and 'Some cats are not

---

[1] For an account of some of the difficulties see P. T. Geach, *Reference and Generality* (Ithaca, N.Y., 1962) Chap. I, and a review by Leonard Linsky in *Mind*, Vol. 73, 1964, p. 575.

black' are not about every animal that could properly be called a cat, so the term 'cats' is undistributed in both. The word 'some' indicates this.

It is not so easy to see immediately which of the predicates of the four types of statement are distributed and which are undistributed.

It is perhaps easiest to start with universal negative (*E*) statements. The statement 'No cats are reptiles' asserts that all the animals properly called cats are distinct from all animals properly called reptiles. It is therefore about every animal which could be properly called a reptile. The term 'reptiles' is distributed.

The universal affirmative (*A*) statement 'All cats are mammals' asserts that all the animals properly called cats are also properly called mammals but not that they are the only animals properly so called. This is easy to see because we happen to know that there are other mammals besides cats but this information is not necessary in making the point at issue. What is necessary is to see that in saying 'All *S*s are *P*' we are not saying anything about everything which may be properly called a *P*; the statement leaves open the question whether all *P*s are also *S*s. Thus the statement itself is not about everything which could properly be called a *P*. Therefore, *P* in this general form and 'mammals' in our example are undistributed.

The particular affirmative (*I*) statement 'Some cats are white' is similar in this respect. It asserts that some of the animals properly called cats are also properly called white without implying that they are the only things properly called white or white animals. It is not about everything which could properly be called white and so the term 'white (things, animals)' is undistributed.

Particular negative (*O*) statements are rather more difficult to deal with. In 'Some cats are not black' at least those cats which the statement is about are said to be distinct from all those things properly called black. Thus the statement is about all those things and the term 'black (things, animals)' is distributed. The difference between the particular negative statement and the particular affirmative statement may be emphasized by pointing out that

> Some cats are not black

may be regarded as meaning

> Some cats are not *any* black things

which indicates that the statement is about *every* black thing. On the other hand, we cannot in this way introduce 'any' into the particular affirmative statement. 'Some cats are any white things' does not make sense and 'Some cats are all white things' is just false if understood

138

in the requisite way to make the predicate a distributed term. We may, however, say that the particular affirmative statement means 'Some cats are some of the white things', if we do not object to a little artificiality.

According to one general account of deductive inference the notion of distribution is a central one. If we say that the one thing deductive inference cannot do is to 'go beyond the evidence' we may interpret this as saying that no term which is undistributed in the premisses may be distributed in the conclusion. If our information concerns only some cats we cannot deductively infer a conclusion about all cats. It must be noted, however, that this interpretation can be applied only to inferences containing statements whose terms can sensibly be said to be either distributed or undistributed. It can be applied to traditional syllogisms and to the traditional immediate inferences but there are many other deductive inferences to which it cannot be applied. For example, the inferences

$$4 > 3$$
$$3 > 2$$
$$\therefore\ 4 > 2$$

and

Gold is more valuable than silver
Silver is more valuable than iron
∴ Gold is more valuable than iron

are valid deductive inferences but it makes little sense even to ask whether their terms are distributed or undistributed.

Sometimes the traditional doctrine of distribution is criticized by showing that there are statements, which figure in inferences, about which it is difficult to say whether the terms are distributed or undistributed using the tests I have outlined. It is important in considering such criticisms to be prepared to reply that the inferences in question are not syllogisms. It is a serious mistake to suppose that the analysis of inferences in syllogistic terms is a more powerful or a more generally applicable tool than it in fact is.

In discussing both the immediate inferences and the traditional syllogism I propose to accept the principle already enunciated that if a term is undistributed in the premiss or premisses then it may not be distributed in the conclusion. The basic immediate inferences of traditional logic are called

(a) conversion
(b) obversion

139

and from these may be derived two others called

    (c) contraposition
    (d) inversion.

I shall discuss these in that order.

a. CONVERSION

We *convert* a statement in which the terms are arranged in the order *S–P* when we derive from it a statement in which the terms are arranged in the order *P–S*. The derived statement need not have exactly the same meaning as the original statement but it must follow logically from it alone. The possible conversions are determined by the distribution of the terms in the original statement and our principle of deductive inference.

Consider, first, universal negative (*E*) statements. Since any statement of the form 'No *S*s are *P*' has both its subject and its predicate distributed and since it asserts that they apply to two distinct kinds of things, we may infer from it 'No *P*s are *S*', which is called its converse. If the things properly called *S* totally exclude the things properly called *P* then the things properly called *P* must exclude the things properly called *S*. Total exclusion is a symmetrical relationship. Thus, from

        No cats are reptiles

it follows that

        No reptiles are cats.

We may use Euler's circles to illustrate this. 'No *S*s are *P*' will be represented by two circles which do not overlap, thus,

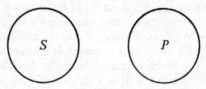

This clearly also represents a statement of the form 'No *P*s are *S*'. These two forms are equivalent since either can be inferred from the other.

Next, consider particular affirmative (*I*) statements. In statements of the form 'Some *S*s are *P*' both terms are undistributed and since they may be taken to assert that some things called *S* are properly called *P* it follows that some things called *P* can also be called *S*. The original statement gives no information about all things called *P* in relation to *S*, since *P* is undistributed.

For example, from

> Some cats are white

it follows that

> Some white animals are cats.

If we illustrate this using Euler's circles, 'Some Ss are P' will be represented either by two circles overlapping

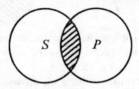

where the shaded portion indicates the Ss and Ps in question or by one circle inside the other or coinciding with the other, thus,

However, since the original statement gives no grounds for choosing one of these rather than the others we are not entitled to make any inference which depends on one but is inconsistent with the others. We can allow only inferences which are consistent with all four diagrams. Thus the only inference which can be made with certainty is to 'Some Ps are S'.

These two conversions, of 'No Ss are P' and 'Some Ss are P', in which nothing is changed except the order of S and P in the statements, are called *simple conversions*.

The conversion of universal affirmative (A) statements is slightly more complex. Statements of the form 'All Ss are P' have S distributed and P undistributed and assert that all the things called S are properly called P. However, they leave open the question whether all the things called P can also be called S. The most that we can infer with certainty is that 'Some Ps are S'. Thus from

> All cats are mammals

we can infer

> Some mammals are cats

but *not*

> All mammals are cats.

141

This would be to distribute 'mammals' which was undistributed in the premiss. Using Euler's circles, a statement of the form 'All Ss are P' can be represented by either of two diagrams

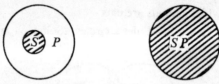

We have no grounds for choosing between them so the only statement which we can infer, because it is the only statement consistent with both diagrams, is 'Some Ps are S'.

This kind of conversion in which we move from a universal to a particular statement is called *conversion by limitation* or *conversion per accidens*.

Particular negative (*O*) statements have no converses. A statement of the form 'Some Ss are not P' has its subject undistributed and its predicate distributed and asserts that some Ss are distinct from every P but leaves open the questions whether all are distinct from every P and whether every or any P is an S. We cannot, therefore, infer from it any statement with S and P in the reverse order. The Euler's circle diagrams which can represent 'Some Ss are not P' are

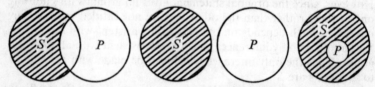

and the original statement gives no grounds for choosing between them. There is no statement of traditional form with the terms in the order *P–S* which is consistent with all three diagrams. So a converse is unobtainable.

We may summarize the results of this discussion in the following table.

	Original Statement					Converse			
		D	U				U	U	
A	All Ss are P	S a P	⟶		Some Ps are S		P i S		*I*
		D	D				D	D	
E	No Ss are P	S e P	⟷		No Ps are S		P e S		*E*
		U	U				U	U	
I	Some Ss are P	S i P	⟷		Some Ps are S		P i S		*I*
		U	D						
O	Some Ss are not P	S o P			None				

The double-headed arrows indicate that we can infer in both directions, that is, that we have simple conversion; the single-headed arrow indicates that we can infer in only one direction, that is, that we have conversion *per accidens*. It should be noted that in no case is a term distributed in the conclusion and undistributed in the premiss.

b. OBVERSION

We *obvert* a statement of the general form *S–P* when we derive from it a statement of the form *S–non-P*. The derived statement is logically equivalent to, and means the same as, the original statement. It is clear that other changes have to be made in the original statements besides those indicated by the general schema. This form of inference involves what has been called *the principle of double negation* according to which we regard 'John is bald' as equivalent to 'John is not not bald'. We can give a general rule for obversion which is: *negate the whole statement and negate the predicate-term*. In the traditional forms of statement we negate the whole of a universal statement by changing 'all' to 'no' and 'no' to 'all' and we negate the whole of a particular statement by adding or removing 'not'. We negate the predicate-term by adding the negative particle 'non-' to the term or removing it if it is already there. In the former case, the term with its new particle, becomes the new predicate.

The obverse of a universal affirmative statement of the form

> All *S*s are *P*   (*A*)

is a statement of the form

> No *S*s are non-*P*.   (*E*)

For example, the obverse of

> All snakes are vertebrates

is

> No snakes are non-vertebrates.

The obverse of a universal negative statement of the form

> No *S*s are *P*   (*E*)

is a statement of the form

> All *S*s are non-*P*.   (*A*)

For example, the obverse of

> No snakes are mammals

is

> All snakes are non-mammals.

The obverse of a particular affirmative statement of the form

> Some Ss are P　　　　　(*I*)

is a statement of the form

> Some Ss are not non-P.　　(*O*)

For example, the obverse of

> Some snakes are poisonous

is

> Some snakes are not non-poisonous.

Finally, the obverse of a particular negative statement of the form

> Some Ss are not P　　　　(*O*)

is a statement of the form

> Some Ss are non-P.　　　(*I*)

For example, the obverse of

> Some snakes are not poisonous

is

> Some snakes are non-poisonous.

In this last case, we negate the whole statement by removing 'not' and we negate the predicate-term by adding 'non-' to it. The result is an *affirmative* statement since the effect of 'non-' is only to make the predicate-term into a negative term and not to make the whole statement negative. The statement asserts that the subject *has* the (negative) predicate.

When we add a negative particle to a term we produce a new term; *P* and non-*P* are different terms. An analogy may help to illuminate this. In everyday discourse we have negative particles which we may attach to words with the same effect as adding 'non-'. For example, we may say that a parcel is opened or unopened. 'Opened' and 'unopened' are, like *P* and non-*P*, in contradictory opposition. That is, a parcel may be unopened or opened but it must be one or the other and cannot be both.

It is important to note, however, that there are other uses of 'un-', and similar particles in everyday discourse, which are different. We may say of a man that he is kind or unkind but because he is not kind it does not follow that he is unkind. There are people to whom we would hesitate to apply either term. To say of a man that he is kind is to say that he does kind actions and to say that he is unkind

144

is to say that he does unkind actions. However, a man may go through life never doing actions which are either kind or unkind; all his actions are 'neutral' in this respect. 'Kind' and 'unkind' are in contrary opposition; an action cannot be both but it may be neither.

In logic we use '*P*' and 'non-*P*' in the way in which, in ordinary speech, we use 'opened' and 'unopened' and not in the way in which we use 'kind' and 'unkind'. '*P*' and 'non-*P*' exhaust the possibilities and are mutually exclusive.

We may summarize our conclusions about obversion in the following table. The symbol $\bar{P}$ is used for 'non-*P*'.

	Original Statement		*Obverse*	
		D U		D D
A	All *S*s are *P*	$S\,a\,P$ ⟷ No *S*s are non-*P*	$S\,e\,\bar{P}$	*E*
		D D		D U
E	No *S*s are *P*	$S\,e\,P$ ⟷ All *S*s are non-*P*	$S\,a\,\bar{P}$	*A*
		U U		U D
I	Some *S*s are *P*	$S\,i\,P$ ⟷ Some *S*s are not non-*P*	$S\,o\,\bar{P}$	*O*
		U D		U U
O	Some *S*s are not *P*	$S\,o\,P$ ⟷ Some *S*s are non-*P*	$S\,i\,\bar{P}$	*I*

It is obvious that these inferences are valid and that we may infer in either direction, hence the double-headed arrows. Once again, no term which is undistributed in the premiss is distributed in the conclusion. It may look, at first sight, as if this rule is broken in the first and third cases but this is not so. In both cases *P* is undistributed in the premiss but it is non-*P* that is distributed in the conclusion. This is not forbidden by our principle and it is the change in the quality of the statement as a whole which allows it in these two cases. We must remember that *P* and non-*P* are different terms.

I have referred to these two basic immediate inferences as both 'inferences' and 'operations'. If we think of them as operations it is clear that we may begin with a statement and apply them successively and in various orders to the original statement and to the statement resulting from each operation. For example, we may begin with the statement

> All cats are vertebrates

and obvert it to obtain

> No cats are non-vertebrates.

We may now convert this to obtain

> No non-vertebrates are cats

145

and obvert that to obtain

> All non-vertebrates are non-cats.

Similarly, we may begin with

> No cats are reptiles

and convert it to obtain

> No reptiles are cats.

We may then obvert this to obtain

> All reptiles are non-cats

and then convert that to obtain

> Some non-cats are reptiles.

It is by applying these operations in various such ways that we derive the other two immediate inferences, contraposition and inversion.

c. CONTRAPOSITION

In contraposition we infer from a statement of the general form *S–P* a statement of the general form non-*P*–*S*. We do this by first obverting the given statement and then converting the result. This yields the *first contrapositive*. If we then obvert this we obtain the *second contrapositive*. These operations can be regarded as purely mechanical applications of obversion and conversion. They may be represented generally in the following ways.

(o = obversion
c = conversion)

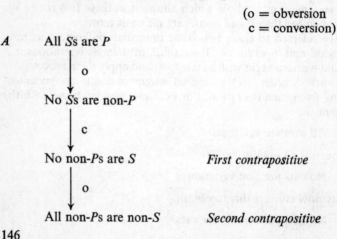

A	All *S*s are *P*	
	No *S*s are non-*P*	
	No non-*P*s are *S*	*First contrapositive*
	All non-*P*s are non-*S*	*Second contrapositive*

146

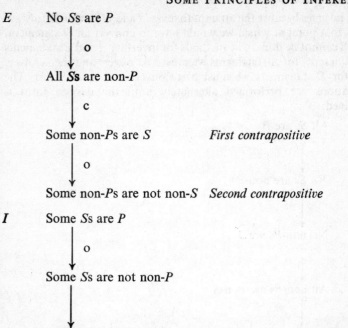

E   No *S*s are *P*

           o

All *S*s are non-*P*

           c

Some non-*P*s are *S*   *First contrapositive*

           o

Some non-*P*s are not non-*S*   *Second contrapositive*

I   Some *S*s are *P*

           o

Some *S*s are not non-*P*

Conversion is impossible ∴ no contrapositive obtainable.

Here, if we attempt to obtain a contrapositive by first converting and then obverting we are again faced with the necessity of converting an *O* statement, which cannot be done.

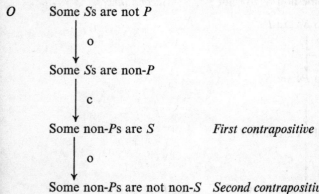

O   Some *S*s are not *P*

           o

Some *S*s are non-*P*

           c

Some non-*P*s are *S*   *First contrapositive*

           o

Some non-*P*s are not non-*S*   *Second contrapositive*

d. INVERSION

In inversion we infer from a statement of the general form *S–P* a statement of the general form non-*S–P*. Only *A* and *E* statements

147

yield inverses because the attempt to invert I and O statements always leads to a point at which we would have to convert an O statement, which cannot be done. The methods for inverting A and E statements are different; for A statements we must first obvert and then convert but for E statements we must first convert and then obvert. The operations are performed alternately until the desired form is obtained.

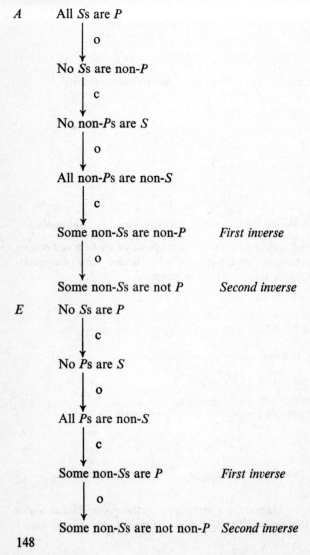

A All Ss are P

         o

No Ss are non-P

         c

No non-Ps are S

         o

All non-Ps are non-S

         c

Some non-Ss are non-P *First inverse*

         o

Some non-Ss are not P *Second inverse*

E No Ss are P

         c

No Ps are S

         o

All Ps are non-S

         c

Some non-Ss are P *First inverse*

         o

Some non-Ss are not non-P *Second inverse*

These immediate inferences have here been treated in the manner of the traditional logic, that is, as applying only to the four types of statement which could appear in syllogisms. It might be supposed that they could be generalized so that these operations could be applied to any sort of statement. For example, from the statement

$$4 > 3$$

we can infer

$$3 < 4.$$

This is an immediate inference if we define immediate inferences as inferences from single premisses. At first sight it might seem to be an example of conversion. However, it differs in an important respect from conversion since the change in the order of the terms involves also a change in the relationship holding between them, from 'is greater than' to 'is smaller than'. A similar thing may be said for one possible inference from 'Paul is the father of John'.

We may, of course, move from

Paul is the father of John

to

The father of John is Paul

which seems to be a mere re-wording of a more trivial kind than that involved in moving from

No Ss are P

to

No Ps are S.

However, we may also move from

Paul is the father of John

to

John is the son of Paul
(assuming that John is always a masculine name)

which is a less trivial inference and which involves a change in the relation said to hold.

There are, therefore, numbers of immediate inferences which do not fall under the traditional classification and which are in effect studied by studying the logical properties of relations, which will be introduced in Section 4 of this chapter.

It should be mentioned that there is a modern use of the term 'contrapositive' which looks different from the traditional use but which is in fact the same. According to this use a hypothetical statement of the form

> If p then q

has a contrapositive which is

> If not q then not p.

This is related to the traditional use in the following way. Suppose that

> If p then q

when further analysed becomes

> If $(x$ is $S)$ then $(x$ is $P)$

which is equivalent to

> All Ss are P.

Under these conditions

> If not q then not p

becomes

> If not $(x$ is $P)$ then not $(x$ is $S)$

which is equivalent to

> If x is not P then x is not S

which is in turn equivalent to

> All non-Ps are non-Ss.

This, however, is the traditional contrapositive of 'All Ss are P' so 'If p then q' and 'If not q then not p' are related exactly as a traditional universal affirmative statement and its contrapositive.

I now wish to turn to some problems which arise in connection with the traditional treatment of the immediate inferences. Conversion and obversion are very simple and seem obviously valid. Contraposition and inversion depend only upon conversion and obversion; every step in each process seems trivially obvious so that the new student is often led to wonder why these inferences are worth mentioning at all. In none of them is any term distributed in the conclusion but undistributed in the premiss. Yet, in spite of the intuitive obviousness of each step, there are reasons for questioning the validity of some of the inferences.

It is easy to construct examples of contrapositives and inverses which are invalid. For example, the contrapositive of

No purple cow is a black animal

is

Some non-black animals are purple cows.

The original statement appears to be true, there being no purple cows, while its contrapositive appears to be false. However, the definition of validity excludes this; if an inference is valid the conclusion must be true if the premisses are true. This conclusion appears to be valid if we stress its derivation from the original statement by a series of valid and obvious steps but it appears to be invalid if we consider the truth values of the premiss and conclusion.

Similar situations arise in connection with some inverses. For example, the inverse of

No Russian has landed on the moon

is

Some non-Russian has landed on the moon,

and the inverse of

No mathematician has squared the circle

is

Some non-mathematician has squared the circle.

In the first of these, the conclusion appears to be false, at the time of going to press, and the premiss is true since no one has landed on the moon. The second is an even stronger case since we believe the conclusion to be false because it is *logically impossible* that anyone should ever square the circle.

It seems clear that we cannot accept that these inferences are valid, as they stand, since that would be directly to contradict our definition of deductive validity. This would seem to leave us only two alternatives.

(i) We may say that the inferences are indeed invalid because some step in the immediate inferences of contraposition and inversion is unwarranted.
(ii) We may say that the inferences are valid but that they were not strictly made from one premiss and involved the tacit use of at least one other premiss.

In fact, this puzzle can be seen to give some support to the idea that universal statements do not have existential import while particular statements do have existential import. This idea was

151

discussed earlier (Chap. III, Section B(iii)) but historically these immediate inferences were seen to be problematical before this distinction between universal and particular statements was current. The introduction of the distinction has the advantage of throwing light on these traditional inferences and this is partly what it was intended to do.

In each of the puzzling inferences we have moved from a universal premiss to a particular conclusion. Why, precisely, are the conclusions unacceptable? Because they appear to assert the existence of purple cows, people who have landed on the moon and people who have squared the circle, respectively. We do not think there are such things, so we think the conclusions false.

Consider the third example. When we say that no mathematician has squared the circle we do not presuppose that someone *has* squared the circle. In fact, we may think the first statement true just because we know that no one has squared the circle or could square the circle. We regard the statement as perfectly meaningful, in spite of this, or else we could not regard it as true. Thus it is surprising when we arrive by apparently valid steps at the false conclusion that someone, after all, has squared the circle. We do usually, of course, presuppose the existence of mathematicians in making such statements. However, if we now consider the first example we have 'purple cows' as the subject of the premiss. We do not, and need not, presuppose the existence of purple cows in regarding this premiss as meaningful and true but the conclusion asserts the existence of purple cows.

We could just say that inversion and contraposition are invalid because they take a step from a universal statement, having no existential import, to a particular statement, having existential import. This, however, is awkward since some contrapositions and inversions seem perfectly valid. For example, the contrapositive of

> No cats are reptiles

is

> Some non-reptiles are cats

and the inverse of

> No frogs are mammals

is

> Some non-frogs are mammals.

Here the operations used are the same as in the puzzling examples and yet the premiss and the conclusion are true in each example. Are there differences between the various examples which explain this? Should the move from universal statements to particular statements be allowed in some cases and not in others?

In formal logic we wish to arrive at principles which are as general as possible without doing violence to everyday arguments which fall under these principles. Thus, if we can give an account of the immediate inferences which covers satisfactorily all the examples we have considered this is better than producing *ad hoc* principles covering the different examples. We may approach this by considering again the puzzling examples.

What would make them into valid inferences? In the third example, if we were to presuppose, along with the stated premiss, that there are non-mathematicians as well as mathematicians *and* those who have squared the circle as well as those who have not, then we should have all we needed. The conclusion was invalid because we began by presupposing the non-existence of those who had squared the circle. Of course, the original presupposition was true and the new one false but that is beside the point when we are considering only what is necessary to make the inference valid; if it *were* true that somebody had squared the circle and that no mathematician had done so, then it would follow that some non-mathematician had squared the circle and it would be true.

Now, if we write the new presupposition as an extra premiss, our argument becomes

> There are mathematicians, non-mathematicians, those
> who have squared the circle and those who have not
> No mathematician has squared the circle
> ∴ Some non-mathematician has squared the circle

which is valid. (It must be noted that the presupposition must exhaust the universe of discourse. See page 109.)

When we argue, in the non-puzzling examples, like this

> No frogs are mammals
> ∴ Some non-frogs are mammals

and we see nothing wrong with it, we are not stating in the premiss that there are frogs, non-frogs, mammals and non-mammals but we are presupposing this. Because we never stop to question the correctness of this presupposition we do not even notice that we are making it. Our puzzling examples show that we are presupposing it and that

153

it can again be set out as an extra premiss. Thus, if we are being quite precise, our inference should be set out in the following way.

> There are frogs, non-frogs, mammals and non-mammals
> No frogs are mammals
> ∴ Some non-frogs are mammals.

We may now say one of two things about these inferences. We may say that the immediate inferences are all valid given the pre-supposition that all the terms in them name existent things, or we may say that they are valid only if we add, wherever a particular is inferred from a universal, further premisses to the effect that every term mentions existent things. If we take the second course we are in effect saying that some of these inferences are not, after all, im-mediate inferences since they require not one but two premisses. The step which causes the trouble is the conversion *per accidens* of an *A* statement to give an *I* statement. This occurs in the contraposition of *E* statements and the inversion of both *A* and *E* statements. Thus, on the second alternative, it must be said that these so-called immediate inferences, at least, are not strictly immediate inferences. It is true in this case, also, that the conversion of an *A* statement itself requires an extra premiss and so is not an immediate inference.

The general point involved here is that universal statements may be meaningful, and so true or false, without any assertion or pre-supposition of existence, whereas particular statements cannot. Thus, we cannot say *generally* that a statement of the form 'All *S*s are *P*' or 'No *S*s are *P*' asserts, or carries any assumption of, existence. Clearly, we often do make presuppositions of existence when making such statements but we do not always do so and we therefore cannot treat them as if they always carry these presuppositions.[2]

All this can be expressed in another way and used to support another conception of the character of the four traditional types of statement. This amounts to the giving of a different interpretation of everyday statements which can be put in one of the traditional forms and it has the advantage that it can be extended to other kinds of statements, and so other kinds of inferences, than the traditional ones. This new interpretation will be introduced in the next section and developed in later sections.

3. CLASSES

An alternative interpretation of the traditional logic became important during the nineteenth century owing to the work of several

---

[2] See Otto Bird, *Syllogistic and its Extensions* (Englewood Cliffs, N.J., 1964) for further possibilities.

logicians including George Boole, Augustus de Morgan, W. S. Jevons and C. S. Peirce.[3] This interpretation takes the four traditional types of statement as relating *classes* or parts of classes.

A class is simply a collection of things which may be specified either by enumerating those things or by mentioning some property which the things to be included in the class must have. The things comprising a class are called its *members*. Specified in the second way, the idea may be seen to have its roots in everyday discourse. The description 'the red things in this room' defines a class and determines its members. We may use the expression 'some property in common' in a broad way so as to include both those properties which we normally think of as *belonging to* objects, such as redness, and those 'properties' which are apparently accidental, such as 'being on that table' or 'being thought about by me at this moment'. This is, no doubt, a development of any idea of classes which we use in everyday speech but it is a useful one for logic. Another development which is important is the idea that a class may have only one member or, indeed, no member at all. This may seem strange at first sight but, as we shall see, it is a useful logical device.

We may justify these ideas in the following way. It is close to everyday usage to regard such descriptions as 'red objects' or 'men over six feet tall' as defining classes containing just those objects which answer to those descriptions. It is a short step to regarding the description 'present Queen of England' as defining a class with just one member and 'men over twelve feet tall' as defining a class with no members or, as we say, an *empty class* or *the null class*. That is, any descriptive expression which could conceivably have application can be regarded as defining a class; some classes so defined will turn out to have many members, some will turn out to have only one member and some to have no members.

If we delineate a class in this way, by stating its defining property or properties, we are said to be defining it *in intension* or *intensionally*. We may, as I said, delineate a class simply by enumerating its members and this is to delineate it *in extension* or *extensionally*. It should be noted that even if we delineate a class extensionally it is always possible to mention some defining property (e.g. 'pointed to by *x* at time *t*') and so to define it intensionally. However, it should be clear that if we delineate classes extensionally, that is, in terms of their members, there is considerable difficulty in introducing the idea

[3] George Boole, *The Mathematical Analysis of Log ic* (1847, reprinted Oxford, 1948). Augustus de Morgan, *Formal Logic* (1847, reprinted 1926). W. S. Jevons, *Pure Logic* (London, 1864) and *Elementary Lessons in Logic* (London, 1870). John Venn, *Symbolic Logic* (London, 1881).

of an empty class. Logicians have differed about the relative merits of these two ways of specifying classes but this controversy need not delay us here. It will be convenient, for our purposes, to think of classes intensionally.

I have said that the early interpretation of the four traditional types of statement regarded them as relating *terms*. It is not quite clear what the nature of a term was intended to be and there have been differences of opinion about what a term stands for and whether it should be taken as a merely linguistic entity in the manner of the grammarian. The class interpretation takes terms as standing for or naming classes and so takes statements as relating classes. This interpretation was already implicit in Euler's circles; a circle representing a term can be seen as representing the class of those things to which the term could be applied.

This conception leads to the following interpretations of the four types of statement.

A	All *S*s are *P*:	The class *S* is wholly included in the class *P*.
E	No *S*s are *P*:	The class *S* is wholly excluded from the class *P*.
I	Some *S*s are *P*:	Part (at least) of the class *S* is included in the class *P*.
	or	The class *S* overlaps the class *P*.
O	Some *S*s are not *P*:	Part (at least) of the class *S* is excluded from the class *P*.

Given these interpretations, the validity of inferences involving these types of statement may be explained entirely in terms of the relations between classes determined by the relations said to hold in the premisses.

We now have another way of stating the differences between universal and particular statements in respect of existential import. Universal statements assert relations between classes which may or may not (i.e. *need* not) have members, so we cannot assume merely because a universal statement is meaningful or true that the classes it deals with have members. Particular statements assert relations between classes which have members, so a particular statement cannot be inferred from universal statements alone.

We may apply this to the puzzling examples of immediate inferences. When we move from

> No purple cow is a black animal

to

> Some non-black animals are purple cows

we are moving from a true statement about a class, purple cows, which we take to be empty, to a statement which is false because it asserts that this class is not empty. Similarly, when we move from

No mathematician has squared the circle

to

Some non-mathematician has squared the circle,

we move from a true statement about a class, those who have squared the circle, which is empty, to a statement which is false because it asserts that this class is not empty.

These inferences are, therefore, valid only if we begin with a pre-supposition, or an extra premiss, to the effect that all the classes mentioned have members. This is another way of describing the situation which leads to the same conclusion we reached earlier, namely, that contraposition and inversion cannot be shown formally to be generally valid without bringing out the presupposition or adding an extra premiss, which is to treat them as mediate rather then immediate inferences.

It has been argued[4] that if we adopt a class interpretation of the syllogism we no longer need the doctrine of distribution or, more strongly, that the attempt to combine these two notions leads only to incoherence. Distribution has frequently been explained by saying that a term is distributed or undistributed in a given statement according to whether it names the whole of a class or part of a class, respectively. However, on the class interpretation it is clear that in both

All Ss are P

and

Some Ss are P

the term S *simply names a class* and cannot be regarded as, in the first, naming the whole class and, in the second, naming only part of the class. If it is the *name* of a class then it is the name of a *class*. This is a controversial matter which we cannot settle here. It might perhaps be said that although S simply stands for a class in both statements, the two statements are respectively *about* the whole and part of that class, as is indicated by 'all' and 'some'. On the definition I have used, this allows us to say that S is distributed in the first statement and undistributed in the second because these notions depend upon what the statements are about.

However, this is not a matter of great importance for our purposes since, as we shall see, if we adopt a thoroughgoing class interpretation

[4] P. T. Geach, *loc. cit.*

of the syllogism we can deal with validity and invalidity without using the doctrine of distribution. Thus, even if the fusion of the two ideas is incoherent, we can avoid this fusion.

The idea of class relations can be used to interpret other kinds of inferences besides syllogistic inferences. The various possibilities arising from the inclusion, exclusion and overlapping of classes have been developed into a general calculus or 'algebra' of classes. The possibilities depend upon the general properties of class relations which in turn depend upon certain general properties of all relations, whether between classes or not. I shall discuss these in the next section and later return to a consideration of a calculus of classes.

4. LOGICAL PROPERTIES OF RELATIONS

This subject was introduced, briefly and informally, in Chap. II, Section 2. Here, a slightly fuller and more formal account is necessary.

All relations have certain logical properties which are independent, or relatively independent, of the terms which they relate. These properties govern the kinds of inferences in which the relations may figure. Relations may differ from one another in respect of the numbers of terms they relate. For example,

> John loves Mary

involves a relation between two terms while

> John wrote a *letter* to Mary

involves a relation between three terms and

> John conveyed a *message* from Mary to Paul

involves a relation between four terms. These are called, respectively, *dyadic*, *triadic* and *tetradic* relations.

I shall be concerned here with dyadic relations. We may represent a dyadic relation and its two terms in a general way by

> $x \, R \, y$

where x and y stand for the terms and R for the relation. Any dyadic relation R has a *converse*, which we shall represent by $\breve{R}$; if x has the relation R to y then the converse, $\breve{R}$, is the relation y has to x. That is, given

> $x \, R \, y$

then

> $y \, \breve{R} \, x$

involves the converse of R. The relations R and $\breve{R}$ may be the same or different relations; most often they are different but there is a number of familiar examples in which they are the same. For example, if R is the relation expressed by 'is equal to' then $x \, R \, y$ and $y \, \breve{R} \, x$ involve the same relation, since if x is equal to y then y is equal to x. However, if R is the relation expressed by 'is the father of' then $x \, R \, y$ and $y \, \breve{R} \, x$ involve different relations, since if x is the father of y, y cannot be the father of x but is the son or daughter of x.

There are two groups of logical properties of relations; every dyadic relation has one property from each group.

(a) A dyadic relation is either symmetrical, asymmetrical or non-symmetrical.

(b) A dyadic relation is either transitive, intransitive or non-transitive.

I shall explain these two groups of properties in turn.

(a) (i) *Symmetrical Relations:* A relation R is symmetrical if and only if $x \, R \, y$ implies $y \, R \, x$. In this case R and $\breve{R}$ are the same relation. Examples of symmetrical relations are *equal to* and *married to*.

   (ii) *Asymmetrical Relations:* A relation R is asymmetrical if and only if $x \, R \, y$ implies not $(y \, R \, x)$. In this case R and $\breve{R}$ are different relations. Examples of asymmetrical relations are *greater than* and *father of*.

   (iii) *Non-symmetrical Relations:* A relation R is non-symmetrical if and only if $x \, R \, y$ does not imply either $y \, R \, x$ or not $(y \, R \, x)$. In this case R and $\breve{R}$ may or may not be the same relation, depending upon which terms R holds between. Examples of non-symmetrical relations are *brother of* and *in love with*.

(b) (i) *Transitive Relations:* A relation R is transitive if and only if $x \, R \, y$ and $y \, R \, z$ together imply $x \, R \, z$. Examples of transitive relations are *greater than* and *ancestor of*.

   (ii) *Intransitive Relations:* A relation R is intransitive if and only if $x \, R \, y$ and $y \, R \, z$ together imply not $(x \, R \, z)$. Examples of intransitive relations are *father of* and *half of*.

   (iii) *Non-transitive Relations:* A relation R is non-transitive if and only if $x \, R \, y$ and $y \, R \, z$ together do not imply either $x \, R \, z$ or not $(x \, R \, z)$. Examples of non-transitive relations are *loves* and *different from*.

159

Any dyadic relation has one property from each group. Since the groups are independent, any property from group *a* may be found along with any property from group *b*. It will be seen that *father of* appears as an example of an asymmetrical relation and as an example of an intransitive relation; it is said to be an *asymmetrical intransitive relation*. On the other hand, *greater than* is an *asymmetrical transitive* relation and *equal to* a *symmetrical transitive* relation.

It is obvious that these properties are important in determining the possible kinds of inferences. In particular, non-symmetry and non-transitivity give very little scope for inference whereas symmetry gives more and transitivity a great deal more. It is by virtue of the transitivity of *greater than* (symbol $>$) that we can argue

$$a > b, b > c, c > d, d > e \text{ therefore } a > e$$

and it is by virtue of the transitivity of the relation *implies* that we can argue

p implies q, q implies r, r implies s, therefore p implies s.

Implies is, in fact, a non-symmetrical transitive relation. In general, the fact that we can have chains of deductive inferences in this way, depends upon the transitivity of the relations involved.

There are various other logical properties of relations which are not directly relevant to our present purpose and which I shall not deal with here.[5]

5. RELATIONS BETWEEN CLASSES

One celebrated treatment of classes, to which most versions of the calculus of classes are indebted, is called the Boolean Algebra of Classes, after its inventor George Boole. He saw certain important analogies between relations between classes and relations dealt with in mathematics, and especially in algebra. He set out to give symbolical representations of classes and their relations which would enable us to treat inferences as mechanical calculations. I shall begin to discuss relations between classes in a way that owes much to Boole's treatment, although I shall not follow it exactly.

We have seen that we may define a class by mentioning a property or set of properties which its members have. For every class defined in this way there is a *complementary* class defined by the absence of that property or set of properties. For example, the *complement* of the class of mammals is the class of non-mammals, containing the animals which lack the properties defining mammals. I shall represent

[5] For a fuller treatment of these properties see, e.g. L. S. Stebbing, *A Modern Introduction to Logic*, 3rd edition (London, 1942), Chap. X.

classes by capital letters A, B, C ... and capital letters with superscripts A', B' C', ..., where A' is the complement of A, and so on.

This notion of a class and its complement is, however, ambiguous without further explanation. Consider the class of cats. This contains every animal, defined in a certain way, which is correctly called a cat. What does its complement contain? The class of non-cats would seem to contain everything in the world apart from cats, for example, books and stars as well as horses and wolves. This, however, would not be a very useful kind of division to make; there are few purposes for which we should need to classify stars and books, along with horses, in the same class. When we are concerned with such classes as those of cats, dogs and non-cats we are usually concerned to classify animals. We should regard the class of cats as containing all animals having certain properties and the class of non-cats as containing all other animals. Following de Morgan we may call animals, here, our *universe of discourse*. In general, the universe of discourse is the total range of things we are considering when we make these classifications.

Our universe of discourse may vary from time to time even when we are talking of the same classes. I may be thinking of cats as mammals or as animals or as living organisms, that is, in the context of different universes of discourse. Which I am in fact concerned with will be determined by what I am prepared to include in the complementary class, the class of non-cats. If I include plants then my universe of discourse must be at least as wide as living organisms; if I include snakes but not plants then it is probably animals; if I include only other animals which are mammals then it is mammals.

It should be clear from this that a class and its complement *exhaust* the universe of discourse. If we are considering the class A then its complement, A', must contain everything contained in the universe of discourse except what A contains. This way of putting it suggests a diagrammatic representation such as that introduced by John Venn. We may represent the universe of discourse by a rectangle and classes by circles within it. Thus a class A and its complement A' are represented by

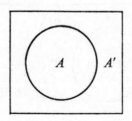

A' is just that part of the rectangle outside A. Thus A and A' together make up the whole of the rectangle and so exhaust the universe of discourse. The universe of discourse is usually symbolized by '1'. If we add the classes A and A' we get the universe of discourse; we may thus write $A + A' = 1$. It is important to notice how the '+' sign functions here. The universe of discourse contains all those things which are either members of A or members of A'. Thus the so-called *logical sum* is analogous to the connective 'either . . . or'.

In general, the logical sum of any two classes, A and B is the class of those things which are members of A or of B or of both and is represented by '$A + B$'.

The *logical product* of two classes, A and B, is the class containing those things common to A and B and may be represented by '$A \times B$' or 'AB'. Putting this in another way AB is the class of those things which are members of both A and B. Thus the logical product is analogous to the connective 'and'. Clearly, there can be no members common to a class, say 'cats', and its complement, 'non-cats'. We may nevertheless represent the product of A and A' by 'AA'' but because this class has no members, is empty, we write $AA' = 0$.

We may represent the logical sum and the logical product of two classes by a Venn diagram. The basic diagram is

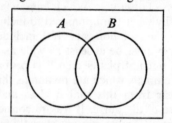

in which the rectangle, as before, represents the universe of discourse and the circles represent two overlapping classes, A and B. Now we may label each separate area in the diagram with a class product, i.e. we can regard each space as representing the members common to two classes. We then obtain

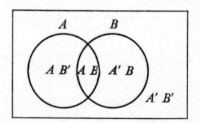

We can easily construct an example to make clear what each class is.

Example: Let the universe of discourse = cats

Let A = fierce cats

Let B = black cats

Then AB = fierce black cats (those cats which are both fierce and black)

AB' = fierce non-black cats

$A'B$ = black non-fierce cats

$A'B'$ = non-black non-fierce cats.

Those cats which are either fierce or black (or both) would then be represented by $A + B$, that is cats which are contained in circle A or circle B (or, of course, both). It follows that

$$A + B = AB' + AB + A'B.$$

There are two important relations involving classes which must now be explained and distinguished. These are *class inclusion* and *class membership*.

Class inclusion is a relation which can hold only between classes. A class A is included in another class B if and only if all the members of A are also members of B. For example, we may regard 'All cats are mammals' as stating the inclusion of the class 'cats' in the class 'mammals'. Every cat is a mammal, that is, every member of the first class is a member of the second. If class A is included in class B then class B may not be included in class A; it is so included only if the two classes coincide. The two possibilities are represented by the following two diagrams.

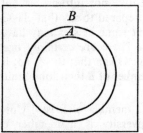 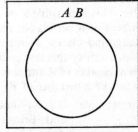

In the first, A is included in B but B is not included in A; in the second A is included in B and B is included in A. Thus, if A is included in B it may or may not be true that B is included in A. The relation of class inclusion is therefore non-symmetrical. I shall use the symbol '$\subset$' for class inclusion; the expression '$A \subset B$' is to be read 'Class A is included in class B'.

This relation is transitive, as should be obvious. If all cats are mammals and all mammals are vertebrates then all cats are vertebrates. If one class is included in another and that in a third, then the first is included in the third. In symbols

$$(A \subset B \cdot B \subset C) \supset (A \subset C).$$

The relation of class inclusion is therefore non-symmetrical and transitive.

Class membership is a different relation with different logical properties and must not be confused with class inclusion. This relation is a little more difficult to explain; it is the relation between a class and its members so what we say about it depends upon what we are prepared to consider as a member of a class. In everyday speech we use the idea somewhat loosely and allow both individuals and classes as members of classes. Most obviously, individuals may be members of classes. 'John Smith is an inhabitant of Bristol' may be taken as saying that the individual John Smith is a member of the class 'inhabitants of Bristol'. 'Inhabitants of Bristol are inhabitants of England' must be treated as a class-inclusion statement because the class 'inhabitants of Bristol', being a class, cannot be an inhabitant of England, that is, a member of the class 'inhabitants of England'. The members of that class are individual people and not classes. John Smith is of course a member of both classes.

John Smith is a member of the class 'inhabitants of Bristol' but, of course, the class 'inhabitants of Bristol' cannot be a member of John Smith. The relation is asymmetrical. Is it transitive, intransitive or non-transitive? The answer to this depends on what we are prepared to count as classes and members. I am inclined to say that in everyday discourse it is neither transitive nor intransitive but non-transitive. This is possible if we are prepared to say that classes may be members of other classes and that some classes may have both individuals and classes as members. There are certainly organizations which satisfy this last condition. Given that this is so, if John Smith is a member of A and A is a member of B then John Smith may or may not be a member of B.

> For example: if John Smith is a member of Bristol University and Bristol University is a member of the Aristotelian Society then John Smith may or may not be a member of the Aristotelian Society.

This is because the Aristotelian Society admits to membership both individuals and institutions. Thus, in somewhat loose everyday uses we can perhaps say that class membership is asymmetrical and non-transitive.

164

Logicians have differed in the way in which they have sought to tighten up this relationship. If only individuals are admitted to membership of classes the relation of class membership must be intransitive. In some systems[6] individuals are excluded altogether and only classes accepted, in which case the relation is non-transitive.[7]

We shall use small letters from the end of the alphabet for *individual variables* and small letters from the beginning of the alphabet for *individual constants*. That is to say, '*x*' for example, will represent indifferently any one of a certain range of individuals whereas '*a*', for example, will represent a particular individual from that range. We use the symbol '$\in$' for the class-membership relation. We may then write '$x \in A$' to indicate that each individual of the given range is a member of the class A and '$a \in A$' to indicate that a particular individual is a member of the class A.

We have seen that class inclusion may be defined in terms of class membership. To repeat: A is included in B if and only if every member of A is a member of B. We may represent this symbolically by

$$A \subset B =_{df.} (x)\{(x \in A) \supset (x \in B)\}.$$

If two classes have all their members in common then these classes may be said to be *identical*, represented by $A = B$. This is defined by saying that all members of A are members of B and all the members of B are members of A. Symbolically

$$A = B =_{df.} (A \subset B) \cdot (B \subset A)$$

or

$$A = B =_{df.} (x)\{((x \in A) \supset (x \in B)) \cdot ((x \in B) \supset (x \in A))\}.$$

It should be noted that this presents no problems if the classes are defined extensionally, that is, simply in terms of their members, but that if they are defined intensionally we must be careful in our interpretation of $A = B$. The two properties 'having a heart' and 'having a liver' may determine exactly the same membership of the two classes but we should still want to say that the two descriptions have different meanings or are not identical in *that* respect.

Singular statements, such as 'John Smith is a man' may be treated in two different ways. We have seen that the most natural way to treat this is as a class-membership statement. We have also seen that it makes sense to talk of a class with only one member. This points to the alternative treatment of this and any other singular statement as a class-inclusion statement. Thus, if we regard 'John Smith' as the

---

[6] See W. V. Quine, *Set Theory and its Logic* (Cambridge, Mass., 1963), Chaps. I and II.

name of an individual our statement must be interpreted as 'John Smith is a member of the class "men" '; but we may treat it as the name of a class with only one member, or a *unit class*, in which case our statement is to be interpreted as 'The class "John Smith" is included in the class "men" '. Of course, 'John Smith' may be the name of more than one individual but when we take our statement to be singular we are taking 'John Smith' as naming some unique individual. We shall see later that it is important not to confuse an individual with a unit class; its importance appears in considering syllogisms involving singular statements.

I have said that a class with no members may be referred to as 'an empty class' or '*the* null class'. The point of this second expression is that if we define a class by its members and define two classes as equivalent if and only if they have the same members then it follows that any two empty classes are identical since there is no member of one that is not a member of the other. Thus there can be only one empty class, the null class.

We have used the figure 1 to refer to the universe of discourse or, as we may call it, the *universal class* for a given context and the figure 0 to represent the null class. It is worth noting a difference between 1 and 0 as they are used here. The expression '$A = 0$' indicates that the class A has no members and the expression '$A \neq 0$' can therefore be used to indicate that it *has* members. However, the expression '$A + A' = 1$' indicates that the whole universe of discourse is exhausted by '$A + A'$' and does not tell us whether or not these have members. For example, if our universe of discourse is 'unicorns' and A stands for white unicorns and A' for non-white unicorns, then A and A' together exhaust the universe of discourse even though neither has members.

We are now in a position to represent the four traditional types of statement in terms of the emptiness or the non-emptiness of classes and also in terms of the inclusion and non-inclusion of classes.

a. *All S*s *are P*

We have seen that this form of statement may be regarded as excluding something and so may be put in the form 'Nothing is both S and non-P'. If we now think of this in terms of class membership we can put it as asserting that there are no members in the class SP' or that the class which is the logical product of S and P' is empty, that is, $SP' = 0$.

We may also think of statements of this form in terms of the class-inclusion relation. The original statement is then regarded as saying that the class S is wholly included in the class P, that is $S \subset P$.

166

b. *No Ss are P*

Statements in this form may also be taken as excluding something and so may be put in the form 'Nothing is both S and P'. This may be taken as saying that there are no members in the class SP or that the class which is the logical product of S and P is empty, that is, $SP = 0$.

In terms of class inclusion the original statement may be regarded as saying that the class S is wholly excluded from the class P, that is wholly included in the class P', that is, $S \subset P'$.

c. *Some Ss are P*

We have seen that this form of statement may be put in the form 'Something is both S and P'. Thinking of it now in terms of class-membership we may take it to say that the class SP is not empty, i.e. has at least one member, and so we may represent the original statement by $SP \neq 0$.

In terms of class inclusion we may regard it as saying that it is not the case that the class S is included in the class P', that is, $\sim (S \subset P')$.

d. *Some Ss are not P*

This form of statement may be put in the form 'Something is both S and P''. In terms of class membership, SP' is not empty, or it has at least one member, so we may represent the original statement by $SP' \neq 0$.

In terms of class inclusion, we may regard it as saying that it is not the case that the class S is included in the class P, that is, $\sim (S \subset P)$.

Summarizing this, we have two alternative ways of giving a class interpretation of the four standard types of statement, namely,

All Ss are P	$SP' = 0$	$S \subset P$
No Ss are P	$SP = 0$	$S \subset P'$
Some Ss are P	$SP \neq 0$	$\sim (S \subset P')$
Some Ss are not P	$SP' \neq 0$	$\sim (S \subset P)$.

There is a third way of representing the traditional types of statement, using the relation of class membership together with quantifiers as follows.

All Ss are P $\quad (x)\{(x \in S) \supset (x \in P)\}$

This is read: for any x, if x is a member of class S then it is a member of class P.

No Ss are P $\quad (x)\{(x \in S) \supset (x \in P')\}$

167

This is read: for any x, if x is a member of class S then it is a member of class P'.

Some Ss are P $(\exists x)\{(x \in S) \cdot (x \in P)\}$

This is read: there is at least one x such that x is a member of class S and a member of class P.

Some Ss are not P $(\exists x)\{(x \in S) \cdot (x \in P')\}$

This is read: there is at least one x such that x is a member of class S and a member of class P'.

I shall shortly return to these topics in connection with the syllogism but first I shall outline briefly the traditional treatment of the syllogism.

6. THE SYLLOGISM

Some traditional logicians hoped that all deductive arguments would eventually be shown to be either obviously or covertly syllogistic. The aim of logic was to generalize as much as possible the forms of valid deductive argument. There are many different kinds of deductive argument to be found in everyday discourse; it was hoped that each of them would be shown to be equivalent to one of the various types of valid syllogism. It was further hoped that all these types of syllogism would be shown to be covered by one general principle of deductive reasoning. Thus the aim was eventually to subsume every valid deductive argument under one general logical principle. In fact this aim, expressed in just this way, can fairly easily be seen to be unattainable although the less specifically stated aim of generalizing as much as possible is one that most logicians would accept.

One principle which was intended to cover all forms of the syllogism was the *dictum de omni et nullo*. There has been considerable controversy about the history of the principle. It has frequently been said to be Aristotle's syllogistic principle but it is clear that Aristotle neither stated it nor used it.[7] Indeed, there are reasons for thinking that Aristotle did not feel strongly the need for *one* basic principle for all syllogisms; he used a number of principles for various different types of syllogism.

Some writers have distinguished categorical and hypothetical syllogisms. The form

All Ms are P
All Ss are M
∴ All Ss are P

[7] W. and M. Kneale, *The Development of Logic* (Oxford, 1962).

being one kind of categorical syllogism and the form

$$\text{If } p \text{ then } q$$
$$p$$
$$\therefore \quad q$$

being one form of hypothetical syllogism. This terminology is not, however, much used nowadays and I shall always mean by 'syllogism' what was meant by 'categorical syllogism'.

The categorical syllogism has, by definition, three statements only and three terms only. Each statement must be of the subject-predicate form, that is, it must have just two terms joined by some part of the verb 'to be'. It follows that the two premisses must have one term in common and each must have a term which does not appear in the other. The terms which the premisses do not share are brought together in the conclusion. Using the traditional symbols for the terms, in any syllogism we must have some combination of the three terms S, P and M, such that S and M appear in one premiss, P and M in the other and S and P in the conclusion. There are four such possibilities, namely,

I	II	III	IV
M–P	P–M	M–P	P–M
S–M	S–M	M–S	M–S
S–P	S–P	S–P	S–P

By convention, we always represent the conclusion by S–P, S standing for 'subject' and P for 'predicate'. M stands for 'middle term', the term shared by the premisses. Another convention is that we always put the premiss containing P first. These four arrangements are called the *figures* of the syllogism and are referred to by the numbers shown.

S is called the *minor term* and the premiss containing it the *minor premiss*; P is called the *major term* and the premiss containing it the *major premiss*. Which are the major and minor premisses is thus determined by the order of the terms in the conclusion.

Each statement represented here by a pair of letters must be of the traditional A, E, I or O type. In each figure there are several valid syllogisms differing from one another in the types of statement comprising them. Not every combination of types of statement is valid. Whether we have a valid syllogism depends upon

(1) which of the four schemata (figures) it fits into and (2) which combination of types of statement it has. The valid syllogisms in each figure are called the *moods* of that figure.

The *dictum de omni et nullo*, which has been claimed to be the one principle governing the validity of syllogisms, may be stated thus: whatever is predicated, whether affirmatively or negatively, of a distributed term may be predicated in like manner (i.e. affirmatively or negatively) of anything falling under it.

Stated in this way, the *dictum* applies directly only to the first figure. Consider the schema, which is a valid first figure form,

> All *M*s are *P*
> All *S*s are *M*
> ∴ All *S*s are *P*.

In the first premiss *P* is predicated affirmatively of the distributed term *M*. In the second premiss the third term *S* is said to fall under, or be contained in, the term *M*, which was distributed in the first premiss. In the conclusion, the term *P* is predicated in like manner, that is, affirmatively, of the term *S*.

It seems obvious that any argument which conforms to this principle is valid. At least, that has been claimed. Another way of putting it is to say that valid syllogisms in the first figure are quite obviously valid and that they quite clearly fall under this principle. This has also been claimed. That both these views have been criticized need not delay us here. Various objections can be levelled against the theory of the syllogism but we can at least say that it is helpful for analysing certain familiar types of argument. It is worth examining because of this and also because a knowledge of it assists in the understanding of later developments in logic.

There is a set of *general rules* for the syllogism. In so far as they apply to the first figure they are directly derivable from the *dictum*. Some further operations are needed, as we shall see, to show that they *are* general, that is, that they apply to the other three figures as well. There are various ways of stating these rules, one of which is as follows.

(1) *The syllogism has three and only three terms.*

(This rule follows from the *dictum* which requires one distributed term, one term predicated of it and one term falling under it.)

(2) *The syllogism has three and only three statements.*

(The *dictum* requires one statement predicating a term of the distributed term, one asserting a term to fall under the distributed term and one predicating the first term of this contained term.)

(3) *The middle term must be distributed in at least one premiss.*

(The 'distributed term'. In the first figure it is always distributed in the first premiss.)

(4) *No conclusion is possible from two negative premisses.*

(One of them must assert that a term is contained in the distributed term. In the first figure this is always the second premiss.)

(5) *If a term is distributed in the conclusion it must also be distributed in its premiss.*

(*P* is distributed in the conclusion only if it is negative; 'in like manner' indicates that the major premiss is negative so *P* is distributed there. *P* can be predicated of *S* only *in so far as S* is contained in the middle term: if *S* is distributed in the conclusion it must be *wholly* contained in the middle term, so *S* must be distributed in its premiss.)

(6) *If one premiss is negative then the conclusion must be negative.*

(This is required by predication 'in like manner'.)

In relation to Rule (5) it must be noted that it does not disallow syllogisms in which a term is distributed in a premiss and undistributed in the conclusion.

Since the *dictum* applies directly to the first figure only, these rules have so far been shown to apply only to that figure. In order to regard them as general rules we must prove that they apply also to the other three figures and this was the object of the traditional *reduction of the syllogism* to the first figure. This process is of purely theoretical interest, being part of the project of generalizing as much as possible about deductive inferences. It would only have a practical function if it were indeed the case that syllogisms in the first figure are always more perspicuous and obviously valid than syllogisms in the other figures. Here, the reduction of the syllogism will be treated as having a purely theoretical point.

Using only the general rules we may quite easily prove three corollaries which are also shown to apply to all figures when the reduction has been carried out. These corollaries are

(a) At least one premiss must be universal;
(b) If one premiss is particular the conclusion must be particular;
(c) If the major premiss is particular the minor premiss cannot be negative.

As an indication of the way in which these are proved I give here a proof of the third corollary.

Proof:

The major premiss contains the middle term, M, and the predicate P.

(i) Given that it is particular, then if it is negative one of these terms will be distributed, and if it is affirmative neither will be distributed. (By the rules of distribution.) *If it is negative then the minor premiss cannot be negative.* (Rule (4).)

(ii) If it is affirmative P will be undistributed. If the minor premiss were negative the conclusion would be negative. (Rule (6).) In that case P would be distributed in the conclusion but not in the major premiss.

But this is forbidden by Rule (5).

∴ *The minor premiss cannot be negative.*

The other corollaries can be proved in similar ways by considering the distribution of terms.

Methods of reduction are to be found in detail in many standard textbooks of logic[8] so they will not be dealt with fully here. One method will be briefly outlined simply to give some idea of the way in which this may be carried out. This method depends upon the use of the immediate inferences, conversion and obversion.

We may represent the various moods of the syllogism by stating the number of the figure and indicating the types of statement it contains by writing the symbol for the type of statement thus: $I\,A\,I$ or thus

I
A
$I.$

In these representations, the first letter stands for the type of the major premiss, the second for the type of the minor premiss and the third for the type of the conclusion. Thus, for example, 'Fig. III, $I\,A\,I$' stands for a syllogism having the form

$M\,i\,P$
$M\,a\,S$
_____
$S\,i\,P.$

I shall take this as the first example for reduction. The general method is to consider the original syllogism and show either that it is equivalent to a first figure syllogism or that it can be derived from one.

[8] e.g. L. S. Stebbing, *A Modern Introduction to Logic*, Chap. VI.

Example 1

Fig. III, *I A I*

The form of the syllogism is

$$M \ i \ P$$
$$M \ a \ S$$
$$\overline{}$$
$$S \ i \ P$$

If we wish to transform it into a first figure syllogism we have to re-arrange it, by a series of valid steps, so that the middle terms are arranged thus

$$M-$$
$$\quad -M$$

It appears that one of the premisses must be *converted*, to move M from the subject position to the predicate position. If we were to convert the minor premiss, $M \ a \ S$, we should obtain an I statement $S \ i \ M$. The resulting syllogism would have two particular premisses and so could not be valid. The alternative is to convert the major premiss and then change the order of the premisses.

$$
\begin{array}{ccccc}
M \ i \ P & \equiv & P \ i \ M & & M \cdot a \ S \\
M \ a \ S & & M \ a \ S & \nearrow\!\!\!\!\!\searrow & P \ i \ M \\
\hline
S \ i \ P & & S \ i \ P & & S \ i \ P
\end{array}
$$

This is almost in the first figure form. We can achieve this by converting the conclusion, when we obtain

$$M \ a \ S$$
$$P \ i \ M$$
$$\overline{}$$
$$P \ i \ S$$

This is the form of the first figure syllogism $A \ I \ I$. It does not look right because wherever we have P we should have S and wherever we have S we should have P. However, the essential features of the first figure are that the middle term be the subject of the first premiss and the predicate of the second, with the predicate of the conclusion as the predicate of the first premiss and the subject of the conclusion as the subject of the second premiss. We have this arrangement. Since S and P are simply arbitrary symbols for terms we may, in the

173

last syllogism, replace S by P and P by S wherever they occur. We thus obtain

$$M \ a \ P$$
$$S \ i \ M$$
$$\overline{}$$
$$S \ i \ P$$

which is clearly a first figure syllogism, and as it obeys all the rules it is a valid one.

In this process we have used only simple conversion. Thus the new syllogism is *equivalent* to the original one, which accordingly is valid.

It is convenient at this point to indicate what syllogisms are valid in the various figures, that is, to state the results of all the reductions to the first figure which can be validly carried out. I shall then return to further examples of reduction.

Given the schemata for the four figures and the four types of statement that may be used in them, there are 256 possible combinations. Of these, only 24 were traditionally regarded as valid. However, 5 of these are *weakened moods* and may be neglected. A weakened mood is a syllogism whose conclusion is particular but whose premisses would allow a universal conclusion. Excluding the weakened moods there are, therefore, 19 valid syllogisms. They are

1st Figure	$A\,A\,A, E\,A\,E, A\,I\,I, E\,I\,O.$
2nd Figure	$E\,A\,E, A\,E\,E, E\,I\,O, A\,O\,O.$
3rd Figure	$A\,A\,I, I\,A\,I, A\,I\,I, E\,A\,O, O\,A\,O, E\,I\,O.$
4th Figure	$A\,A\,I, A\,E\,E, I\,A\,I, E\,A\,O, E\,I\,O.$

In the thirteenth century these were given names which served as a mnemonic and which are still used today. They are

I	*Barbara, Celarent, Darii, Ferio.*
II	*Cesare, Camestres, Festino, Baroco.*
III	*Darapti, Disamis, Datisi, Felapton, Bocardo, Ferison.*
IV	*Bramantip, Camenes, Dimaris, Fesapo, Fresison.*[9]

It will be noted that the vowels in each word indicate the types of statement in that mood, in order. The initial letter of each indicates

[9] These were part of a mnemonic stanza invented by Peter of Spain (Pope John XXI, *c*. 1210–77) It runs:

> Barbara Celarent Darii Ferio*que prioris*:
> Cesare Camestres Festino Baroco, *secundae*,
> *Tertia*, Darapti Disamis Datisi Felapton
> Bocardo Ferison, *habet*: *Quarta insuper addit*
> Bramantip Camenes Dimaris Fesapo Fresison.

the first figure mood with which it is connected. The letters 's', 'p', 'm' and 'c' give instructions for reduction to the first figure. The remaining consonants have no significance. The example I have taken for reduction is *Disamis* (3rd figure) and the equivalent first figure syllogism is *Darii*. The first 's' in Disamis indicates simple conversion of the first premiss and the final 's' indicates simple conversion of the conclusion. The 'm' indicates that the premisses must be transposed. These are just the operations which we used. The letter 'p' indicates that the statement before it must be converted *per accidens* and the letter 'c' indicates that a special form of reduction is needed.

On examination it will be found that the four moods of the first figure all fit the *dictum de omni et nullo*. It will also be found that no mood other than those in the lists above, in any figure, can be reduced to a first figure syllogism and so brought under the *dictum*. Most of those which do appear in the lists can be reduced in a straightforward way to equivalent first figure syllogisms. Some of them do present problems but the traditional logicians were confident that these could be overcome and all these moods shown to be valid.

In fact, all the second, third and fourth figure moods can be reduced directly, to yield *equivalent* first figure syllogisms, except *A A I* (*Bramantip*) in the fourth figure, *A O O* (*Baroco*) in the second figure and *O A O* (*Bocardo*) in the third figure.

Example 2

Bramantip in the fourth figure can be dealt with by conversion but it does not yield an equivalent first figure syllogism. We have

$$P \ a \ M$$
$$M \ a \ S$$
$$\overline{}$$
$$S \ i \ P$$

If we transpose the premisses we get the correct arrangement of the middle terms.

$$
\begin{array}{ccc}
P \ a \ M & \longrightarrow & M \ a \ S \\
M \ a \ S & \longrightarrow & P \ a \ M \\
\hline
S \ i \ P & & S \ i \ P
\end{array}
$$

The first figure syllogism *Barbara*, the only one with two *A* premisses, has an *A* conclusion but we cannot get an *A* conclusion from *S i P* by conversion or any other means. However, the two premisses give, in the first figure, the valid conclusion *P a S*, which on conversion gives

175

$S i P$ which is the conclusion of our present syllogism. Thus the given fourth figure syllogism can be derived from, but is not equivalent to, the first figure syllogism

$$M a S$$
$$P a M$$
$$\overline{}$$
$$P a S.$$

We can therefore say that the fourth figure mood *Bramantip* is valid and falls under the *dictum*.

The other two cases, *Baroco* in the second figure and *Bocardo* in the third, were traditionally reduced by a process called 'indirect reduction'. This is indicated by the letter 'c' in their names. However, there is a simpler method, using obversion as well as conversion, which will be given here.

Example 3: *Baroco*

The form of this is

$$P a M$$
$$S o M$$
$$\overline{}$$
$$S o P$$

We cannot convert the minor premiss because it is an O statement. If we convert the major premiss we are left with two particular premisses, which cannot give a conclusion. However, we may *obvert* both premisses and obtain

$$P a M \quad \equiv \quad P e \bar{M} \qquad (\text{where } \bar{M} = \text{non-}M)$$
$$S o M \quad \equiv \quad S i \bar{M}$$
$$\overline{} \qquad \overline{}$$
$$S o P \qquad \quad S o P$$

Now we may convert the major premiss to get the middle term in the correct position, obtaining

$$\bar{M} e P$$
$$S i \bar{M}$$
$$\overline{}$$
$$S o P$$

This is a first figure syllogism in the mood *Ferio*, with $\bar{M}$ as the middle term instead of M. This is acceptable since $\bar{M}$ occurs in both premisses. The new syllogism is equivalent to the original one.

176

Example 4: *Bocardo*

The form of this is

$$M \ o \ P$$
$$M \ a \ S$$
$$\overline{\hspace{2cm}}$$
$$S \ o \ P$$

This presents the same difficulties for conversion as *Baroco*. We may, however, *obvert* the major premiss and the conclusion

$$M \ o \ P \quad \equiv \quad M \ i \ \bar{P}$$
$$M \ a \ S \quad \quad \quad M \ a \ S$$
$$\overline{\hspace{1cm}} \quad \quad \quad \overline{\hspace{1cm}}$$
$$S \ o \ P \quad \equiv \quad S \ i \ \bar{P}$$

Now convert the major premiss and the conclusion obtaining

$$\bar{P} \ i \ M$$
$$M \ a \ S$$
$$\overline{\hspace{2cm}}$$
$$\bar{P} \ i \ S$$

Finally, transpose the premisses, obtaining

$$M \ a \ S$$
$$\bar{P} \ i \ M$$
$$\overline{\hspace{2cm}}$$
$$\bar{P} \ i \ S$$

This is a first figure syllogism in the mood Darii with $\bar{P}$ in place of S and S in place of P. It is equivalent to the original syllogism.

It is worth noting that the immediate inferences used in examples (3) and (4) do not involve moving from universal statements to particular statements. Consequently they do not involve any of the immediate inferences which we found to be problematical.

Given that the programme of reduction can be carried out in full, it shows that all valid moods of the syllogism fall under the *dictum de omni et nullo* and therefore that the rules stated above are general rules of the syllogism. These can now be used to test the validity of syllogistic arguments. If an apparently deductive argument can be put into syllogistic form we can examine it to see whether it breaks any of the six rules. If it does break one or more of them then it is not a valid syllogism.

There are certain fallacies which have been given names. If an apparent syllogism has an ambiguous middle term then, strictly, we have four terms and not three; this is called the *fallacy of four terms*.

177

If the middle term is not distributed in either premiss we have the fallacy called *undistributed middle*. If the major term is distributed in the conclusion but not in the major premiss we have the fallacy of *illicit major*; if the minor term is distributed in the conclusion but not in the minor premiss we have the fallacy of *illicit minor*.

In everyday discourse we use arguments from time to time which may be regarded as syllogistic. This means that we use arguments which we take to be conclusive and that their conclusiveness may be made obvious by putting them in traditional syllogistic form. As we ordinarily use these arguments they may not be stated as complete syllogisms. For example, one premiss or the conclusion may be understood rather than stated or a universal quantifier ('all') may be left out. To put such an argument in syllogistic form is to supply what was taken for granted and what is needed to show it to be a conclusive argument.

If, for example, I say 'Badgers are mammals so they don't lay eggs' I am making, or stating, an inference. If I am prepared to stand by it firmly enough I am treating it as a conclusive argument, but 'Badgers don't lay eggs' does not follow from 'Badgers are mammals' alone. What is needed is another premiss 'No mammals lay eggs'. This is now an inference which can clearly be put in syllogistic form, that is, shown to fall under the rules of the syllogism.

How does this help? It would, of course, be a mistake to suppose that our notion of the principle of the syllogism is innate or God-given; that we have this principle is advance of our use of any syllogistic argument and that all we have to do to show that an inference is valid is to show that it can be put in a form which falls under that principle.

The situation is, rather, that in the course of the development of our language and our ways of talking and arguing, certain forms of argument have come to be accepted and the rest rejected. Some of them are roughly syllogistic in form and others are not. The traditional logician attempted to find common features in those roughly syllogistic arguments that we accept, and ultimately a general principle which summarizes those common features, if possible. This was an attempt to extract from many different accepted arguments some principle of validity.

We might demand that this principle should be obviously acceptable or, in some sense, 'self-evident' and we might expect this if the one we propose is one that we, in fact, already use tacitly. However, this need not be an overriding demand because it would be of some value to show that a given principle did distinguish infallibly between all those arguments we regard it as reasonable to accept and all those we regard it as reasonable to reject, even if there were no way of showing that this principle was already tacitly used.

7. CRITICISMS OF SYLLOGISTIC THEORY

One traditional interpretation of the syllogism treated it as relating terms. This raises problems about what terms are. Are they purely linguistic entities or are they to be thought of as symbols for entities such as things and properties or classes?

It will surely not do to regard terms merely as words; we are concerned not just with collections of words, that is, sentences, but with these in so far as they can be used to make statements which can be true or false. We are therefore concerned with certain of the ways in which words can be used; a term must therefore be more than a mark on paper or a spoken sound. There are difficulties, however, in saying that a term is what a word *refers to*, since we may be interested in statements which are true or false just because some of the words used to make them fail to refer to anything or, again, in spite of a failure to refer. We have seen that statements may be meaningful although they refer to nothing actual.

On the other hand, we are often interested in what a word could be used to refer to, even if it does not. It is sometimes said that we are interested in the *senses* of words, which determine what they may be used to refer to, or the *extensions* of words, which may be thought of as everything to which the words *could* properly be applied.[10]

Another more detailed suggestion is that terms should be regarded as naming genera and species, so that the four traditional types of statement state types of relations between a genus and its species. This allows that a genus or species may be 'ideal' or 'empty' and that we may consider relations between them nevertheless.

Aristotle required that any term may be either the subject or predicate of a statement appearing in a syllogism. An examination of the schemata of the figures shows why this is necessary. This requirement made it difficult to allow singular statements such as 'Socrates is a man' in syllogisms since it is difficult to allow that 'Socrates' can appear as a predicate if it is a name of an individual.[11] The class interpretation of statements, including the device of treating 'Socrates' as the name of a unit class, was partly intended to overcome this difficulty. This interpretation is, of course, connected with the genus-species interpretation.

[10] See H. W. B. Joseph, *An Introduction to Logic* (Oxford, 1906), Chap. II. Jan Łukasiewicz, *Aristotle's Syllogistic* (Oxford, 1951), Chap. I.

[11] Jan Łukasiewicz, *Aristotle's Syllogistic*, Chap. I. There are discussions of these points in P. T. Geach, *Reference and Generality*, Chap. II and P. F. Strawson, *Individuals* (London, 1959), Chap. 5.

There are difficulties attached to the idea of distribution and also, therefore, to the *dictum de omni et nullo*. Aristotle used a different principle for each figure of the syllogism and did not attempt to provide one all-embracing principle. He therefore avoided some of the problems introduced by later logicians. Distribution is often defined by means of the *reference* of terms but if we say, as seems sensible, that a term cannot refer to a non-existent thing then there are problems about empty terms and universal statements. I have tried to avoid these problems in the way in which I have defined 'distribution'.

However, the most serious problems concern the generality of syllogistic theory. Logicians have from time to time been over-optimistic about this. In hoping that all deductive inferences could be brought under one principle, namely the *dictum*, they were hoping that all deductive inferences would be shown to be syllogistic. This was a forlorn hope. It led some mediaeval logicians into extraordinary mental contortions in the attempt to show that all statements which could figure in deductive inferences could be put in the *A*, *E*, *I* and *O* forms.

It is clear, however, that there are many statements which cannot be put in these forms and such statements can obviously be used in inferences. I have already mentioned singular statements; it seems artificial and misleading to regard them either as universal or as particular statements. There are also difficulties about the so-called *relational* statements, such as

> London is north of Paris
> Three is greater than two

in which 'is north of' and 'is greater than' express relations between two things. The traditional treatment would divide up such statements into subject-copula-predicate in this way

> London/is/north of Paris
> Three/is/greater than two

as if 'north of Paris' were an attribute of London and 'greater than two' an attribute of three. However, if we do this it is clear that these are attributes in a different sense from that in which 'red' is an attribute in 'This book is red'. In fact, it seems more natural to regard these statements as divisible in this way

> London/is north of/ Paris
> Three/is greater than/two.

This is to regard them as being of the form '*A R B*' rather than '*A* is *B*', where *R* stands for some relation other than that indicated by 'is'.

Some logicians may have been misled by the fact that we use statements of this sort in inferences which look superficially like syllogisms. For example,

$$3 > 2$$
$$4 > 3$$
$$\therefore 4 > 2.$$

This has several features in common with a first figure syllogism. It has three terms and three statements, the arrangement of the terms corresponds to that of the first figure and it appears to have a middle term. But what sense can we give to the question whether the statements are universal or particular? If we say, as seems plausible, that they are universal what could possibly be the corresponding particular statements? If we use the notion of distribution, what sense can be given to the idea that the terms are either distributed or undistributed?

If we interpret the statements in the way that is necessary for syllogistic treatment of the inference we obtain, for example,

Three/is/greater than two

and this gives trouble when we consider the possibilities of immediate inference. We cannot convert it, in the usual way, for that would give us something like

Greater than two/is/three

which does not make very good sense. It might be better to interpret the original statement as

Three/is/a number greater than two

and the converse as

A number greater than two/is/three.

This is true, as long as we do not regard it as saying that *any* number greater than two is three, but it is cumbersome and not very informative. If we treat this in what I have said is the more natural way we have as the original statement

Three/is greater than/two

and as its 'converse'

Two/is less than/three.

This is both more informative and more like inferences we normally use. Moreover, it does not raise spurious problems about the distribution of the terms.

There are various other types of statement which may figure in deductive inferences but which cannot easily be fitted into the traditional types of statement. For example, there are statements with several quantifiers which do not conform with the rules of quantification expressed by the mnemonic word ASEBINOP, such as

> All the men in this room are taller than all the men in the next room
>
> Someone in this room is taller than anyone in the next room.

If we attempt to represent these by '*S* is *P*' we obscure important features of the original statements.

There are many other types of statement, which I shall not discuss in detail, which will not yield to the traditional treatment. I content myself with a list of some examples.

> Paul will not come unless Harry does.
> John believes that there are tigers in Africa.
> James said 'There are tigers in Africa'.
> When John began to speak Mary left.
> Paul was at the cinema during the examination.
> There are ghosts.

We may conclude that not all statements can be put in the traditional forms and that not all deductive inferences are syllogistic. If we accept the theory of the syllogism as useful for dealing with some deductive inferences we must recognize that it lacks the generality it has sometimes been supposed to have. There are many deductive inferences which are non-syllogistic. If we wish to continue the process of generalizing about deductive inferences one way of doing this is to attempt to find principles which cover both syllogistic and non-syllogistic deductive inferences. This would amount to finding more general principles than, for example, the *dictum de omni et nullo*. This would be to regard the theory of the syllogism as not wrong in principle but merely incomplete because it does not cover all deductive inferences.

One way of approaching this is by considering various interpretations of the syllogism which are more general than the traditional interpretation of it as relating terms. This is to look for more general forms of argument of which the syllogism is only one example and which can therefore be used in the analysis of other kinds of inference as well. Apart from the view of syllogisms as relating terms there are three other main possibilities: we may regard them as relating statements or propositions, or as relating classes, or as relating predicates. These are not all equally satisfactory as will emerge. I shall discuss these three possibilities in turn.

In considering this interpretation I rely partly on what was said about hypothetical inferences in Chap. III, Section 2 and on what was said about inference and implication in Chap. I, Section 4.

When we say that a syllogism is valid we mean that if the premisses are true then the conclusion is true or if the premisses were true then the conclusion would be true. I have so far usually represented the syllogism as an inference thus

> All Ms are P
> All Ss are M
> ∴ All Ss are P.

This is to take the two premisses as asserted and to take the conclusion as asserted in consequence of this. However, what is of logical interest is not the truth or falsity of what is asserted but the relations between the statements. We may remove any apparent reference to the truth or falsity of statements by considering only the implication upon which this inference is based. This implication is

> *If* all Ms are P
> *and* all Ss are M
> *then* all Ss are P.

We may now represent the first statement by p, the second by q and the third by r. Then the whole implication may be represented by

> If (p and q) then r,

or

> (p and q) implies r.

The analogous expression in the propositional calculus, using material implication, is

> $(p \cdot q) \supset r$.

Now suppose that we wish to use this relation for an inference. One way of doing so is to follow the pattern for *modus ponens* (see Chap. III, Section 2, p. 117). We then obtain

> p and q implies r
> p and q
> ∴ r

or

$$(p \cdot q) \supset r$$
$$p \cdot q$$
$$\therefore \ r.$$

That is, given the hypothetical statement, the assertion of the antecedent (p and q), or ($p \cdot q$), allows the assertion of the consequent r. In using a syllogism we do, in fact, assert what ($p \cdot q$) represents, that is, the two premisses, and so what r represents, that is, the conclusion. The validity of this move depends on ($p \cdot q$) implying r.

However, the expression

$$(p \cdot q) \supset r$$

is not a valid expression of the propositional calculus; it is not true under every substitution for p, q and r, that is, for any three statements. What the rules of the syllogism ensure is that if p and q satisfy certain conditions as to distribution of terms, and so on, then they do together imply r, given that r also satisfies certain conditions. That is, they give us certain conditions under which (p and q) does imply r. We can derive from this a principle which covers the syllogism, namely,

> If two statements imply a third then if we can correctly assert the first two statements we are entitled to assert the third;

or

> If $\{(p$ and $q)$ implies $r\}$ and (p and q) then r;

or

$$[\{(p \cdot q) \supset r\} \cdot (p \cdot q)] \supset r.$$

Now this principle has the advantage of being more general than the *dictum de omni et nullo* since it covers inferences which are possible whenever two statements, of whatever kind, imply a third. For example, it can be regarded as the principle covering the inferences

$$3 > 2 \quad (p)$$
$$4 > 3 \quad (q)$$
$$\therefore \ 4 > 2 \quad (r)$$

and

> Queen Elizabeth II is the Queen of England $\qquad (p)$
> The Queen of England is the Queen of Canada $\quad (q)$
> $\therefore$ Queen Elizabeth II is the Queen of Canada $\qquad (r)$

both of which are difficult to regard as syllogistic.

However, we always have to pay some price for generality and the price we pay here is particularly high: it gives no guidance about the conditions under which (p and q) *does* imply r. In fact, this 'principle' simply shows one of the ways in which 'implies' or '$\supset$' is correctly used and shows nothing about any particular kind of inference. It does not give us any help in sorting out the valid and invalid inferences because it says nothing about any of the conditions under which two statements do imply a third.

It is true that the expression

$$[\{(p \cdot q) \supset r\} \cdot (p \cdot q)] \supset r$$

is a valid formula of the propositional calculus but it is not very useful for deciding on the validity of actual inferences, for which we have to decide whether the first '$\supset$' holds.

One advantage of the doctrine of the syllogism is that it gives us a further analysis of the statements involved and so throws light on this relation. We have seen that the conditions specified for the syllogism have no bearing on such inferences as

$$
\begin{array}{ll}
3 > 2 & (p) \\
4 > 3 & (q) \\
\therefore 4 > 2 & (r).
\end{array}
$$

About this inference we have to say, for example, that ($p \cdot q$) implies (r) when the terms are arranged according to the pattern

$$
\begin{array}{l}
a \, R \, b \\
c \, R \, a \\
\therefore c \, R \, b
\end{array}
$$

and the relation (R) is the same throughout and is a transitive relation. This will in fact cover a great many deductive inferences having two premisses and a conclusion. However, it is important that this can be extended to cover inferences with any number of premisses having the form

$$
\begin{array}{l}
a \, R \, b \\
b \, R \, c \\
c \, R \, d \\
d \, R \, e \\
\quad \cdot \\
\quad \cdot \\
\quad \cdot \\
x \, R \, y \\
\therefore a \, R \, y.
\end{array}
$$

185

The interesting question now is whether there is any kind of analysis of statement which could throw light on the conditions under which

$$(p \cdot q) \supset r$$

holds but which is more general than the analysis implicit in the theory of the syllogism. The points made in the previous paragraph lead us to the next possibility.

b. THE SYLLOGISM AS RELATING CLASSES

As we have seen, one important transitive relation is that of class inclusion. It can, therefore, figure in valid inferences of the type mentioned at the end of the last section. We have also seen that the four traditional types of categorical statement can be represented as class inclusion or class exclusion statements.

The idea of distribution has often been explained in class-language so that a term is distributed if it refers to the whole of a class and undistributed if it refers to only part of a class. However, even ignoring difficulties about reference, there are further difficulties about supposing that some of the terms said to be undistributed refer to only parts of classes. For example, the predicate in

> All Ss are P

is said to refer to only part of a class but if we say that the statement may be interpreted as

> The class S is included in the class P

then there seems to be no sense in regarding this as a statement about only part, rather than the whole, of class P. We can surely put it

> The class P includes the class S

which appears to be about the whole of the class P.

However, when we consider the ways in which such statements may be given a class interpretation we see that the notion of distribution becomes superfluous, so if it is incoherent that does not matter. It may be put as an advantage of the class interpretation that it avoids the need to use the problematical idea of distribution.

We have seen that there are two ways of representing the traditional types of statement in class language. The first is

All Ss are P	$S P' = 0$
No Ss are P	$S P = 0$
Some Ss are P	$S P \neq 0$
Some Ss are not P	$S P' \neq 0.$

These may be read respectively,

the class of things common to S and P' is empty;
the class of things common to S and P is empty;
the class of things common to S and P is non-empty;
the class of things common to S and P' is non-empty.

These statements appear to deal with the classes in question as wholes; there seems no possibility of regarding some appearances of S as distributed and others as undistributed. The senses of 'all' and 'some' now seem to be absorbed into 'is empty' and 'is non-empty'.

The other way of representing these statements is by means of the class-inclusion sign, thus,

All Ss are P	$S \subset P$
No Ss are P	$S \subset P'$
Some Ss are P	$\sim (S \subset P')$
Some Ss are not P	$\sim (S \subset P)$.

These may be read, respectively,

the class S is included in the class P;
the class S is included in the class P';
the class S is not included in the class P';
the class S is not included in the class P.

These, again, appear to be statements about the classes as wholes and there is no room for the idea of distribution.

The methods of testing the validity of inferences, including syllogisms, which can be derived from these interpretations depend upon the relations of inclusion, exclusion and overlapping of classes and, in particular, upon the transitivity of class inclusion.

I shall first consider briefly a method of testing the validity of syllogisms by means of an elementary *algebra of classes* similar to that invented by Boole and modified by later writers. The general method is to begin with a number of rules, which are presented as self-evident given the notions of classes we have discussed, and to apply them in such a way as to show that the conclusion can be extracted from the premises.

We have seen that an empty class, or the null class, is represented by 0 and the universe of discourse, or universal class, is represented by 1. It will be remembered that there is just one empty class, that is, that all empty classes are identical. I shall first state just those rules which are needed to deal with the validity of syllogisms. There are other rules which will not be needed here.[12] The rules are stated in symbols and an informal explanation of each is given.

[12] A. H. Basson and D. J. O'Connor, *An Introduction to Symbolic Logic* (London, 1953). R. M. Eaton, *General Logic* (New York, 1931).

Rules:

(i) $0\,A = 0$	There are no members common to A and the null class.
(ii) $0 + 0 = 0$	The class of things contained in the null class or the null class is empty.
(iii) $1\,A = A$	The members common to A and the universal class are the members of A.
(iv) $A + A' = 1$	The sum of any class and its complement is the universal class.
(v) $A(B + C) = A\,B + A\,C$	The members common to A and (B or C) are the members common to A and B or the members common to A and C. (The distributive rule.)
(vi) $A\,B = B\,A$	The members common to A and B are the members common to B and A.
(vii) $A + B = B + A$	The members of A or B are the members of B or A.

I shall now consider two examples and use these rules to show that these examples are valid. The use of these rules is purely mechanical.

Example 1

Fig. II *Cesare*

$$P \text{ e } M$$
$$S \text{ a } M$$
$$\overline{\phantom{S \text{ e } P}}$$
$$S \text{ e } P$$

Represented in the class-symbolism this is

$$P\,M = 0 \qquad \text{(a)}$$
$$S\,M' = 0 \qquad \text{(b)}$$
$$\overline{}$$
$$S\,P = 0 \qquad \text{(c)}$$

(a) *Major Premiss*

$$M\,P = 0 \qquad \text{(by Rule (VI) } P\,M = M\,P)$$
$$\therefore S\,M\,P = 0 \qquad \text{(Rule (i) } 0\,A = 0, \; S = A$$
$$\therefore S\,M\,P = 0)$$
$$\text{and } S'\,M\,P = 0 \qquad \text{(Rule (i))}$$
$$\therefore S\,M\,P + S'\,M\,P = 0 \qquad \text{(Rule (ii) } 0 + 0 = 0)$$

(b) *Minor Premiss*
$$S\,M' = 0$$
$$\therefore\ S\,M'\,P = 0 \qquad \text{(Rule (i))}$$
$$\text{and } S\,M'\,P' = 0 \qquad \text{(Rule (i))}$$
$$\therefore S\,M'\,P + S\,M'\,P' = 0 \qquad \text{(Rule (ii))}$$

(c) *Conclusion*
$$S\,P = 0$$
$$S\,M\,P = 0 \qquad \text{(Rule (i))}$$
$$\text{and } S\,M'\,P = 0 \qquad \text{(Rule (i))}$$
$$\therefore S\,M\,P + S\,M'\,P = 0 \qquad \text{(Rule (ii))}$$

We have now arrived at what is called the *expansion* of each statement.

From the major premiss $\qquad S\,M\,P = 0$

From the minor premiss $\qquad S\,M'\,P = 0$

$\therefore S\,M\,P + S\,M'\,P = 0 \quad$ (Rule (ii))

But this is the conclusion; since it was extracted from the *premisses* the syllogism is valid.

Example 2

Fig. III Disamis $\qquad M\text{ i }P$
$$M\text{ a }S$$

$$\overline{}$$

$$S\text{ i }P$$

Represented in the class symbolism this is

$$M\,P \neq 0 \qquad \text{(a)}$$
$$M\,S' = 0 \qquad \text{(b)}$$

$$\overline{}$$

$$S\,P \neq 0 \qquad \text{(c)}$$

(a) *Major Premiss*
$$M\,P \neq 0$$
$$1\,M\,P \neq 0 \qquad \text{(Rule (iii) } 1\,A = A,\ M\,P$$
$$= A \neq 0)$$
$$S + S' = 1 \qquad \text{(Rule (iv))}$$
$$M\,P\,(S + S') \neq 0 \qquad \text{(Since } 1\,M\,P \neq 0)$$
$$\therefore\ S\,M\,P + S'\,M\,P \neq 0 \qquad \text{(Rule (v))}$$

(b) *Minor Premiss*
$$S'\,M = 0 \qquad \text{(Rule (vi))}$$
$$\therefore\ S'\,M\,P = 0 \qquad \text{(Rule (i))}$$
$$\text{and } S'\,M\,P' = 0 \qquad \text{(Rule (i))}$$
$$\therefore\ S'\,M\,P + S'\,M\,P' = 0 \qquad \text{(Rule (ii))}$$

189

From the minor premiss $S'\,M\,P = 0$

∴ Major premiss is $\qquad S\,M\,P + 0 \neq 0.$

∴ $S\,M\,P \neq 0 \qquad$ (Rule (ii))

∴ $S\,P \qquad \neq 0 \qquad$ (If there are members common to S, M and P then there must be members common to S and P. Rule (i).)

This is the original conclusion; it was extracted from the premisses so it must be valid.

The four moods of the syllogism which have two universal premisses and a particular conclusion cannot be shown to be valid in this way. This is not surprising. They can be accepted as valid only if all the classes involved have members and the class algebra does not involve any such assumptions but deals only with relations between classes which hold whether or not they have members.

I shall now show informally how syllogisms may be expressed in the class-inclusion notation and shown to be valid. We may take the implication statement

$$(p \cdot q) \supset r$$

and substitute in it the appropriate class-inclusion statements for the syllogism in question. From our knowledge of the properties of class inclusion, we can see by inspection that many of the syllogisms are valid. I shall consider three examples.

Example 1

The easiest of all is Fig. I. Barbara. This is

All Ms are P
All Ss are M

∴ All Ss are P

which, in the class-inclusion notation, is

$M \subset P$
$S \subset M$

∴ $S \subset P.$

The corresponding implication statement is

$$\{(S \subset M) \cdot (M \subset P)\} \supset (S \subset P).$$

For clarity, I have reversed the order of p and q.

We can see that this simply says that if S is included in M and M in P then S is included in P, which is true owing to the transitivity of the class-inclusion relation. The syllogism is therefore valid.

Example 2

Fig. II Cesare

> No Ps are M
> All Ss are M
> _____
> ∴ No Ss are P

which, in the class-inclusion notation is

> $P \subset M'$
> $S \subset M$
> _____
> ∴ $S \subset P'$.

The corresponding implication statement is

$$\{(S \subset M) \cdot (P \subset M')\} \supset (S \subset P').$$

Clearly, if S is included in M and P is excluded from M then S cannot be included in P, so is included in P'. The syllogism is valid.

Example 3

Fig. III Disamis

> Some Ms are P
> All Ms are S
> _____
> ∴ Some Ss are P

which, in the class-inclusion notation is

> $\sim (M \subset P')$
> $M \subset S$
> _____
> ∴ $\sim (S \subset P')$

The corresponding implication statement is

$$\{\sim (M \subset P') \cdot (M \subset S)\} \supset \sim (S \subset P')$$

If M is not included in P' and M is included in S then it cannot be that S is included in P'. This syllogism is therefore valid.

It must be stressed that these are not rigorous proofs but only intuitively obvious truths about class relations. The various implication statements can be proved formally in the class-calculus by stating rules and showing that the statements can be derived using them. A brief general account of the way in which such proofs are conducted will be found in the next chapter.[13]

This treatment can be applied to any arguments which can be stated in class-inclusion terms, whether or not they are syllogistic.

C. THE SYLLOGISM AS RELATING PREDICATES

If classes are thought of intensionally, that is, as determined by certain defining properties, we can translate statements about relations between classes into statements about relations between properties or *predicates* which name properties.

Consider, for example, the statement

> All men are mortal.

We can interpret this as a class statement by taking it as

> The class of men is included in the class of mortals.

Let F stand for the class of men and G for the class of mortals. We may then represent the class statement by

> $F \subset G$.

In view of our definition of class inclusion in terms of class-membership we may in turn translate this into a statement about the membership of the respective classes, thus

> If anything is a member of the class of men then
> it is a member of the class of mortals.

The word 'anything' introduces the need for a quantifier and the words 'if . . . then' the need for the sign of material implication, if we are to be able to symbolize this completely.

We thus obtain

> $(x) \{(x \in F) \supset (x \in G)\}$

where x stands for everything which is a candidate for class membership. The expression may be read 'For all x, if x is a member of class F then it is a member of class G', or more briefly, 'If anything is a member of F then it is a member of G'.

Now suppose that instead of thinking of the classes F and G we think of the properties defining those classes. I shall represent predicates, which stand for properties, by the corresponding small letters

[13] See R. M. Eaton, *General Logic.*

f and *g*. We may now write, in place of our English class statement,

> If anything has the property of being a man
> then it has the property of being mortal,

or

> If the predicate 'is a man' applies to anything then the
> predicate 'is a mortal' applies to it.

This may be represented by

$$(x)\,(fx \supset gx)$$

which is to be read 'For all *x*, if *x* has *f* then *x* has *g*', or 'If anything has *f* then it has *g*'. We have here eliminated the specific signs for class membership and class inclusion ($\in$ and $\subset$). We need only the quantifiers and the connectives of the propositional calculus. This is the basis of the *predicate calculus* or, as it is sometimes called, *functional calculus*.

We may interpret syllogisms in terms of the ideas of the predicate calculus and this provides another way of showing under what conditions the premisses imply the conclusion. This interpretation is also more general than either the propositional calculus or the elementary class algebra, allowing us to deal with many different kinds of inference.

We may interpret the four traditional types of statement as expressions in the predicate calculus in the following way. We may begin by giving an interpretation in terms of class membership.

All *S*s are *P*	(x)(If *x* is *S* then *x* is *P*)
No *S*s are *P*	(x)(If *x* is *S* then *x* is not *P*)
Some *S*s are *P*	$(\exists x)$(*x* is *S* and *x* is *P*)
Some *S*s are not *P*	$(\exists x)$(*x* is *S* and *x* is not *P*).

This is to regard *S* and *P* as standing for classes, 'is' for 'is a member of' and 'not *P*' for 'the complement of *P*' or '*P*'', Now let *f* stand for the defining properties of *S* and *g* for the defining properties of *P* and we can then represent our statements in the following way.

All *S*s are *P*	$(x)(fx \supset gx)$
No *S*s are *P*	$(x)(fx \supset \sim gx)$
Some *S*s are *P*	$(\exists x)(fx \cdot gx)$
Some *S*s are not *P*	$(\exists x)(fx \cdot \sim gx)$

In these expressions the symbols of the propositional calculus are used according to the usual rules.

An advantage of this method of representation is that it gives a

193

method of interpreting singular statements which shows their difference from universal statements and so conforms better to everyday usage than their interpretation as being about unit classes. We use small letters m, n, o for the names of individuals, that is, for particular instances of x. Thus we may represent 'Socrates is mortal' by gm where m stands for the individual Socrates. If we were to represent this as a universal statement we should have to regard 'being Socrates' as a property and 'being mortal' as another property and write

$$(x)(x \text{ is Socrates} \supset x \text{ is mortal})$$

or

$$(x)(fx \supset gx)$$

where f stands for 'being Socrates'. This symbolic representation does not distinguish 'Socrates is mortal' from 'All men are mortal', which is a weakness. If, however, we represent 'All men are mortal' by

$$(x)(fx \supset gx)$$

and 'Socrates is mortal' by

$$gm$$

then 'gm' may be regarded as an *instance* of 'gx'.

Using this device we can see how certain arguments which were troublesome in syllogistic theory work. Consider

> All men are mortal
> Socrates is a man
> ∴ Socrates is mortal.

We can represent this in the predicate calculus by

$$(x)(fx \supset gx)$$
$$fm$$
$$\therefore gm.$$

This is valid on the reasonable assumption that the universal statement may be applied to any relevant instance and the acceptance of the *modus ponens* rule.

The expression fm stands for a statement that a given individual has a certain property. In connection with the propositional calculus we used $p, q, \ldots$ to stand for any statements whatever; it follows that statements of the form fm may be substituted for $p, q \ldots$ in expressions of the propositional calculus. We are then simply applying the expressions of the propositional calculus to statements of a particular sort.

For example, the formula

$$\{(p \supset q) \cdot (\sim r \supset \sim q)\} \supset (p \supset r)$$

is a valid formula. That is, whatever statements are substituted for p, q and r the relations will still hold and a true statement will result. If we let $p = fm$; $q = gm$ and $r = fn$ we obtain, by substitution

$$\{(fm \supset gm) \cdot (\sim fn \supset \sim gm)\} \supset (fm \supset fn).$$

We can see that this is valid by *modus ponens* and *modus tollens*. Truth tables may also be used to test it. (See Chap. IV, Section 8.)

It should be noted that in these predicate-calculus interpretations of the traditional types of statement, the particular statements are represented as having existential import while the universals are not. It may be wondered why the connective '$\supset$' appears in the universal statements but not in the particular statements. This is connected with the last comment but we may explain it by considering what it means to negate the expression $(x) A$, where A stands for an expression containing x. The negation is written most simply

$$\sim (x) A$$

which may be read 'It is not the case that for any x, A'. This clearly means 'There is at least one x such that not A'. Thus

$$\sim (x) A$$

is equivalent to

$$(\exists x) \sim A.$$

Now suppose that for A we substitute $(fx \supset gx)$, then the expression

$$(\exists x) \sim A$$

becomes

$$(\exists x) \sim (fx \supset gx).$$

But, by the definition of '$\supset$', the expression

$$fx \supset gx$$

is equivalent to

$$\sim (fx \cdot \sim gx).$$

This is A, so $\sim A$ is

$$(fx \cdot \sim gx).$$

195

Therefore

$$(\exists x) \sim (fx \supset gx)$$

is equivalent to

$$(\exists x)(fx \cdot \sim gx),$$

which may be read 'There is at least one thing which has property f and not property g'. The negation of a universal affirmative statement gives us its contradictory, a particular negative statement, as we saw in discussing the square of opposition. Thus the negation of

$$(x)(fx \supset gx)$$

is

$$(\exists x)(fx \cdot \sim gx).$$

which is, therefore, the representation in the predicate calculus of 'Some Ss are not P'.

In general, the negation of a universal statement is an existential statement and the negation of an existential statement is a universal statement. This gives us two ways of representing each traditional type of statement.

All Ss are P	$(x)(fx \supset gx)$
	$\sim (\exists x)(fx \cdot \sim gx)$.
No Ss are P	$(x)(fx \supset \sim gx)$
	$\sim (\exists x)(fx \cdot gx)$.
Some Ss are P	$(\exists x)(fx \cdot gx)$
	$\sim (x)(fx \supset \sim gx)$.
Some Ss are not P	$(\exists x)(fx \cdot \sim gx)$
	$\sim (x)(fx \supset gx)$.

There is then a simple way of putting contradictories. In the above list, the *negation* of the first expression in each pair is the second expression without its initial negation sign. That is

$$\sim (x)(fx \supset gx) \equiv (\exists x)(fx \cdot \sim gx)$$
$$\sim (x)(fx \supset \sim gx) \equiv (\exists x)(fx \cdot gx)$$
$$\sim (\exists x)(fx \cdot gx) \equiv (x)(fx \supset \sim gx)$$
$$\sim (\exists x)(fx \cdot \sim gx) \equiv (x)(fx \supset gx).$$

This means that if we wish to refute a universal statement, such as 'All cats are black', then we can do so only by producing evidence, that is, at least one thing which is a cat and not black. On the other hand, it is not essential to produce evidence to establish every universal statement since a universal statement may be made true by definition. It must be added, however, that many of the universal statements in which we are interested are such that we want them to be supported by evidence and not to be true merely by definition.

Given that the negation of a universal statement is an existential statement, it may be wondered what has happened to the distinction between universal and particular statements on the grounds of existential import. This is preserved since both affirmative and negative universal statements are seen to assert merely the non-existence of certain combinations or properties while particular statements are seen to assert the existence of certain combinations of properties and so to deny the universal connection of certain *other* properties.

We can now go on to consider how syllogistic arguments can be expressed in the predicate calculus and their validity tested. Again there is the advantage that the methods for doing this do not depend upon the idea of distribution. The simplest way of testing predicate-calculus expressions relies heavily on the ideas of the propositional calculus. This is acceptable at least for simple inferences of the syllogistic types. A more sophisticated and rigorous method is by means of formal proofs depending upon the acceptance of a set of rules. The approach to the method of rigorous proof will be outlined in the next chapter; here I shall deal briefly with the simpler method. I shall do this by means of examples.

Example 1

Fig. I   *Barbara*

All mammals are vertebrates
All cats are mammals
∴ All cats are vertebrates.

Let f stand for 'is a mammal', g for 'is a vertebrate' and h for 'is a cat'. We may then represent the syllogism thus

$$(x) (fx \supset gx)$$
$$(x)(hx \supset fx)$$
$$\therefore (x)(hx \supset gx).$$

Writing the whole of this as an implication statement we obtain

$$\{(x)(fx \supset gx) \cdot (x)(hx \supset fx)\} \supset (x)(hx \supset gx).$$

This appears to be a valid formula simply by inspection on the basis of the transitivity of the implication relation or the rule of *modus ponens*. If hx implies fx and fx implies gx then it follows that hx implies gx.

14   197

More formally, we may say that the expression in the predicate calculus is analogous to the following expression in the propositional calculus

$$\{(p \supset q) \cdot (r \supset p)\} \supset (r \supset q).$$

Putting it in another way, the predicate-calculus expression may be regarded as a substitution instance of the expression of the propositional calculus. The expression of the propositional calculus may be shown to be valid by the truth-table method to be discussed in the next section. Because the quantifiers are the same throughout the expression of the predicate calculus, this can be said to be valid by analogy.

Example 2

Fig. IV *Fresison*

$$P \ e \ M$$
$$M \ i \ S$$
$$\overline{}$$
$$\therefore \ S \ o \ P$$

The representation of this in the predicate calculus is

$$(x)(fx \supset \sim gx)$$
$$(\exists x)(gx \cdot hx)$$
$$\therefore (\exists x)(hx \cdot \sim fx).$$

Written as an implication this becomes

$$\{(x)(fx \supset \sim gx) \cdot \exists x(gx \cdot hx)\} \supset \exists x(hx \cdot \sim fx).$$

The second premiss tells us that there is something with both property *g* and property *h*. From the first premiss, using *modus tollens* we can conclude that anything with property *g* does not have property *f*. It follows that there must be something with property *h* and without property *f*, which is the conclusion.

The analogous expression in the propositional calculus is

$$\{(p \supset \sim q) \cdot (q \cdot r)\} \supset (r \cdot \sim p).$$

This can be shown to be valid by truth-table methods. The use of the existential quantifier in the expression of the predicate calculus introduces a complication here. The expression $(p \supset \sim q)$ does not assert or presuppose the existence of anything or the truth of either its components. The expression $(q \cdot r)$ does something analogous to asserting existence since it asserts the truth of both components. This is what allows the assertion of the truth of both components of the

198

conclusion. There is an analogy between asserting existence in the predicate calculus and asserting truth in the propositional calculus.

Example 3

Fig. III *Bocardo*.

This is one of the moods which give trouble in the traditional reduction to the first figure, requiring a special method. Here it may be dealt with in a similar way to other valid moods. Its schema is

$$M \text{ o } P$$
$$M \text{ a } S$$
$$\therefore S \text{ o } P.$$

Its representation in the predicate calculus is

$$(\exists x)(fx \cdot \sim gx)$$
$$(x)(fx \supset hx)$$
$$\therefore (\exists x)(hx \cdot \sim gx).$$

Written as an implication it becomes

$$\{(\exists x)(fx \cdot \sim gx) \cdot (x)(fx \supset hx)\} \supset \exists x(hx \cdot \sim gx).$$

By inspection we can see that the first premiss asserts that there is something with property *f* but not property *g*. The second premiss asserts that anything with property *f* has property *h*. It follows that there is something with property *h* but not property *g*, which is the conclusion.

The analogous expression in the propositional calculus is

$$\{(p \cdot \sim q) \cdot (p \supset r)\} \supset (r \cdot \sim q)$$

which can be shown to be valid by the truth-table method.

Example 4

Fig. IV *Bramantip*.

$$P \text{ a } M$$
$$M \text{ a } S$$
$$\therefore S \text{ i } P$$

Its representation in the predicate calculus is

$$(x)(fx \supset gx)$$
$$(x)(gx \supset hx)$$
$$\therefore (\exists x)(hx \cdot fx).$$

199

Written as an implication this becomes

$$\{(x)(fx \supset gx) \cdot (x)(gx \supset hx)\} \supset (\exists x)(hx \cdot fx).$$

Here it is quite clear that the premisses alone do not give sufficient grounds for asserting the conclusion. What is additionally needed is at least the presupposition that there are things with property f. Without that, the two premisses simply tell us that *if* anything has f then it has g and if anything has g it has h, but not that anything does possess any of these properties. The conclusion, asserting as it does that something does possess properties h and f, fails to follow. This is yet another way of showing that a syllogism with two universal premisses and a particular conclusion is invalid without the assumption that universal statements have existential import. Because this was generally assumed by traditional logicians, they took Bramantip to be a valid syllogism.

The analogous expression of the propositional calculus is

$$\{(p \supset q) \cdot (q \supset r)\} \supset (r \cdot p)$$

which the truth-table method shows to be invalid. Once again we see that $(r \cdot p)$ is analogous to an assertion of existence and no such assertion occurs in the premisses.

The various possible interpretations of the syllogism with which I have dealt amount to different ways of formalizing certain inferences which occur in everyday discourse. They are arrived at by concentrating on different features of the everyday arguments, that is, by abstracting in different ways from these arguments. Which is preferable will depend on one's aim. If the aim is to generalize as much as possible about deductive inferences then the preferable formalization will be that which is capable of covering the greatest number of different kinds of inference. The price we pay for this is that it may blur distinctions between different inferences in everyday discourse, which means that we must exercise care in translating the discoveries we make in the formal systems into everyday language, or in applying these discoveries to everyday inferences. In a context in which we use these inferences it may become important to consider features which are left out of account in the formalism.

The most powerful interpretation with which I have dealt is that in terms of predicates which forms the basis for the predicate calculus. It is the most powerful because it allows the most general test of validity, being applicable to the widest range of different kinds of inference. The class interpretation is of great importance in relation to pure mathematics since it led to the modern branch of mathematics known as set theory which is an immensely more subtle and complex development of the simple class algebra with which I have dealt.[14] This is not the place in which to go into this development. The basis of the formal treatment of the predicate calculus will be outlined in the next chapter.

8. THE TESTING OF VALIDITY BY TRUTH TABLES

Whenever an inference can be represented as a number of statements related by the connectives of the propositional calculus we may test the validity of the inference by constructing a truth table for its symbolic representation. The propositional calculus might be said to be the most general, though not the most revealing, of the logical calculi; the class calculus and the predicate calculus and even, in a limited way, the theory of the syllogism are finer tools for the analysis of inferences. The propositional calculus treats relations between statements without distinguishing between kinds of statement; the other calculi do distinguish between kinds of statement. The propositional calculus, therefore, only allows rather crude tests of validity.

I shall now outline this method of testing validity using the basic truth tables which were explained in Chap. III, Section 2c.

(a) *Negation*

p	$\sim p$
T	F
F	T

(b) *Conjunction*

p	$\cdot$	q
T	T	T
T	F	F
F	F	T
F	F	F

(c) *Disjunction*

p	$\vee$	q
T	T	T
T	T	F
F	T	T
F	F	F

(d) *Material Implication*

p	$\supset$	q
T	T	T
T	F	F
F	T	T
F	T	F

Using these we can construct a truth table for any expression containing just these constants and propositional variables in a purely mechanical way, no matter how complex the expression may be. The expression is shown to be valid if the resulting table has nothing but

[4] See W. V. Quine, *Set Theory and Its Logic* (Cambridge, Mass., 1963).

Ts under the main connective, invalid if it has at least one 'F' under the main connective, and self-contradictory if it has nothing but Fs under the main connective. The main connective is usually an implication sign which corresponds to 'therefore' in the original inference. In other words, it represents the break between premisses and conclusion.

I shall begin to explain the method by using the simplest *modus ponens* argument, that is,

$$\text{If } p \text{ then } q$$
$$p$$
$$\therefore \quad q.$$

We may represent the statements in the notation of the calculus thus

First premiss	$(p \supset q)$
Second premiss	p
Conclusion	$q.$

The two premisses, being both asserted, may be joined by '·' and bracketed together thus,

$$\{(p \supset q) \cdot p\}$$

and since these together are said to imply the conclusion, we may represent the whole inference by

$$\{(p \supset q) \cdot p\} \supset q.$$

We begin to construct its truth table by filling in all the possible combinations of truth values for the variables. We have seen, in Chap. III, Section 2c, that for two variables we need four rows. We then work outwards from the values for the variables, filling in the consequent values for the narrowest bracket, using the basic truth tables, until we have completed the column for the main connective. We have seen that in any given row, a particular variable must keep the same value throughout.

We proceed by the following steps, which I number in order.

(a)	$\{(p$	$\supset$	$q) \cdot$	$p\}$	$\supset$	q
		T		T	T	T
		T		F	T	F
		F		T	F	T
		F		F	F	F
		(1)		(2)	(3)	(4)

(b) $\{(p \supset q) \cdot p\} \supset q$

        T T T
        T F F
        F T T
        F T F
           (5)

This is simply an application of the basic table for '$\supset$'.

(c) $\{(p \supset q) \cdot p\} \supset q$

        T   T T
        F   F T
        T   F F
        T   F F
           (6)

This is an application of the basic table for '$\cdot$'.

(d) $\{(p \supset q) \cdot p\} \supset q$

          T T T
          F T F
          F T T
          F T F
             (7)

The second '$\supset$' is the main connective. Column (6) is the set of values for the whole expression to the left of it. This completes the truth table which, written out in full is

    $\{(p \supset q) \cdot p\} \supset q$
      T T T T T T T
      T F F F T T F
      F T T F F T T
      F T F F F T F
    (1)(5)(2)(6)(3)(7)(4)

Column (7) shows the expression to be valid or a *tautology*. This is the expected result. The connection between an expression's being valid and its being a tautology is this: to show that it is a tautology is to show that the main relation holds under all conditions of truth and falsity of its variables and this means that the part of it taken as representing a conclusion is never false when the part taken as representing the premisses is true. Any argument which has the form of the expression is therefore valid.

Proceeding in a similar way, we may construct the truth table for the following expressions which represents a different inference.

$$\{(p \supset q) \cdot \sim p\} \supset \sim q$$

The steps are again numbered in order.

$$
\begin{array}{c}
\{(p \supset q) \cdot \sim p\} \supset \sim q \\
\text{T T T F F T T F T} \\
\text{T F F F F T T T F} \\
\text{F T T T T F F F T} \\
\text{F T F T T F T T F} \\
(1)(7)(2)(8)(5)(3)(9)(6)(4)
\end{array}
$$

The single 'F' in the final column (9) is enough to establish the invalidity of the expression.

Finally, as a last introductory example we will construct the truth table for the expression

$$(p \supset q) \cdot (p \cdot \sim q)$$

where the main connective is '·' rather than '⊃'. We obtain

$$
\begin{array}{c}
(p \supset q) \cdot (p \cdot \sim q) \\
\text{T T T F T F F T} \\
\text{T F F F T T T F} \\
\text{F T T F F F F T} \\
\text{F T F F F F T F} \\
(1)(6)(2)(8)(3)(7)(5)(4)
\end{array}
$$

This expression is shown by the entire absence of Ts in the final column to be self-contradictory. We might have expected this result since the expression in the right-hand bracket is the negation of one definition of the expression in the left-hand bracket (see Chap. III, Section 2c).

In presenting these simple examples I have not made clear any principles about the use of brackets and the order in which the tables are to be constructed. I must now do this.

The principal use of brackets is to avoid ambiguity and to make clear, if we are dealing with inferences, what is intended to follow from what. In representing an inference in the propositional calculus it is essential to use brackets correctly if there is any possibility of ambiguity. Ideally, if we regard this calculus as a *system*, we should state formal rules for the use of brackets but this presents considerable difficulty and here I shall deal with this matter informally.

The formula '$p \cdot q$' is quite unambiguous without brackets. However, suppose we add a negation sign and write

$\sim p \cdot q.$

Unless we have some agreed convention, this is ambiguous since '$\sim$' may be intended to negate just 'p' or to negate the whole conjunction '$p \cdot q$'. We distinguish these possibilities by taking the unbracketed expression in the first way and using brackets when we wish to negate the whole conjunction thus:

$\sim (p \cdot q).$

Consider next the expression

$p \supset q \supset r.$

That this is seriously ambiguous, as it stands, may be shown by an example. There is an important difference between

(a) If John works hard then if he takes the examination he will pass,

and

(b) If John's working hard implies that he will take the examination then he will pass.

The first is a reasonable thing to say but the second is odd: in any case, they are quite different and should be represented, respectively, by

(a) $p \supset (q \supset r)$
(b) $(p \supset q) \supset r.$

These have different truth tables.

Similarly the expression

$p \lor q \supset r$

is ambiguous and may be bracketed in two different ways, namely,

(a) $(p \lor q) \supset r$

and

(b) $p \lor (q \supset r).$

These would distinguish between the two different statements

(a) If John is stupid or he is lazy then he will not pass

and

(b) Either John is stupid or if he is lazy then he will not pass.

These also have different truth tables.

However, the expressions

$$p \lor q \lor r$$

and

$$p \cdot q \cdot r$$

are unambiguous as they stand and so they strictly need no brackets. This may be verified by constructing truth tables for the two possible bracketings of each expression. The members of each pair will be found to have identical truth tables. It is often helpful, however, to bracket such expressions in an arbitrary way as this makes clear the order of procedure in constructing truth tables. We may indicate this arbitrary bracketing thus

$$\overline{p \lor q} \lor r.$$

Closely related to the use of brackets is the idea of the *scope* of connectives. Crudely, the scope of a connective is that part of the whole expression to which the connective applies. This is what is indicated by brackets. In the expression '$\sim p$' the scope of '$\sim$' is 'p'; in the expression '$(p \cdot q)$' the scope of '$\cdot$' is 'p, q'; in the expression '$\sim (p \cdot q)$' the scope of '$\sim$' is '$(p \cdot q)$' and the scope of '$\cdot$' is 'p, q'. In this last expression the scope of '$\sim$' is said to be wider than the scope of '$\cdot$'.

Consider a more complex expression which might be understood as representing an inference

$$\{(p \supset q) \cdot r\} \supset \{(r \supset p) \lor (s \supset p)\}.$$
$$(1) \quad (2) \ (4) \qquad\qquad (3)$$

The scope of each numbered connective is as follows.

(1) p, q.
(2) $(p \supset q), r$.
(3) $(r \supset p), (s \supset p)$.
(4) $\{(p \supset q) \cdot r\}, \{(r \supset p) \lor (s \supset p)\}$.

The material implication sign (4) is the connective which has as its scope the whole of the rest of the expression; it is thus the *main connective*. If the expression represents an inference, this connective stands for 'therefore' joining premisses and conclusion. It is the connective which would be dealt with last in constructing a truth table.

In constructing a truth table we should always begin by putting in the possible truth values for the variables, then proceed with the values for the connectives of narrowest scope, then the values for the connectives of next widest scope and so on until we reach the connective of widest scope, which is always the main connective.

The principle underlying the truth table is that it shows what truth value the whole expression has for each possible combination of the truth values of its variables. It is therefore essential, in constructing a truth table, that we put in at the beginning every possible combination of values for the variables. We can ensure that we do this by a simple mathematical calculation according to the following two rules.

Rule 1 Given that we have *n* variables the number of *rows* needed will be 2^n.

If we have just two variables, *p* and *q*, each of which may be true or false, then the possible combinations (rows) are four (2^2), thus,

p	q
T	T
T	F
F	T
F	F

If we now add another variable, *r*, we need eight (2^3) rows, thus,

p	q	r
T	T	T
T	T	F
T	F	T
T	F	F
F	T	T
F	T	F
F	F	T
F	F	F

If we omit any one of these rows it is clear that one possible combination is missing. On the other hand, inspection shows that these eight rows omit no possible combinations.

It is clear that the size of the truth table increases rapidly as we increase the number of variables. Thus for an expression containing 10 different variables we need 2^{10} rows, that is 1024 rows.

Rule 2 It is difficult to state this rule in a way that is both short and clear so I will explain it informally.

The first rule simply tells us the number of rows we need but it does not determine how the Ts and Fs are to be arranged in these rows.

It is convenient to consider the composition of the *columns*. A convenient rule of thumb is: if by Rule 1 we have calculated that we need *m* rows then the column under the first variable will consist of $m/2$ Ts followed by $m/2$ Fs; the column under the second variable will consist of $m/4$ Ts followed by $m/4$ Fs followed by the same pattern repeated. We continue in this way, halving the number of Ts and Fs in the first group in each successive column until the last column contains T and F alternately. Thus, for four variables we obtain the pattern

p	*q*	*r*	*s*
T	T	T	T
T	T	T	F
T	T	F	T
T	T	F	F
T	F	T	T
T	F	T	F
T	F	F	T
T	F	F	F
F	T	T	T
F	T	T	F
F	T	F	T
F	T	F	F
F	F	T	T
F	F	T	F
F	F	F	T
F	F	F	F

We have four variables so we need $2^4 = 16$ rows. The first column contains $\frac{16}{2} = 8$ Ts followed by 8 Fs, and so on. It will be noted that the portion of this table marked by dotted lines is the table for two variables and the portion marked by broken lines is the table for three variables.

I will now show the construction of two more truth tables, this time with three variables each, indicating the order of procedure by a number under each column.

Example 1

$$(p \lor q \lor r) \supset \{(\sim p \supset r) \cdot (\sim q \supset r)\}.$$

It will be convenient to bracket the first expression arbitrarily thus, $(\overline{p \lor q} \lor r)$, to remind us that the first '$\lor$' is being treated first. As we have three variables we need 2^3 rows, that is, 8 rows. We obtain

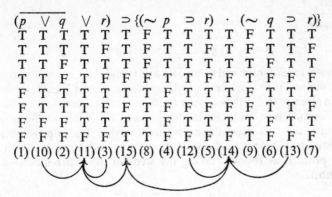

$(p$	$\lor$	q	$\lor$	$r)$	$\supset$	$\{(\sim$	p	$\supset$	$r)$	$\cdot$	$(\sim$	q	$\supset$	$r)\}$
T	T	T	T	T	T	F	T	T	T	T	F	T	T	T
T	T	T	T	F	T	F	T	T	F	T	F	T	T	F
T	T	F	T	T	T	F	T	T	T	T	T	F	T	T
T	T	F	T	F	F	F	T	T	F	F	T	F	F	F
F	T	T	T	T	T	T	F	T	T	T	F	T	T	T
F	T	T	T	F	F	T	F	F	F	F	F	T	T	F
F	F	F	T	T	T	T	F	T	T	T	T	F	T	T
F	F	F	F	T	T	T	F	F	F	T	F	F	F	F
(1)	(10)	(2)	(11)	(3)	(15)	(8)	(4)	(12)	(5)	(14)	(9)	(6)	(13)	(7)

The two Fs in the final column show the whole expression to be invalid. In constructing this truth table we construct columns (4), (5), (6) and (7) simply by copying the values from the relevant column (1), (2) or (3).

Example 2

$\{(p$	$\supset$	$q)$	$\cdot$	$(q$	$\supset$	$r)\}$	$\supset$	$(p$	$\supset$	$r)$
T	T	T	T	T	T	T	T	T	T	T
T	T	T	F	T	F	F	T	T	F	F
T	F	F	F	F	T	T	T	T	T	T
T	F	F	F	F	T	F	T	T	F	F
F	T	T	T	T	T	T	T	F	T	T
F	T	T	F	T	F	F	T	F	T	F
F	T	F	T	T	T	T	T	F	T	T
F	T	F	T	F	T	F	T	F	T	F
(1)	(7)	(2)	(10)	(3)	(8)	(4)	(11)	(5)	(9)	(6)

The column under the main connective is entirely Ts so the expression is valid, that is, a tautology.

Note that a sufficient condition for the invalidity of an expression is the appearance of just one F in the final column of the truth table, that is, under the main connective. This allows the development of a *short method* for testing validity, which is based upon the truth table but obviates the necessity of constructing the full table. This is of considerable value in testing expressions containing more than three variables since, at this stage, truth tables become very cumbersome. It is unfortunate, however, that the short method does not work effectively for every expression.

Consider first the simple expression

Example 1

$$(p \lor q) \supset (p \supset q).$$

If this is *invalid* there will be at least one F under the main connective. The method is to work backwards from an assumed F in this column in an attempt to construct a row which gives this result. If we succeed, the formula is invalid. On the other hand, if it is impossible to construct such a row then the expression is valid. The impossibility of constructing this row is shown if the attempt leads to a contradiction. We proceed as follows, taking the steps in the order indicated by number.

$$(p \lor q) \supset (p \supset q)$$

(1)			F			
(2)	T					F
(3)				T		F
(4)	T		F			

There is no contradiction here so the formula is invalid because we have shown that the full table would contain the row

$$(p \lor q) \supset (p \supset q)$$
$$\text{T T F} \quad \text{F T F F.}$$

If we consider again the basic truth tables

p	$\lor$	q		p	$\cdot$	q		p	$\supset$	q
T	T	T		*T	T	T		T	T	T
T	T	F		T	F	F		*T	F	F
F	T	T		F	F	T		F	T	T
*F	F	F		F	F	F		F	T	F

we see that the starred row in each table is unique in that it is the only row giving one particular value (T or F) for that connective. This is the fact upon which we rely in the short method. In deciding at each stage what step to take next we look for a value under a connective which is produced under only one set of conditions, that is, for F under '$\supset$' or '$\lor$', or for T under '$\cdot$'. It follows that there is no alternative for the next step from that value. Thus in step (3) we dealt with the F under '$\supset$' rather than the T under '$\lor$'. Once we get a value for a variable we can fill it in wherever that variable occurs, as indicated by arrows.

210

Now consider a more complex example.

Example 2

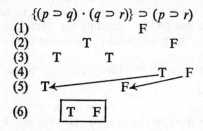

$$\{(p \supset q) \cdot (q \supset r)\} \supset (p \supset r)$$

(1)			F
(2)	T		F
(3)	T	T	
(4)			T F
(5)	T	F	
(6)	T F		

Here we have a contradiction, indicated by the rectangle, because q is given different values, which is impossible in the same row. We arrive at this result in the following way. In step (3) we have shown that both $(p \supset q)$ and $(q \supset r)$ must be true. Step (5) shows p to be true, so to preserve the truth of $(p \supset q)$ it is necessary that q be true. Step (5) also shows r to be false, so to preserve the truth of $(q \supset r)$ it is necessary that q be false. This is a contradiction. Thus no row having F under the main connective can be constructed so the expression is valid.

We may use these techniques of the propositional calculus for testing arguments in everyday English if the argument can be represented adequately by an expression of the propositional calculus. We first represent the arguments in this form and then construct a truth table or apply the short method. If the expression in the propositional calculus turns out to be invalid then the original argument is invalid, as long as it cannot be represented by any other expression which can be shown to be valid. The point of this last reservation will be explained in the next section. If the expression in the propositional calculus turns out to be valid then the original argument is valid, assuming that nothing has been lost in representing it in the propositional calculus. As I have said, considerable caution must be exercised in this matter.

I shall now consider two examples of arguments in everyday English to show how the short method may be applied.

Example 1

> *If* Smith cheated *or* the judges are in doubt, *then either* Smith will bribe the judges *or* he will forfeit the title. *Therefore, if* Smith does *not* forfeit the title *or* the judges are in doubt, *then it is false that* he *both* cheated *and* is *not* bribing the judges.

211

Clearly, the first sentence is intended to constitute the premisses and the second sentence the conclusion, as is indicated by 'therefore'. The words which are to be represented by connectives of the propositional calculus are italicized. Since there is no explicit indication that the uses of 'or' are exclusive, we take them to be inclusive. The main connective will be '$\supset$', standing for 'therefore'. We represent each statement in the premisses by a letter, as follows.

(Smith cheated)   or   (the judges are in doubt)

$$p \qquad\qquad \vee \qquad\qquad q$$

(Smith will bribe the judges)   or   (he will forfeit the title)

$$r \qquad\qquad \vee \qquad\qquad s$$

These two compound premisses are joined by 'if ... then' so we represent the whole of the premisses by

$$(p \vee q) \supset (r \vee s).$$

The conclusion contains just these statements or their negations, so they will be represented as follows.

(Smith does not forfeit the title) or (the judges are in doubt)

$$\sim s \qquad\qquad \vee \qquad\qquad q$$

(he (Smith) cheated)   and (he is not bribing the judges)

$$p \qquad\qquad \cdot \qquad\qquad \sim r$$

The first of these is said, in the conclusion, to imply the negation of the second, so we have as the whole of the conclusion

$$(\sim s \vee q) \supset \sim (p \cdot \sim r).$$

The whole premiss is said to imply the whole conclusion, so we represent the whole argument thus

$$\{(p \vee q) \supset (r \vee s)\} \supset \{(\sim s \vee q) \supset \sim (p \cdot \sim r)\}.$$

We may now apply the short method to this, each step being numbered as before.

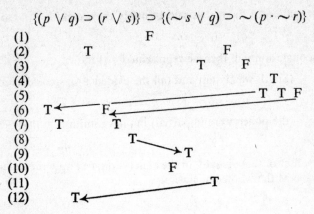

$$\{(p \lor q) \supset (r \lor s)\} \supset \{(\sim s \lor q) \supset \sim (p \cdot \sim r)\}$$

[Explanations

Step (7)   T under 'p' is enough to ensure T under '$\lor$' in the first bracket; this together with T under the first '$\supset$' necessitates T under '$\lor$' in the second bracket.

Step (8)   In the second bracket F under 'r' and T under '$\lor$' necessitates T under s.

Step (11) In '$(\sim s \lor q)$', T under '$\lor$' and F under $\sim$'s' necessitates T under 'q'.]

We have here arrived at values for all the variables which will give F under the main connective without any contradiction. The expression is therefore invalid. If no other way of showing the original argument to be valid is possible and it is not distorted by its representation in the propositional calculus, then the original argument is invalid.

Example 2

If it is false that Smith's lying *implies* Smith's guilt *then if* all the evidence was considered, the police were not impartial. *Therefore,* if Smith was lying *and* all the evidence was considered *then if* the police were impartial, Smith is guilty.

The premises may be represented in the following way.

(Smith was lying) implies (Smith is guilty)

$p \qquad\qquad\qquad \supset \qquad\qquad\qquad q$

(All the evidence was considered) implies (the police were
not impartial)

$r \qquad\qquad\qquad\qquad\qquad \supset \qquad\qquad s.$

15

213

The negation of the first is said to imply the second so we have

$$\sim (p \supset q) \supset (r \supset s).$$

The conclusion will then be represented as follows.

(Smith was lying) and (all the evidence was considered)

$$p \qquad \qquad \cdot \qquad \qquad r$$

(the police were impartial) implies (Smith is guilty)

$$\sim s \qquad \qquad \supset \qquad \qquad q.$$

The first of these is said, in the conclusion, to imply the second, so we have as the whole conclusion

$$(p \cdot r) \supset (\sim s \supset q).$$

The whole argument is then represented by

$$\{(\sim p \supset q) \supset (r \supset s)\} \supset \{(p \cdot r) \supset (\sim s \supset q)\}$$

We apply the short method using the numbered steps.

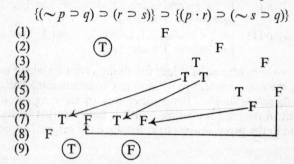

The three circled values give a contradiction since we cannot have T under '$\supset$' and T and F in that order under the expressions it joins. Thus, with the reservations we have noted, we may say that the original argument is valid.

The truth-table methods for testing the validity of expressions has here been applied only to expressions of the propositional calculus. I mentioned, in the last section, that these can be extended to allow their use in connection with simple expressions, at least, of the predicate calculus.[15] I conclude this section by saying a little more about this.

We cannot apply these methods directly to expressions involving quantifiers but we can apply them indirectly to expressions involving

[15] See W. V. Quine, *Methods of Logic* (2nd Edn., London, 1958), Part III.

such elementary uses of quantifiers as we have considered. As I have indicated, the method is to find an expression of the propositional calculus which is analogous to the expression of the predicate calculus and then to test the analogous expression by truth-table methods.

For example, in the expression

$$\{(x)(fx \supset gx) \cdot (x)(gx \supset hx)\} \supset (x)(fx \supset hx)$$

each expression of the form 'fx' can be regarded as a statement-variable and is represented by 'p', 'q', 'r' etc. Thus our expression is analogous to

$$\{(p \supset q) \cdot (q \supset r)\} \supset (p \supset r)$$

which, as a truth table will show, is valid.

We may treat certain simple expressions containing both universal and existential quantifiers in a similar way. For example, the expression

$$((x)fx \cdot (\exists x)gx) \supset (x)fx$$

is analogous to the expression

$$(p \cdot q) \supset p$$

which is shown to be valid by truth-table methods.

It must be noted that '$(x)fx$' and '$(\exists x)fx$' must be treated quite differently in these constructions of analogous expressions, in spite of the presence of 'fx' in both. 'All xs have f' and 'There is an x such that it has f' are quite different statements and so must be represented by different propositional variables. This leads to some difficulties in the attempt to find analogous expressions for expressions in the predicate calculus which contain both quantifiers.

For example, the expression

$$\{(x)(fx \supset gx) \cdot (\exists x)fx\} \supset (\exists x)gx$$

must be represented by

$$\{(p \supset q) \cdot r\} \supset s.$$

This expression in the propositional calculus is not a valid formula but the original expression in the predicate calculus is valid. Its validity is evident when we examine the inner structures of the statements represented by p, q, r and s. Thus the simple method of analogy which we have used so far has serious limitations.

However, some of these limitations may be overcome if we accept certain rules relating various types of quantified and unquantified expressions. I shall mention here just two of these rules; they will be dealt with formally in the next chapter.

For these rules we need a new conception, that of an *individual arbitrarily selected from a given range*. I shall use the letters '*a*', '*b*', '*c*', . . . for abritrarily selected individuals. If we can prove something to be true of any arbitrarily selected thing then it is true of everything, as long as our proof did not depend upon our having selected the thing we did select. A related conception is that of the *ambiguous name* and I shall use the same symbols for these; if we know that there is some individual having a certain property but we don't know which individual this is, we can use an ambiguous name to stand for it, rather as lawyers use 'John Doe' as the name of an unspecified individual who logically could be specified but for our ignorance.

(i) *Rule of Universal Instantiation*
Under certain conditions

$$(x)fx \text{ implies } fa.$$

Explanation. Any universally quantified expression may be said to imply any of its instances; if something is true of every individual then it is true of any arbitrarily selected individual.

Consider the expression

$$\{(x)(hx \supset ix) \cdot (x)(gx \supset hx)\} \supset (x)(gx \supset ix).$$

Using our rule, where *a* is any arbitrarily selected individual, we obtain

$$\{(ha \supset ia) \cdot (ga \supset ha)\} \supset (ga \supset ia).$$

The analogous expression in the propositional calculus may be written

$$\{(q \supset r) \cdot (p \supset q)\} \supset (p \supset r)$$

which may be shown to be valid by a truth-table method.

(ii) *Rule of Existential Instantiation*
Under certain conditions

$$(\exists x)fx \text{ implies } fa$$

where *a* is an ambiguous name.

Explanation: The assertion that there is something satisfying a certain condition implies the assertion that this given condition is satisfied by some nameable individual. Here we are letting '*a*' stand for one of the things having property *f*.

216

Now consider again the expression with which we had difficulty above, namely,

$$\{(x)(fx \supset gx) \cdot (\exists x)fx\} \supset (\exists x)gx.$$

Using the rule of Universal Instantiation we may write in place of the first, universally quantified, expression

$$fa \supset ga.$$

Using the rule of Existential Instantiation we may write in place of the existentially quantified expressions 'fa' and 'ga', respectively. Thus we may write, in place of the whole expression,

$$\{(fa \supset ga) \cdot fa\} \supset ga.$$

The analogous expression in the propositional calculus may be written

$$\{(p \supset q) \cdot p\} \supset q$$

which is shown to be valid by truth-table methods. It is, in fact, just *modus ponens*. Note that the result of the application of our two rules was useful just because we could regard our arbitrarily selected individual as being one of the individuals having property f and so represent both by 'a'.

This method of testing validity is available only for very simple and special relations between quantified expressions. As soon as we extend the use of quantifiers so that quantifiers may occur within quantified expressions, testing for validity becomes very much more difficult because there is no means of taking account of this complication in the propositional calculus. We need this device even for so simple a statement as

All who keep cows keep mammals.

For certain purposes this would have to be represented by some such expression as

$$(x)\{(\exists y)(fy \cdot hxy) \supset (\exists y)(gy \cdot hxy)\}.$$

This may be read 'For all x, there is a y such that y is a cow and x keeps y, implies that there is a y such that y is a mammal and x keeps y'.

What has been involved in this short discussion of ways of establishing validity is the fact that all tautologies are valid formulae of the predicate calculus but not all valid formulae are tautologies. For example, the formula

$$(x)fx \supset fa$$

217

is valid, as we have seen, but we cannot show its validity by constructing a truth table for it, as it stands, and showing it to be a tautology. (In such expressions as the last quoted the quantifier applies only to '*fx*', in the absence of further brackets.)

It has in fact been proved[16] that there is no general *mechanical* method, such as the truth-table method, for testing the validity of expressions in the predicate calculus. This means that the only way of establishing validity for certain expressions is to construct for them formal proofs from the basic rules or postulates of the system in which we are working. When it is said that the test of validity cannot be mechanized this means that there is no mechanical method of discovering the proof; we have to search for it and no one can be sure of finding it. Of course, once a proof has been discovered, the deductions it involves can be checked mechanically.

It is at this point, at which logic ceases to be mechanical, that it becomes interesting and creative. The next chapter will deal with the beginnings of non-mechanical logic.

9. VALIDITY AND INVALIDITY

The techniques which we have so far considered for testing the validity of arguments give rise to certain problems about what precisely is the power of formal systems in relation to arguments expressed in everyday English.

It might be said, for example, that it is a doubtful step to argue from the validity of a formula in the propositional calculus to the validity of an argument in everyday English of which that formula is a representation. This is owing to the differences already noticed between the connectives '$\lor$', '$\cdot$' and '$\supset$' and the everyday words 'or', 'and' and 'if . . . then' and to the fact that formulae of the propositional calculus are interpreted truth-functionally. We have seen that the conditions for the holding of '$\supset$' are necessary conditions for the holding of the 'if . . . then' relations, so that if '$\supset$' does *not* hold it seems safe to conclude that the 'if . . . then' relations do not hold. However, these conditions are not sufficient conditions for the holding of the 'if . . . then' relations so we cannot argue from the fact that '$\supset$' holds to the conclusion that the 'if . . . then' relations hold. It therefore looks as if we can use the truth table method for concluding to the invalidity of an argument in everyday discourse but not for concluding to its validity.

---

[16] By Alonzo Church, 'A Note on the Entscheidungsproblem', *Journal of Symbolic Logic*, Vol. I 1936, pp. 40–41 and 101–102. There is a helpful informal account of this in Barkley Rosser's 'An Informal Exposition of Proofs of Godel's Theorem and Church's Theorem', *Journal of Symbolic Logic*, 1939, Vol. IV, pp. 53–60.

An extreme example to illustrate what may go wrong can be constructed using the equivalence between $p \supset q$ and $\sim (p \cdot \sim q)$. Since these are equivalent we may write

$$\sim (p \cdot \sim q) \supset (p \supset q)$$

and be sure that it is a valid formula of the propositional calculus. The construction of a truth table should remove any doubts. Now the whole expression should be true if any two true statements are substituted for p and q. For example, substitute for 'p' the true statement 'St Paul's Cathedral is in London' and for 'q' the true statement 'Galileo was born in Pisa'. Then the whole expression becomes

> It is not true that both St Paul's Cathedral is in London and Galileo was not born in Pisa. Therefore, if St Paul's Cathedral is in London then Galileo was born in Pisa.

We should not in the ordinary way accept this as a valid argument. The normal reaction of the intelligent layman would be to say that is was a *non sequitur*. Nevertheless, if we started with this argument and set out to test it by expressing it in the propositional calculus and constructing its truth table we should naturally express it in the way indicated and find that the formula was valid. We should therefore be tempted to conclude that the original argument was valid, which appears to conflict with common sense.

This is, to some extent, a controversial point since it has been argued[17] that the relation of material implication is closer to the relation we indicate by 'if . . . then' than I have allowed or, to make the point in a rather different way, that material implication is all that we are justified in meaning by 'if . . . then' since this gives the only clear interpretation of those words. However, whatever we conclude about the possibility of establishing the validity of everyday arguments by the techniques of formal logic, it is clear that we must exercise great care in representing them by logical formulae. We must ensure that the representation does not distort or omit some feature of the original argument upon which its validity or invalidity depended.

These problems arise from concluding that an argument is valid from the fact that its representing formula in the propositional calculus is valid. I suggested, as logicians usually do, that there were no problems connected with concluding that an argument is invalid on the basis of an invalid representing formula in the propositional calculus. However, there are reasons for thinking this assumption

[17] e.g. by J. A. Faris, *Truth-Functional Logic* (London, 1964).

unjustified. These are implicit in some of the considerations of the last section and this was the point of some reservations I mentioned there. A full discussion of this would lead us into questions of considerable complexity but the substance of the matter can be indicated fairly simply using some of our earlier examples.

We saw that any syllogism could be represented by

$$(p \cdot q) \supset r$$

where 'p' and 'q' are the premisses and 'r' the conclusion. However, this formula is invalid. We cannot conclude from this that every syllogism is invalid. The syllogism in question might be representable by

$$M \ a \ P$$
$$S \ a \ M$$
$$\overline{}$$
$$\therefore S \ a \ P$$

or by

$$(M \subset P)(S \subset M) \supset (S \subset P)$$

both of which are valid.

Consider the argument

All Frenchmen are Europeans and
Pierre is French, therefore Pierre is European.

Since we can regard 'All Frenchmen are Europeans' as equivalent to 'If anyone is French then he is European' we might represent this argument by

$$\{(p \supset q) \cdot r\} \supset s,$$

which is an invalid formula. However, we cannot conclude that the original argument is invalid since it can also be represented by

$$\{(x)(fx \supset gx) \cdot (\exists x)fx\} \supset (\exists x)gx$$

or by

$$\{(x)(fx \supset gx) \cdot fm\} \supset gm$$

both of which are valid formulae of the predicate calculus. We might represent it also as a formula of the class calculus, thus,

$$\{(F \subset G) \cdot a \in F\} \supset (a \in G)$$

which is also valid.

In general, concerning these techniques we must say that the invalidity of the formal representation of an argument shows the argument to be invalid *only if* there is no other formal representation of the argument which is valid.

We may sum this up by saying that it is necessary to distinguish between the validity of *forms* of arguments and the validity of arguments. A form of argument is valid if and only if no instance of that form has true premisses and a false conclusion. An argument is valid if and only if it is an instance of a valid form. When we turn to invaldity in the light of our discussion we have to say that an argument is invalid only if it is an instance of *no* valid form. A form of argument is invalid if and only if there are instances of it with true premisses and false conclusions.[18]

---

[8] I am indebted to an article by J. W. Oliver entitled 'Formal Fallacies and other Invalid Arguments', in *Mind*, Vol. 76 (1967), p. 463, for this way of putting the matter, although there are other parts of this article with which I find difficulties.

CHAPTER V

Systems and Proofs

1. GENERAL CONSIDERATIONS

I have so far introduced a number of conceptions of modern logic, informally and in a piecemeal fashion, just as each became necessary. I have done this mainly in the course of setting up methods of testing types of inferences which we might encounter in our everyday pursuits; I have treated these logical conceptions as being derived from, or as analogous to, various features of everyday inferences. From time to time I have referred obliquely to the idea of a logical system, an idea which is implicit in that of a logical calculus.

One of the most important features of modern logic is the idea that we can construct logical systems in an abstract way, that we have considerable freedom in choosing how to do this and that these systems may be developed in great numbers and considerable variety. We may approach the construction of systems from the opposite point of view from that I have adopted; that is, we may start by constructing a system and then consider whether, and how well, it reflects the inferences we actually use, rather than by examining those inferences and abstracting from them the basis of our system.

The idea of a system is not new; indeed, it is to be found in a recognizable form in Aristotle's work. However, in recent years there has emerged an interest in the study of systems as such, in their own right and from various points of view. We may be interested in discovering how the deductive arguments we use in, for example, science or pure mathematics rest on underlying logical systems or we may be interested in simply constructing new abstract systems for the sake of investigating their powers and limitations and their applications, if there are any. This last approach is one of the possible pursuits of logicians which I mentioned in Chapter I and is relatively distinct from the approach which has occupied most of our attention, namely, the critical examination of types of argument in everyday use.

Nevertheless, these two approaches are not ultimately separable. The *justification* for a good deal of what has gone before can be found in the systematic nature of various branches of logic upon

222

which I have implicitly relied. This point may be used in leading up to an account of what is meant by a system in this context.

We have seen that we may test the validity of a syllogism by seeing whether or not it conforms to certain rules about the distribution of terms. This was a comparatively late addition to syllogistic logic. Aristotle proceeded differently. If we take it as evident that a syllogism in *Barbara* is valid and can then show that some other syllogism is equivalent to, or derivable by acceptably obvious steps from, a syllogism in *Barbara*, then we have shown that other syllogism to be valid. If we can show that every acceptable syllogism is connected in this way with, say, two evidently valid syllogisms then we have a system in which every syllogism is connected logically with those two syllogisms and is covered by one of the principles governing the validity of those two syllogisms. In fact, Aristotle stated principles for the moods *Barbara* and *Celarent* and then showed that every other acceptable syllogism with which he dealt could be reduced, directly or indirectly, to one or other of those moods.[1] He thus showed that every acceptable syllogism was covered ultimately by just two principles. This allows us to test the validity of syllogisms without relying on the notion of distribution. Moreover, Aristotle saw that he might do the same using as basic other pairs of syllogisms besides Barbara and Celarent. This means that it is possible to construct a variety of systems each of which covers the same acceptable syllogisms.

Later developments in syllogistic logic were also attempts to show that syllogistic reasoning was reasoning within a system. The *dictum de omni et nullo* was a principle intended to cover all acceptable syllogisms in a more economical way, replacing the two principles of Aristotelian theory by one principle. The class interpretation of the syllogism was a further attempt to show syllogistic theory to be just a portion of a more general system covering other types of arguments as well. Similar things can be said about the developments at which we have glanced.

At this point it is important to note that there are two different notions of satisfactoriness for logical formulae corresponding to the two different ways of testing arguments which I have mentioned. There is a difference between showing an expression to be *valid* by a truth-table method and showing an expression to be *derivable*, or a *theorem*, in a system.

As I indicated at the end of the last chapter, the testing of arguments by truth tables rests on the idea that an argument is valid if and only if it is an instance of a valid form and that a form is valid if and

[1] See William and Martha Kneale, *The Development of Logic* (Oxford, 1962).

223

only if no instance of that form has true premisses and a false conclusion. Putting this more formally we may say that a logical formula is valid if and only if every substitution instance of it is true. A substitution instance is a statement obtained from the logical formula by substituting appropriately for all the variables in it, that is, by substituting propositions for propositional variables, predicates for predicate variables, and so on.

When we show that a formula is derivable, or is a theorem, in a system we are not directly concerned with the truth of substitution instances. We merely show that the formula is obtainable in the system using only the accepted formulae and rules of that system.

This distinction is important because it has been shown that in the lower reaches of logic the two methods of testing formulae give the same results but that in the higher reaches this is not so. That is, whether all derivable formulae in a system are valid and all valid formulae are derivable is something that has to be proved. This is a complex matter upon which much has been written[2] but which cannot be pursued here.

In current logic, there are two broad types of system; they may conveniently be referred to as *axiomatic systems* and *systems of natural deduction*. Examples of axiomatic systems are Aristotle's syllogistic and the system of Whitehead and Russell's *Principia Mathematica*[3]. The original system of natural deduction was that of G. Gentzen.[4]

In an axiomatic system we first set up the basic concepts of our system and then decide to accept a few expressions built up out of these as unquestionable 'truths' or axioms for our system. They can be regarded as statements which are accepted without proof or other support for the purpose of furnishing a starting point for the development of our system. From these, using clearly stated rules of deduction, we derive other statements which are the theorems, or 'derived truths', of our system. Ordinary school geometry is a system of this kind with which we are all familiar.

Systems of natural deduction are built on the belief that our ordinary habits of reasoning do not involve accepting statements as axiomatic but do involve the use of accepted rules of deduction in conjunction with assumptions which we make and test from time to

---

[2] See, e.g. W. V. Quine, *Methods of Logic*, Sections 32 and 41; S. C. Kleene, *Introduction to Metamathematics*, Chap. VIII; and note (6) below.

[3] A. N. Whitehead and B. Russell, *Principia Mathematica* (Cambridge, 1910–13); abridged text of volume 1 (Cambridge, 1962).

[4] Gerhard Gentzen, 'Untersuchungen über das logische Schliessen', *Mathematische Zeitschrift* 39 (1934), pp. 176–210, 405–431. French translation by R. Feys and J. Zadriëre, *Recherches sur la Deduction Logique* (Paris, 1955).

time. In such systems we accordingly begin by accepting specified rules of deduction but no axioms. According to this view a system is constituted, not by a set of statements, basic and derived 'truths', but by a set of deducibility relations between possible statements.

Of course, both types of system require rules for the deduction of formulae from other formulae. It is approximately true for axiomatic systems that the more complex the axioms we accept, the simpler may be our rules for deduction. In constructing systems of natural deduction we may regard ourselves as reducing the axioms to zero and being prepared to accept a fairly complex set of rules.

In setting up a system of either sort, rigour demands that we specify, precisely, every symbol which may appear in the system, every rule according to which symbols may be combined and every move which may be made from one combination of symbols to others. In general we require the following elements.

(i) *Primitive symbols*
   (a) variables (like x, y, in algebra);
   (b) constants (like $+$, $=$, in algebra);
   (c) brackets (like brackets in algebra).
(ii) *Rules of formation* which determine what combinations of primitive symbols are allowable or 'grammatically correct'. (Like the tacit rules in algebra which allow, for example, '$x + y = o$' but not '$xy + o = $'.) An allowable combination is called a *well-formed formula*, or *wff* for short.
(iii) *Rules of derivation* or *deduction* which determine how we may derive wffs from one another to discover which wffs are theorems of our system. These rules are often called *rules of procedure*.

We may also need one or both of the following.

(iv) *Definitions*, which may be regarded as mere abbreviations or as specifying equivalent formulae which may replace one another.
(v) *Axioms*, that is, statements which are accepted without proof. These will not, of course, be necessary if our system is one of natural deduction.

It should be noted that I am here distinguishing between *allowable* formulae (wffs) and *accepted* formulae. Accepted formulae are either axioms or theorems and comprise only some of the allowable formulae. The distinction is comparable to that between the grammatically correct sentences of a natural language (wffs) and those

225

sentences of the language which can be used to make true statements (axioms or theorems).

Once we have established the basis of our system, its symbols and rules, we may say that the system *exists*. It is true that, having done just this much, we have not stated, and are not yet able to state, all that it contains, but we have determined what it contains and made it possible to discover, if we wish, all it contains. At this stage, whether or not we proceed to derive its theorems is a matter for our choice but what theorems are derivable is not.

It should be clear, also, that although once we have decided upon the basis of our system we have removed this possibility of choice, we have considerable freedom of choice before we have done this. For example, if we are constructing an axiomatic system we are free, within certain wide limits, to decide what formulae to regard as axioms and the kind of system we create will depend upon how we make this choice. As I pointed out, Aristotle saw this when he saw that it was possible to take other pairs of syllogisms besides *Barbara* and *Celarent* as basic for syllogistic theory.

We have from time to time considered the testing of the validity of arguments and expressions in symbolic form. The truth table is the outstanding device for such testing; for expressions of the propositional calculus it allows us to show, in a completely mechanical way, whether a formula is valid or invalid. We can rely absolutely on this method to distinguish between valid and invalid formulae, given only time and patience on our part or a suitable computer. That is, it constitutes what is called a *decision procedure* for the propositional calculus. There is no such decision procedure for the predicate calculus; indeed, it has been proved that there *can be* no such procedure.[5]

There are, as we have seen, certain types of expression of the predicate calculus which we can test by truth-table methods. The procedure is to find an expression of the propositional calculus which is testable and which parallels the expression in question. However, there are many types of expression which are derivable (provable) in the predicate calculus but which do not parallel tautologies in the propositional calculus. For example, using the symbols explained in Chap. IV, Section 7c, the expression

$$((x)fx \supset fa) \lor (fa \supset (x)fx)$$

is derivable in the systems we consider, and is analogous to

$$(p \supset q) \lor (q \supset p)$$

[5] See footnote 16 on p. 218.

which is a tautology. However, the expression

$$(x)fx \supset fa$$

is also derivable but the analogous expression

$$p \supset q$$

is not a tautology.

In such a situation, the only way in which we can test for acceptability is by showing that the expression in question is derivable in our system. This means that we have to discover a proof for it and there may be no mechanical means of discovering a proof. It is an important fact that it makes sense to look for a proof of any wff but it does not make sense to look for a disproof. Suppose we have a wff which is not a theorem of our system. We might be able to show that it contradicted a wff already known to be a theorem or that it had logical consequences which contradicted a theorem but this is a rare situation and we should be exceedingly lucky to find it. Suppose that we tried to find a proof for this formula and failed; this could never show it to be unprovable, however diligent our search and however prolonged our failure, since we can never take the failure to find a proof to show that there is no proof to be found. Thus, the derivability test cannot constitute a decision procedure which is like the truth-table method in being mechanical.

I must now confess to a fault in what has gone before which should by now be obvious to the reader. I have frequently referred to various expressions in the propositional calculus and the predicate calculus as valid without having set up systems in which they can be seen, or shown to be, valid. This has been a sort of confidence trick which it has been convenient to use but which is strictly illegitimate and can no longer be allowed to pass. I have relied upon the fact that expressions which are 'seen' to be acceptable and which represent, or are analogous to, types of expressions we would accept in everyday discourse are also expressions which are derivable in certain well-known logical systems.

When we embark on the construction of logical systems we leave behind the idea of expressions being 'seen' to be acceptable or, as it is sometimes misleadingly called, the idea of 'intuitive' acceptability; we accept no expression without either rigorous derivation or the explicit understanding that it is being accepted without proof as an axiom. The beginner in modern logic will find things being asserted and proved which seem so trivial as not to be worth writing down and other things being proved which seem to have no application. This is because we wish to take as little as possible for granted and because we are moving on to a view of logic where applicability to everyday reasoning is not the primary concern. When we come to the point of studying the powers and the limitations of systems, as such, we may be interested in proving whatever can be proved, whether or not we see any immediate application for it. Logicians are interested in 'experimenting' with systems just for the purpose of seeing what happens when they assume something, or some combination of things, which no one has previously thought of assuming. It was in this way that, in pure mathematics, systems of non-Euclidian geometry were constructed. The interest lies at least as much in the fact that such systems can be constructed and in the properties they have as in their possible applications.

There are two conditions, which I have not so far mentioned, to which it is desirable that logical systems conform. They are as follows.

(i) Our system must be *consistent*. Crudely, we do not want contradictory statements to be derivable. More precisely, to say that a system is consistent is to say one of three different but related things, namely,

   (a) that every derivable formula is valid;
   (b) that if P is derivable then $\sim P$ is not derivable, where P is any wff;
   (c) that there are formulae that are not derivable. (The formulae that are not derivable would be direct negations of formulae that are derivable.)

(ii) We should like our system to be *complete*.[6] This has been explained in various ways. It may mean that in the system one may derive from any given set of statements any consequence of that set. It may also mean that if we add any axioms to the system we would produce inconsistency. If we accept this last statement then we have three senses of 'completeness' corresponding to the three senses of 'consistency' noted above.

In axiomatic systems it is also desirable, though not essential, that our axioms be independent of one another, that is, that no one of them be derivable from the others, using the rules of the system. This is a matter of economy; if an axiom is not independent then it is not needed as an *axiom* since it can be proved.

Proofs have been devised for the consistency and completeness of systems and the independence of axioms. These proofs will not be

---

[6] There are serious problems here. See E. Nagel and J. R. Newman, 'Gödel's Proof' in I. M. Copi and J. A. Gould (eds.) *Contemporary Readings in Logical Theory* (N.Y., 1967).

given, or even sketched, here, as they are readily available in some of the books referred to and many others.[7]

There are many excellent textbooks of logic in which various systems are developed rigorously and in detail, so it would be superfluous to attempt to develop one such system in detail here. It is not the main purpose of this book to consider this aspect of logic or to help the reader to become an expert in logical manipulations; its purpose is rather to help him to grasp logical principles. Nevertheless, partly because the different aspects of logic cannot be sharply separated and partly because what I have already said may illuminate, and be illuminated by, more formal considerations, I propose to show how the development of logical systems proceeds. This will necessarily be a somewhat informal and unrigorous account since I wish to roam widely among systems which have been explored in depth by others. I propose, therefore, to sketch both axiomatic systems and systems of natural deduction for both the propositional calculus and the predicate calculus.

I shall introduce a number of new ideas in the course of each of the four sketches which are to follow. These ideas will not necessarily be relevant only to the systems in connection with which they are introduced; there are alternative ways of doing things in each system and the various alternatives will not be considered in each sketch. For example, the symbol '⊢' will be introduced in the sketch of the system of natural deduction for the propositional calculus but it can equally well be used in any of the other systems sketched. Similarly, the idea of *free and bound variables* is used here only in connection with axiomatic predicate calculus but it could be used also in the system of natural deduction for the predicate calculus; for purely pedagogic reasons it is here replaced by the device of the *arbitrary name*.

2. AXIOMATIC SYSTEMS

a. PROPOSITIONAL CALCULUS

The system I shall outline is a modified version of that expounded by Whitehead and Russell in *Principia Mathematica*.

(i) *Primitive Symbols*
(a) Propositional Variables: The letters 'p', 'q', 'r' . . . are used as propositional variables, that is, as marking spaces which may be filled by any propositions whatever.

---

[7] See e.g. A. H. Basson and D. J. O'Connor, *Introduction to Symbolic Logic* (London, 1957), and I. M. Copi, *Symbolic Logic* (New York, 1967), Chaps. 7 and 9.

(b) Constants: The symbols '$\sim$', '$\cdot$', '$\vee$', '$\supset$' and '$\equiv$' are used as logical constants. They may be regarded as operations performed on propositions or as ways of combining propositions.

(c) Brackets: The left-hand bracket '(' and the right-hand bracket ')' are used together to mark the scope of constants.

[I shall also use the letters 'P', 'Q', 'R' ... not as symbols of the system but as convenient symbols for *talking about* the system. They are often referred to as *metalogical symbols*. Such a symbol may be used to stand for any wff of the system whatsoever, without specification of its structure.]

(ii) *Rules of Formation*

RF1*. (a) Every propositional variable is a wff.
   (b) If P is a wff, then $\sim P$ is a wff.
   (c) Any two wff's joined by a *binary constant* (that is, '$\cdot$' or '$\vee$' or '$\supset$' or '$\equiv$') is a wff.

Strictly, we should also have rules for the punctuation of complex expressions, that is, rules of formation governing the use of brackets and the scope of constants. However, it is exceedingly difficult to give watertight rules and I shall not here attempt to do so. I will assume that the reader's knowledge of the use of brackets in mathematics, together with the explanation given in Chap. IV, Section 8, will suffice for our present, unrigorous approach. We may simplify matters somewhat by stipulating that any pair of brackets round a whole expression may be omitted.[8] It is clear that this omission is harmless. There is, for example, no important difference between the expression

$$(((p \supset q) \cdot (q \supset r)) \supset (p \supset r))$$

---

* The rule is numbered in this way, although only one rule is given, because further rules will be added for the following sketches.

[8] There is another device which is often used for simplifying the use of brackets, namely, the device of *ranking* constants. It is usual to rank them thus:

   $\cdot \ \vee \supset \ \equiv$

moving from the narrowest to the widest scope.
   Thus the unbracketed expressions

   (a) $p \cdot q \vee r \supset s$
   (b) $p \vee q \equiv r \cdot s$
   (c) $p \supset q \vee r \cdot s$

would be read as if bracketed thus:

   (a) $((p \cdot q) \vee r) \supset s$
   (b) $(p \vee q) \equiv (r \cdot s)$
   (c) $p \supset (q \vee (r \cdot s))$.

In fact, in working with complex expressions it is usually helpful to have the brackets written in.

230

and the expression

$$((p \supset q) \cdot (q \supset r)) \supset (p \supset r).$$

(iii) *Rules of Procedure*

R1. *Rule of Substitution*. In any expression, any wff may be substituted for any propositional variable as long as the substitution is carried throughout the expression.

Thus, for

$$(p \lor q) \supset p$$

we may write

$$((r \cdot s) \lor q) \supset (r \cdot s)$$

or we may write

$$((p \cdot q) \lor q) \supset (p \cdot q).$$

We indicate these substitutions by writing $r \cdot s / p$ and $p \cdot q / p$, respectively, to the right of the new expression in the derivation. Since propositional variables are themselves wffs, one propositional variable may be substituted for another.

R2. *Rule of Replacement*. In any axiom or theorem we may replace any part of the formula by an expression which is equivalent to it by an accepted definition, or by an expression which has been proved to be equivalent to it. This replacement need not be made throughout the original formula.

For example, as we shall see, we accept the definition

$$P \supset Q =_{df.} \sim P \lor Q.$$

Thus, for the expression

$$(p \supset q) \lor (q \supset p)$$

we may write

$$(\sim p \lor q) \lor (q \supset p)$$

and for the expression

$$((p \supset q) \cdot p) \supset q$$

we may write

$$\sim ((p \supset q) \cdot p) \lor q.$$

We indicate this move in a derivation by writing 'Def' to the right of the new expression followed by the number of the definition used.

R3. *Rule of Detachment.* If $P \supset Q$ is derivable and P is derivable then Q is derivable. We indicate this by writing *P, which may be read 'Detach P', to the right of the new expression. This is the rule of *modus ponens*.

We shall also accept another rule which will greatly simplify our proofs.

R4. *Rule of Adjunction.* If P is derivable and Q is derivable then $P \cdot Q$ is derivable.

It should be noted that this rule is not theoretically necessary, since it can be proved separately for each separate case.

It will be convenient, but not theoretically necessary, to accept three definitions.

(iv) *Definitions*

Def 1. $P \cdot Q =_{\text{df.}} \sim (\sim P \vee \sim Q)$
Def 2. $P \supset Q =_{\text{df.}} \sim P \vee Q$
Def 3. $P \equiv Q =_{\text{df.}} (P \supset Q) \cdot (Q \supset P)$

We shall also accept four axioms.

(v) *Axioms*

A1 $(p \vee p) \supset p$
A2 $p \supset (p \vee q)$
A3 $(p \vee q) \supset (q \vee p)$
A4 $(q \supset r) \supset ((p \vee q) \supset (p \vee r))$

Whitehead and Russell used these axioms together with a fifth which was later shown[9] to be derivable from these four, so is superfluous.

It is worth noting that the definitions of logical constants by means of truth tables is not necessary once we have established the system. Theorems that can be proved in fact result in definitions for the constants which are the same as the truth-table definitions.

I shall now use examples to show how derivations or proofs are constructed. It is important, first, to say what a proof is. Suppose that we consider a formula X, which is not an axiom. We prove X if we can exhibit it as the last member of a chain of formulae of which each member is either an axiom or a theorem already proved or

[9] P. Bernays in *Mathematische Zeitschrift*, Vol. 25 (1926), pp. 305–320.

obtained from previous members of the chain by the use of one of our rules of procedure.

There are various conventional ways of setting out proofs. I set out the steps of a proof in a column. To the left of each line I write the number of that line. To the right of each line I write the authority for it: if it is an axiom I write its number; if it is derived from an earlier line I write the number of that line followed by the rule of procedure by which it was derived; if it is a theorem already proved I write its number. I shall use the letter 'D' ('derived'), followed by a number, to indicate a theorem.

D1.   To prove: $(p \supset \sim p) \supset \sim p$

Proof:

1	$(p \lor p) \supset p$	A1
2	$(\sim p \lor \sim p) \supset \sim p$	R1, $\sim p/p$
3	$(p \supset \sim p) \supset \sim p$	R2, Def 2.

Explanation: We begin with Axiom 1. In it we substitute $\sim p$ for p. The information to the right of the line may be read 'Take line 1 and using our first rule of procedure, substitute $\sim p$ for p.' We then apply our second rule of procedure and our second definition to line 2 to give us line 3, that is we replace $(\sim P \lor Q)$ in 2 by $(P \supset Q)$, where $P = p$ and $Q = \sim p$. Line 3 is what we intended to prove and the proof is therefore complete.

D2.   To prove: $(q \supset r) \supset ((p \supset q) \supset (p \supset r))$

Proof:

1	$(q \supset r) \supset ((p \lor q) \supset (p \lor r))$	A4
2	$(q \supset r) \supset ((\sim p \lor q) \supset (\sim p \lor r))$	1, R1, $\sim p/p$
3	$(q \supset r) \supset ((p \supset q) \supset (p \supset r))$	2, R2, Def. 2

D3.   To prove: $p \supset (p \lor p)$

Proof:

1	$p \supset (p \lor q)$	A2
2	$p \supset (p \lor p)$	1, R1, p/q

D4.   To prove: $p \supset p$

Proof:

1	$(q \supset r) \supset ((p \supset q) \supset (p \supset r))$	D2
2	$((p \lor p) \supset p) \supset ((p \supset (p \lor p)) \supset (p \supset p))$	1, R1, $p \lor p/q$, p/r
3	$(p \lor p) \supset p$	A1
4	$(p \supset (p \lor p)) \supset (p \supset p)$	2, R3, *3
5	$p \supset (p \lor p)$	D3
6	$p \supset p$	4, R3, *5

233

D5.   To prove: $\sim p \lor p$
       Proof:

  1 $p \supset p$ D4
  2 $\sim p \lor p$ R2, Def. 2

D6.   To prove: $p \lor \sim p$
       Proof:

  1 $(p \lor q) \supset (q \lor p)$ A3
  2 $(\sim p \lor p) \supset (p \lor \sim p)$ 1, R1, $\sim p/p$, p/q
  3 $\sim p \lor p$ D5
  4 $p \lor \sim p$ 2, R3, *3

We must prove both D5 and D6 because we have no rule by which $(\sim p \lor p)$ is equivalent to $(p \lor \sim p)$.

D7.   To prove: $p \supset \sim \sim p$
       Proof:

  1 $p \lor \sim p$ D6
  2 $\sim p \lor \sim \sim p$ 1, R1, $\sim p/p$
  3 $p \supset \sim \sim p$ 2, R2, Def. 2

D8.   To prove: $p \lor \sim \sim \sim p$
       Proof:

  1 $(q \supset r) \supset ((p \lor q) \supset (p \lor r))$ A4
  2 $(\sim p \supset \sim \sim \sim p) \supset ((p \lor \sim p)$
       $\supset (p \lor \sim \sim \sim p))$ 1, R1, $\sim p/q$,
                                       $\sim \sim \sim p/r$
  3 $p \supset \sim \sim p$ D7
  4 $\sim p \supset \sim \sim \sim p$ 3, R1, $\sim p/p$
  5 $(p \lor \sim p) \supset (p \lor \sim \sim \sim p)$ 2, R3, *4
  6 $p \lor \sim p$ D6
  7 $p \lor \sim \sim \sim p$ 5, R3, *6

D9.   To prove: $\sim \sim p \supset p$
       Proof:

  1 $(p \lor q) \supset (q \lor p)$ A3
  2 $(p \lor \sim \sim \sim p) \supset (\sim \sim \sim p \lor p)$ 1, R1, $\sim \sim \sim p/q$
  3 $p \lor \sim \sim \sim p$ D8
  4 $\sim \sim \sim p \lor p$ 2, R3, *3
  5 $\sim \sim p \supset p$ 4, R2, Def. 2

We have now proved: D7. $p \supset \sim \sim p$
           and   D9. $\sim \sim p \supset p$

From these we can see by Def. 3 that a further theorem can be proved, namely,

$$D10. \ p \equiv \ \sim \sim p.$$

This will be used in the next proof.

D11.   To prove: $(p \supset q) \supset (\sim q \supset \sim p)$

Proof:

1	$(p \lor q) \supset (q \lor p)$	A3
2	$(\sim p \supset q) \supset (\sim q \supset p)$	1, R2, Def. 2
3	$(\sim \sim p \supset q) \supset (\sim q \supset \sim p)$	2, R1, $\sim p/p$
4	$(p \supset q) \supset (\sim q \supset \sim p)$	3, R2, D10.

This last theorem is, of course, the principle of *modus tollens*. It can also be proved that

D12. $(\sim q \supset \sim p) \supset (p \supset q)$ and therefore that

D13. $(p \supset q) \equiv (\sim q \supset \sim p)$

D14.   To prove: $(p \cdot q) \supset p$

Proof:

1	$p \supset (p \lor q)$	A2
2	$\sim p \supset (\sim p \lor \sim q)$	1, R1, $\sim p/p, \sim q/q$
3	$(p \supset q) \supset (\sim q \supset \sim p)$	D11
4	$(\sim p \supset (\sim p \lor \sim q)) \supset (\sim (\sim p \lor \sim q)$ $\supset \sim \sim p)$	3, R1, $\sim p/p, \sim p$ $\lor \sim q/q$
5	$\sim (\sim p \lor \sim q) \supset \sim \sim p$	4, R3, *2
6	$\sim (\sim p \lor \sim q) \supset p$	5, R2, D10
7	$(p \cdot q) \supset p$	6, R2, Def. 1

By an exactly parallel proof we can derive

D15. $(p \cdot q) \supset q$.

It is also possible to prove

D16. $\quad (p \lor q \lor r) \equiv (q \lor p \lor r)$

This will be used in the next proof.

D17. To prove: $((p \supset q) \cdot (q \supset r)) \supset (p \supset r)$
Proof:

1	$(q \supset r) \supset ((p \supset q) \supset (p \supset r))$	D2
2	$\sim(p \supset r) \lor ((p \supset q) \supset (p \supset r))$	1, R2, Def. 2
3	$\sim(q \supset r) \lor \sim(p \supset q) \lor (p \supset r)$	2, R2, Def. 2
4	$\sim(p \supset q) \lor \sim(q \supset r) \lor (p \supset r)$	3, R2, D16
5	$\sim((p \supset q) \cdot (q \supset r)) \lor (p \supset r)$	4, R2, Def. 1
6	$((p \supset q) \cdot (q \supset r)) \supset (p \supset r)$	5, R2, Def. 2

D18. To prove: $(q \supset r) \supset ((p \cdot q) \supset (p \cdot r))$
Proof:

1	$(q \supset r) \supset ((p \lor q) \supset (p \lor r))$	A4
2	$(q \supset r) \supset (\sim(\sim p \cdot \sim q)$ $\supset \sim(\sim p \cdot \sim r))$	1, R2, Def. 1
3	$(q \supset r) \supset ((\sim p \cdot \sim r) \supset (\sim p \cdot \sim q))$	2, R2, D13
4	$(\sim r \supset \sim q) \supset ((\sim p \cdot \sim r)$ $\supset (\sim p \cdot \sim q))$	3, R2, D13
5	$(q \supset r) \supset ((p \cdot q) \supset (p \cdot r))$	4, R1, $q/\sim r, r/\sim q,$ $p/\sim p$

It is also possible to prove the following theorems.

D19. $\quad (p \supset q) \supset ((p \supset r) \supset (p \supset (q \cdot r)))$

D20. $\quad (p \cdot q) \equiv (q \cdot p)$

D21. $\quad (p \lor q) \equiv (q \lor p)$

D22. $\quad (p \supset (q \supset r)) \equiv (q \supset (p \supset r))$

D23. $\quad (p \supset (q \supset r)) \equiv ((p \cdot q) \supset r)$.

b. PREDICATE CALCULUS

An important feature of the predicate calculus is that it is made to rest, as far as possible, on the propositional calculus. There are clear analogies between the two and the proofs already constructed in the propositional calculus will be brought into service in the predicate calculus if the appropriate propositional formulae can be obtained from predicate formulae.

I shall here deal only with what is known as the *first-order predicate calculus*, that is, the calculus in which quantifiers are applied only to individual variables and not to predicates.

As we have seen, predicates differ in the number of their 'places'. Thus, if we symbolize 'This apple is red' by 'fm', f is a one-place predicate whereas if we symbolize 'Mary loves John' by $f m n$', f is a two-place predicate. In order to apply the predicates to individuals we have to mention one or two individuals respectively. Theoretically, we may have predicates of any finite number of places. An alternative way of putting this is to say that a predicate has one, two or more *arguments* or *argument-places*, where 'm', 'n', 'o', etc. are called arguments. The first-order predicate calculus can deal with predicates of any finite number of places.

I now outline the apparatus of one well known axiomatic system of predicate calculus. It is derived from a system put forward by Hilbert and Ackermann.[10]

(i) *Primitive Symbols*

    (a) Propositional Variables: 'p', 'q', 'r' . . . as   e   ositional calculus.

    (b) Individual Variables: The letters 'x', 'y', 'z', 'x_1', 'y_1' . . . are individual variables, that is, they mark spaces which may be filled by any appropriate object or individual. (By 'appropriate' I mean, here, 'of a kind under consideration'.)

    (c) Individual Constants: The letters 'm', 'n', 'o' . . . stand for specific individuals, that is, they function like proper names in merely indicating objects.

    (d) Predicate Variables: The letters 'f', 'g', 'h' . . . stand for predicates, which may be thought of as the names of properties.*

    (e) Quantifiers: The symbols '(x)', '(y)' . . . shall be universal quantifiers and the symbols '$(\exists x)$', '$(\exists y)$' . . . shall be existential quantifiers. It should be noted that the brackets are integral parts of these symbols and that the small letters inside them are individual variables.

    (*f*) Logical Constants: The symbols '$\sim$', '$\lor$', '$\cdot$', '$\supset$' and '$\equiv$' shall be logical connectives or constants. They function here in the same way as in the propositional calculus.

[10] D. Hilbert and W. Ackermann, *Principles of Mathematical Logic*, English translation (New York, 1950).
* Capital letters F, G, H . . . are now frequently used for predicate variables. I prefer to keep these capital letters for classes.

(g) Brackets: The left-hand bracket '(' and the right-hand bracket ')' shall together indicate the scope of constants.

[It is also convenient to use Greek letters 'α', 'β' . . . as metalogical symbols for constants and variables and the letters 'A', 'B' . . . for wffs. It must be remembered that these do not appear in the system but are used for talking about it. The expressions '$A(x)$', '$B(y)$', '$A(xy)$' indicate wffs containing the variables x, y and x and y, respectively.]

Free and Bound Variables: It is important to explain at this point the distinction between *free* and *bound variables*. This concerns the operation of quantifiers but it is a distinction which is not indispensable. As we shall see, there is another device which can be used in its place. A variable is said to be 'free' unless it is restricted or 'bound' by a quantifier. In the expression 'fx', x is a free variable, but in the expressions '$(x)fx$' and '$(\exists x)fx$', x is a bound variable. Quantifiers bind only the variables they mention; thus in the expression '$(\exists x)(fx \supset fy)$' the variable x is bound, the variable y is free. A free variable is one that is free for substitution.

(ii) *Rules of Formation*

We use RF1 of the propositional calculus and in addition the following rules.

RF2. (a) Any predicate variable followed by an appropriate number of individual constants or variables is a wff.
   (b) If A is a wff, then $\sim A$ is a wff.
   (c) If A and B are wffs such that the same individual variable does not occur bound in one of them and free in the other then $A \cdot B$, $A \lor B$, $A \supset B$ and $A \equiv B$ are wffs.
   (d) If A is a wff in which α occurs as a free variable, then $(\alpha)A$ and $(\exists\alpha)A$ are also wffs.

Once again, for complete rigour we should have rules of formation for brackets. The same remarks apply here as were made in connection with the propositional calculus. In addition, in an unbracketed expression the universal and existential quantifiers shall be taken to be narrower in scope than the logical constants of the propositional calculus. For example,

$(x)fx \cdot A$

shall be taken as equivalent to

$$((x)fx) \cdot A$$

and not equivalent to

$$(x)(fx \cdot A).$$

That is, the quantifier binds the variable x only in fx.

(iii) *Rules of Procedure*

We need R1, 2, 3 and 4 of the propositional calculus and, in addition, the following rules.

R5. *Rules of Substitution*

(a) Any wff may be substituted in any wff for any propositional variable as long as the substitution is performed throughout the expression. This substitution is permitted only when the wff to be substituted contains no individual variable which appears as a bound variable in the original expression.

(b) A free individual variable may be substituted by any other individual variable provided that the substitution be made simultaneously at all the occurrences of the free variable and that the substituted variable have no bound occurrence in the original formula.

(c) A predicate variable of n places may be substituted by a well-formed predicate expression of n places, provided that the substitution is carried throughout the expression and that no variable which was free in the original expression is bound in the new one, or vice versa.[11]

For example, in the axiom

$$(x)fx \supset fy$$

---

[11] This rule has been the subject of much discussion and the present statement of it will not do for more advanced work. Hilbert and Ackermann in their *Mathematical Logic* (N.Y., 1950) gave a much more complex rule which, however, came under much criticism from other logicians. For some account of this see Hilbert and Ackermann, p. 69, and Alonzo Church, *Introduction to Mathematical Logic* (Princeton, N. J., 1956), pp. 193 and 289.

we may substitute $(fx \supset gx)$ or $(fx \cdot gx)$, or any other well-formed predicate-expression, for fx, and $(fy \supset gy)$ or $(fy \cdot gy)$, or any other well-formed predicate-expression, for fy.

R6. *Rules for Quantifiers*
  (a) Given the formula $A \supset B(x)$ where $B(x)$ contains the free variable x, while x does not occur in A, we may accept $A \supset (x) B(x)$.
  (b) Under the same conditions for A and $B(x)$, given that $B(x) \supset A$ we may accept $(\exists x) B(x) \supset A$.

R7. *Rules for Bound Variables*. We may replace a bound variable occurring in a formula by any other bound variable. This replacement must be made simultaneously in the universal or existential quantifier involved in all argument places in its scope. The result must be a wff. The substitution need be made in one scope only where the variable replaced occurs in more than one scope.

(iv) *Axioms*

We use the four axioms (A1–4) of the propositional calculus together with the following axioms.

A5 $(x)fx \supset fy$
A6 $fy \supset (\exists x)fx$

These axioms are reasonable because y, being free, may be regarded as standing for any arbitrarily selected individual. Thus, the first may be regarded as saying that if f applies to very individual then it applies to any arbitrarily selected individual; the second may be regarded as saying that if f applies to some arbitrarily selected individual then there is an individual to which it applies.

Using the material we now have, there are certain *derived rules* which can be proved. We shall here use only one.

DR If a formula $A(x)$, containing the free variable x, is derivable then $(x) A(x)$ is derivable.

I shall now use some examples to show how theorems of the predicate calculus may be proved. I shall indicate a theorem by 'T' followed by a number. Proofs will be set out in the manner adopted for the propositional calculus. Theorems which have been proved, or stated to be provable, in the propositional calculus will be used freely according to the rules now available.

240

T1.   To prove: $(y)fy \supset fx$

Proof:

1	$(x)fx \supset fy$	A5
2	$(x)fx \supset fz$	1, R5b, z/y
3	$(y)fy \supset fz$	2, R7, y/x
4	$(y)fy \supset fx$	3, R5b, x/z

T2.   To prove: $p \supset (x)(p \lor fx)$

Proof:

1	$p \supset (p \lor q)$	A2
2	$p \supset (p \lor fx)$	1, R5a, fx/q
3	$p \supset (x)(p \lor fx)$	2, R6a

T3.   To prove: $(y)(p \cdot fy) \supset (p \cdot fx)$

Proof:

1	$(y)fy \supset fx$	T1
2	$(q \supset r) \supset ((p \cdot q) \supset (p \cdot r))$	D18
3	$(q \supset r) \supset ((q \cdot p) \supset (r \cdot p))$	2, D20, R2
4	$((y)fy \supset fx) \supset (((y)fy \cdot p) \supset (fx \cdot p))$	3, R5a, $(y)fy/q, fx/r$
5	$((y)fy \cdot p) \supset (fx \cdot p)$	4, R3, *1
6	$(y)(p \cdot fy) \supset (p \cdot fx)$	5, D20, R2

T4.   To prove: $(x)(fx \lor \sim fx)$

Proof:

1	$p \lor \sim p$	D6
2	$fx \lor \sim fx$	1, R5a, fx/p
3	$(x)(fx \lor \sim fx)$	2, DR

T5.   To prove: $(x)fx \supset (\exists x)fx$

Proof:

1	$(x)fx \supset fy$	A5
2	$fy \supset (\exists x)fx$	A6
3	$((p \supset q) \cdot (q \supset r)) \supset (p \supset r)$	D17
4	$(((x)fx \supset fy) \cdot (fy \supset (\exists x)fx)) \supset ((x)fx$ $\supset (\exists x)fx)$	3, R5a, $(x)fx/p, fy/q,$ $(\exists x)fx/r$

241

5	$((x)fx \supset fy) \cdot (fy \supset (\exists x)fx)$	1, 2, R4
6	$(x)fx \supset (\exists x)fx$	4, R3, *5

T6.   To prove: $(x)(p \cdot fx) \supset (p \cdot (x)fx)$

Proof:

1	$(y)(p \cdot fy) \supset (p \cdot fx)$	T3
2	$(p \cdot q) \supset q$	D15
3	$(p \cdot fx) \supset fx$	2, R5a, fx/q
4	$((y)(p \cdot fy) \supset (p \cdot fx)) \cdot ((p \cdot fx) \supset fx)$	1, 3, R4
5	$((p \supset q) \cdot (q \supset r)) \supset (p \supset r)$	D17
6	$(((y)(p \cdot fy) \supset p \cdot fx) \cdot ((p \cdot fx) \supset fx))$ $\supset ((y)(p \cdot fy) \supset fx)$	5, R5a, $(y)(p \cdot fy)/p,$ $p \cdot fx/q, fx/r$
7	$(y)(p \cdot fy) \supset fx$	6, R3, *4
8	$(y)(p \cdot fy) \supset (x)fx$	7, R6a
9	$(x)(p \cdot fx) \supset (x)fx$	8, R7
10	$(p \cdot fx) \supset p$	D14, R5a, fx/q
11	$((p \supset q) \cdot (q \supset r)) \supset (p \supset r)$	D17
12	$(((y)(p \cdot fy) \supset (p \cdot fx)) \cdot ((p \cdot fx)$ $\supset p)) \supset ((y)(p \cdot fy) \supset p)$	11, R5a, $(y)(p \cdot fy)/p,$ $p \cdot fx/q, p/r$
13	$((y)(p \cdot fy) \supset (p \cdot fx)) \cdot (p \cdot fx \supset p)$	1, 10, R4
14	$(y)(p \cdot fy) \supset p$	12, R3, *13
15	$(x)(p \cdot fx) \supset p$	14, R7, x/y
16	$(p \supset q) \supset ((p \supset r) \supset (p \supset (q \cdot r)))$	D19
17	$((x)(p \cdot fx) \supset p) \supset (((x)(p \cdot fx)$ $\supset (x)fx) \supset ((x)(p \cdot fx) \supset (p \cdot (x)fx)))$	16, R5a, $(x)(p \cdot fx)/$ $p, p/q, (x)fx/r$
18	$((x)(p \cdot fx) \supset (x)fx) \supset ((x)(p \cdot fx)$ $\supset (p \cdot (x)fx))$	17, R3, *15
19	$(x)(p \cdot fx) \supset (p \cdot (x)fx)$	18, R3, *9

We can also prove

T7. $(p \cdot (x)fx) \supset (x)(p \cdot fx)$

and from T6 and T7 together follows

T8. $(x)(p \cdot fx) \equiv (p \cdot (x)fx)$.

T9.   To prove: $(x)(fx \supset gx) \supset ((x)fx \supset (x)gx)$
       Proof:

1	$(y)fy \supset fx$	T1
2	$(y)(fy \supset gy) \supset (fx \supset gx)$	1, R5c, $(fy \supset gy)/$ fy, $(fx \supset gx)/fx$
3	$(p \supset (q \supset r)) \supset (q \supset (p \supset r))$	D22
4	$((y)(fy \supset gy) \supset (fx \supset gx)) \supset (fx \supset$ $((y)(fy \supset gy) \supset gx))$	3, R5a, $(y)(fy \supset$ $gy)/p$, fx/q, gx/r
5	$fx \supset ((y)(fy \supset gy) \supset gx)$	4, R3, *2
6	$(y)fy \supset fx$	T1
7	$((p \supset q) \cdot (q \supset r)) \supset (p \supset r)$	D17
8	$(((y)fy \supset fx) \cdot (fx \supset ((y)(fy \supset gy)$ $\supset gx))) \supset ((y)fy \supset ((y)(fy \supset gy)$ $\supset gx))$	7, R5a, $(y)fy/p$, $fx/$ q, $((y)(fy \supset gy)$ $\supset gx)/r$
9	$(y)fy \supset ((y)(fy \supset gy) \supset gx)$	8, R3, *(6·5)
10	$(p \supset (q \supset r)) \supset ((p \cdot q) \supset r)$	D23
11	$((y)fy \supset ((y)(fy \supset gy) \supset gx)) \supset$ $(((y)fy \cdot (y)(fy \supset gy)) \supset gx)$	10, R5a, $(y)fy/p$, $(y)(fy \supset gy)/q$, gx/r
12	$((y)fy \cdot (y)(fy \supset gy)) \supset gx$	11, R3, *9
13	$((y)fy \cdot (y)(fy \supset gy)) \supset (x)gx$	12, R6a
14	$((x)fx \cdot (x)(fx \supset gx)) \supset (x)gx$	13, R7, x/y
15	$((p \cdot q) \supset r) \supset (p \supset (q \supset r))$	D23
16	$(((x)fx \cdot (x)(fx \supset gx)) \supset (x)gx)$ $\supset ((x)fx \supset ((x)(fx \supset gx) \supset (x)gx))$	15, R5a, $(x)fx/p$, $(x)(fx \supset gx)/q$, $(x)(gx)/r$
17	$(x)fx \supset ((x)(fx \supset gx) \supset (x)gx)$	16, R3, *14
18	$(p \supset (q \supset r)) \supset (q \supset (p \supset r))$	D22
19	$((x)fx \supset ((x)(fx \supset gx) \supset (x)gx))$ $\supset ((x)(fx \supset gx) \supset ((x)fx \supset (x)gx))$	18, R5a, $(x)fx/p$, $(x)(fx \supset gx)/q$, $(x)gx/r$
20	$(x)(fx \supset gx) \supset ((x)fx \supset (x)gx)$	19, R3, *17

This proof has been slightly abbreviated at step 9; it is easy to see how it should be completed. It is important to note that in this proof step 13 must be made before step 14. This is because R6a specifies that if $A \supset B(x)$ is accepted then $A \supset (x)B(x)$ may be accepted but only if A does not contain x. Thus, if the substitution of x for y in step 14 were carried out first we would not then be able to apply R6a.

T10.   To prove: $(\exists x)fx \supset \sim(x)\sim fx$
        Proof:

1	$(y)fy \supset fx$	T1
2	$(y)\sim fy \supset \sim fx$	1, R5c, $\sim fy/fy,$ $\sim fx/fx$
3	$(p \supset q) \supset (\sim q \supset \sim p)$	D11
4	$((y)\sim fy \supset \sim fx) \supset (\sim\sim fx \supset$ $\sim(y)\sim fy)$	3, R5a, $(y)\sim fy/p,$ $\sim fx/q$
5	$\sim\sim fx \supset \sim(y)\sim fy$	4, R3, *2
6	$\sim\sim p \equiv p$	D10
7	$fx \supset \sim(y)\sim fy$	5, D10, R2, $fx/\sim$ $\sim fx$
8	$(\exists x)fx \supset \sim(y)\sim fy$	7, R6b
9	$(\exists x)fx \supset \sim(x)\sim fx$	8, R7

T11.   To prove: $\sim(x)\sim fx \supset (\exists x)fx$
        Proof:

1	$fy \supset (\exists x)fx$	A6
2	$fx \supset (\exists y)fy$	1, R5b, R7, $x/y, y/x$
3	$\sim(\exists y)fy \supset \sim fx$	2, D13, R2, $fx/p,$ $(\exists y)fy/q$
4	$\sim(\exists y)fy \supset (x)\sim fx$	3, R6a
5	$\sim(\exists x)fx \supset (x)\sim fx$	4, R7, x/y
6	$\sim(x)\sim fx \supset \sim\sim(\exists x)fx$	5, D13, R2
7	$\sim(x)\sim fx \supset (\exists x)fx$	6, D10, R2

T10 and T11 together give us

T12. $\sim(x)\sim fx \equiv (\exists x)fx.$

We can also prove

T13. $(x)fx \equiv \sim(\exists x)\sim fx$

T14.   To prove: $(x)(fx \supset gx) \supset ((\exists x)fx \supset (\exists x)gx)$
        Proof:

1	$(p \supset q) \supset (\sim q \supset \sim p)$	D11
2	$(fx \supset gx) \supset (\sim gx \supset \sim fx)$	1, R5a, $fx/p, gx/q$
3	$(x)((fx \supset gx) \supset (\sim gx \supset \sim fx))$	2, DR
4	$(x)(fx \supset gx) \supset ((x)fx \supset (x)gx)$	T9
5	$(x)((fx \supset gx)$ $\supset ((x)(fx \supset gx) \supset (x)(\sim gx \supset \sim fx))$	4, R5c, $(fx \supset gx)/$ $fx, (\sim gx \supset$ $\sim fx)/gx$
6	$(x)(fx \supset gx) \supset (x)(\sim gx \supset \sim fx)$	5, R3, *3

7 $(x)(fx \supset gx) \supset ((x)fx \supset (x)gx)$ T9

8 $(x)(\sim gx \supset \sim fx) \supset ((x) \sim gx \supset (x)$ 7, R5c, $\sim gx/fx$,
    $\sim fx)$ $\sim fx/gx$

9 $(x)(fx \supset gx) \supset ((x) \sim gx \supset (x) \sim fx)$ 6, 8, D17, R3* (6·8)

10 $(p \supset q) \supset (\sim q \supset \sim p)$ D11

11 $((x) \sim gx \supset (x) \sim fx) \supset (\sim (x)$ 10, R5a, $(x) \sim gx/p$,
    $\sim fx \supset \sim (x) \sim gx)$ $(x) \sim fx/q$

12 $(x)(fx \supset gx) \supset (\sim (x) \sim fx \supset$ 9, 11, D17
    $\sim (x) \sim gx)$

13 $\sim (x) \sim fx \equiv (\exists x)fx$ T12

14 $(x)(fx \supset gx) \supset ((\exists x)fx \supset (\exists x)gx)$ 12, 13, R2, $(\exists x)fx/$
                                                  $\sim (x) \sim fx$

It will be noted that this proof, by comparison with earlier proofs, has been slightly abbreviated, for example, at step 9. The earlier proofs have usually been set out in the fullest possible way, in order that the method shall be perfectly clear. Familiarity with the methods enables one to abbreviate proofs even further by taking several steps on one line. Enough information must, however, be given on the right-hand side for it to be perfectly clear what the steps are. For example, the proof of T9 may be considerably shortened wherever a theorem of the propositional calculus is used. A shortened version of the proof may be written in the following way.

To prove: $(x)(fx \supset gx) \supset ((x)fx \supset (x)gx)$
Proof:

1 $(y)(fy \supset gy) \supset (fx \supset gx)$ T1, R5c, $(fy \supset gy)/fy$,
                                              $(fx \supset gx)/fx$

2 $fx \supset ((y)(fy \supset gy) \supset gx)$ D22, R5a, $(y)(fy \supset gy)/p$,
                                            fx/q, gx/r; R3, *1

3 $(y)fy \supset ((y)(fy \supset gy) \supset gx)$ D17, R5a, $(y)fy/p$, fx/q,
                                            $((y)(fy \supset gy) \supset gx)/r$;
                                            R3, *(T1·2)

4 $((y)fy \cdot (y)(fy \supset gy)) \supset gx$ D23, R5a, $(y)fy/p$, (y)
                                            $(fy \supset gy)/q$, gx/r; R3,
                                            *3

5 $((y)fy \cdot (y)(fy \supset gy)) \supset (x)gx$ 4, R6a

6 $((x)fx \cdot (x)(fx \supset gx)) \supset (x)gx$ 5, R7, x/y

7 $(x)fx \supset ((x)(fx \supset gx) \supset (x)gx)$ D23, R5a, $(x)fx/p$, (x)
                                            $(fx \supset gx)/q$, $(x)gx/r$;
                                            R3, *6

8 $(x)(fx \supset gx) \supset ((x)fx \supset (x)gx)$ D22, R5a, $(x)fx/p$, (x)
                                            $(fx \supset gx)/q$, $(x)gx/r$;
                                            R3, *7.

245

If this proof is compared with the original proof, it will be noted that, where important abbreviations have been made, the authority at the end of the new step indicates two operations; first, there is substitution in a formula of the propositional calculus and, second, a detachment from the substituted formula, of a formula established on an earlier line. This occurs at steps 2, 3, 4, 7 and 8 in the abbreviated proof. The two operations are separated by a semicolon in the right-hand column. In the abbreviated proof step 2 replaces steps 3, 4 and 5 and step 3 replaces 7, 8 and 9 in the original proof, and so on.

3. SYSTEMS OF NATURAL DEDUCTION

The essential difference between these systems and axiomatic systems is that no axioms are used in systems of natural deduction. This means that more rules of procedure are required and also that, having no axioms with which to begin our proofs, we have to start with *assumptions* or *suppositions*. I shall comment on these two points in turn.

It is important to understand the relations between axioms and rules. To accept a statement as an axiom is to accept it, at least for the time being for the purposes of the system, as a statement which is true whatever else may be the case. On the other hand, to accept a rule is to accept it as an instruction for doing something or, at least, as permission to do something. However, when we accept an axiom it would be open to us to accept, instead, a corresponding rule. For example, in the propositional calculus we have accepted the axiom

$$(p \lor p) \supset p$$

which, when we accept it as an axiom, must be read 'If p or p is true then p is true'. We are thus accepting it as a true statement. However, we could, instead, regard it as a rule and read it 'If we accept p or p then we may (*or* must) accept p' or 'From (p or p) derive p'. This is not a statement that is true or false but an instruction or permission that is convenient.

Another distinction to be made is that between a statement and an inference pattern. An axiom is a statement, a rule is an instruction but an inference pattern is neither of these. It is not true or false, it is not merely convenient, it is valid or invalid. The inference pattern corresponding to our axiom is

$$p \lor p$$
$$\therefore p.$$

In systems of natural deduction this inference pattern may be regarded as allowed by our rule.

A theorem is a formula which is derivable in a given system. In an axiomatic system it is derivable from our axioms with the help of rules of procedure and is, like the axioms, true. In the propositional calculus, theorems are tautologies, but we cannot say this of the predicate calculus.

In systems of natural deduction we cannot say that theorems are derived from axioms since there are no axioms. Here, we use the method of supposition or assumption. Among the rules we need one which allows us to write down a supposition at any stage of a proof. These suppositions temporarily take the place of axioms since a proof then involves deriving an expression from one or more suppositions. If we can then show that this expression is derivable without making these suppositions we thereby show it to be a theorem.

It will be convenient now to introduce a new sign '⊢'. This is sometimes misleadingly called the 'assertion sign'. It may be used in two ways. We may write

$$p \vdash (p \cdot q) \vee (p \cdot \sim q)$$

when the new sign may be read as 'therefore'. It is perhaps more revealing, however, to read the whole expression thus: 'On the supposition p, the formula $(p \cdot q) \vee (p \cdot \sim q)$ is derivable'.

As we have noted, theorems are those expressions which are derivable without suppositions, so we may also write

$$\vdash p \vee \sim p$$

where what follows '⊢' is a theorem and we read the expression 'It is a theorem that $(p \vee \sim p)$'. It is therefore best to call the new sign 'the sign of derivability'.

Although '⊢' is introduced here for the first time, it could have been used in the axiomatic method. We have proved that

D17. $((p \supset q) \cdot (q \supset r)) \supset (p \supset r)$

is a theorem. We could write this

$$\vdash ((p \supset q) \cdot (q \supset r)) \supset (p \supset r)$$

but if we were using the suppositional method we could also write

$$(p \supset q) \cdot (q \supset r) \vdash (p \supset r).$$

This does not say that the whole expression is a theorem but rather 'On the supposition of $(p \supset q)$ and $(q \supset r)$, the formula $(p \supset r)$ is derivable'.

247

I shall now outline, in turn, systems of natural deduction for the propositional calculus and the predicate calculus.

a. PROPOSITIONAL CALCULUS

We shall use the same primitive symbols and rules of formation as those used for the axiomatic system. We need a much larger collection of rules of procedure. The rules adopted will be sufficient for our purposes here but further rules may be adopted if necessary.

(i) *Primitive Symbols*

(a) Propositional variables: 'p', 'q', 'r' ...
(b) Constants: '$\sim$', '$\cdot$', '$\vee$', '$\supset$' and '$\equiv$'.
(c) Brackets: as for the axiomatic system.

(ii) *Rules of Formation*

RF1 (a) Every propositional variable is a wff.
(b) If P is a wff, then $\sim P$ is a wff.
(c) Any two wffs joined by a binary constant is a wff.
The same conventions are used for brackets.

(iii) *Rules of Procedure*

As so many rules are needed it is clearer to refer to rules by their initial letters, as indicated below.

(a) *Rule of Supposition* (S). Any wff may be introduced as a supposition at any stage of the proof.

(b) *Modus Ponendo Ponens* (MPP). Given P and $P \supset Q$, we may derive Q as a conclusion. Q depends upon any supposition upon which either P or $P \supset Q$ depends.

(c) *Modus Tollendo Tollens* (MTT). Given $\sim Q$ and $P \supset Q$, we may derive $\sim P$ as a conclusion. $\sim P$ depends upon any suppositions upon which either $\sim Q$ or $P \supset Q$ depends.

(d) *Double Negation* (DN). Given P, we may derive $\sim \sim P$ and vice versa. The conclusion depends upon the same suppositions as the premiss.

(e) *Conditional Proof* (CP). Given a proof of Q from P as supposition, we may derive $P \supset Q$ as conclusion on any remaining suppositions.

(f) *Conjunction* (C). Given P and Q, we may derive $P \cdot Q$. $P \cdot Q$ depends upon any suppositions upon which either P or Q depends.

(g) *Conjunction Elimination* (CE). Given $P \cdot Q$, we may derive either P or Q separately. The conclusion depends upon the same suppositions as the premiss.

(h) *Disjunction* (D). Given either P or Q separately, we may derive $P \lor Q$ as conclusion. The conclusion depends upon the same suppositions as the premiss.

(i) *Disjunction Elimination* (DE). Given $P \lor Q$ and a proof of R from P as supposition and a proof of R from Q as supposition, we may derive R as conclusion. R depends upon any suppositions upon which $P \lor Q$ depends or upon which R depends in its derivation from P, apart from P, and upon which R depends in its derivation from Q, apart from Q.

(j) *Reductio ad Absurdum* (RA). Given a proof of $Q \cdot \sim Q$ from P as supposition, we may derive $\sim P$ as conclusion upon any remaining suppositions.

The sign '$\equiv$' for logical equivalence is introduced by the following definition.

$$(P \equiv Q) =_{\text{df.}} (P \supset Q) \cdot (Q \supset P)$$

It is worth noting the connection between these rules and the axioms and theorems of the axiomatic system. The Rule of Supposition corresponds, roughly, to the unstated rule that an axiom may be introduced at any point in a proof. The remaining rules, indicated by their letters, correspond to the axioms or theorems written in the right-hand column

MPP	$((p \supset q) \cdot p) \supset q$
MTT	$((p \supset q) \cdot \sim q) \supset \sim p$
DN	$p \equiv \sim \sim p$
CP	$p \supset (q \supset (p \supset q))$
C	$p \supset (q \supset (p \cdot q))$
CE	$(p \cdot q) \supset p ; (p \cdot q) \supset q$
D	$p \supset (p \lor q) ; q \supset (p \lor q)$
DE	$((p \lor q) \cdot (p \supset r) \cdot (q \supset r)) \supset r$
RA	$(p \supset (q \cdot \sim q)) \supset \sim p$

These expressions are all derivable in the axiomatic system, although they have not all been derived in this book.

It will be noticed, and may be thought strange, that the Rule of Supposition puts no restriction on suppositions that can be made. If we are allowed to make any suppositions we like, we can prove almost anything by making the appropriate suppositions. However, the logician is primarily interested in discovering what can be proved from what, in the validity of inferences rather than in the truth of assumptions and conclusions. One of the features of this method is

17

249

that it makes explicit any assumptions that are being made and it shows what assumptions are necessary to prove a given conclusion. Given a proof based on certain assumptions we are always free to attempt to prove it from different assumptions, from fewer assumptions or from no assumptions at all. Our success or failure in this will itself be instructive.

I shall here introduce a method of setting out proofs which is different from, and clearer than, that previously used. It is based on a method invented by P. Suppes.[12] Each step is written on a separate line and numbered in sequence on the left-hand side by a number in brackets. To the left of that number will be written an unbracketed number indicating the suppositions upon which that line depends. Each line will be either a supposition or a conclusion drawn from earlier lines with the help of accepted rules. To the right of each line will be written 'S' if it is a supposition, or the grounds for that line, for example, the number of a line used as premiss together with the initial letters of the rule used. The number of the suppositions on the extreme left-hand side must include the numbers of any suppositions upon which any premisses for that line depend.

As an example, we may write a simple *modus ponens* inference as a proof, thus,

1	(1)	$p \supset q$	S
2	(2)	p	S
1, 2	(3)	q	1, 2, MPP

The first line, numbered '(1)', is a supposition as indicated. Since it is a supposition it depends only upon itself so '1' is written in the first column to indicate this. The second line is treated similarly. The third line depends upon both suppositions, so we write '1, 2' in the first column. This line is derived from lines (1) and (2) with the help of rule MPP, so we write '1, 2, MPP' in the last column. What we have proved is

$$(p \supset q), p \vdash q,$$

that is, 'on the suppositions $(p \supset q)$ and p, q is derivable'.

As we deal with longer proofs, we will find that on some lines we have numbers in the extreme left-hand column which are different from those in the extreme right-hand column. This is because the line is derived from previous lines which are not suppositions and the numbers of those lines are put in the right-hand column while the numbers in the left-hand column are the numbers of suppositions only.

[12] P. Suppes, *Introduction to Logic* (Princeton, N.J., 1957).

There are two rules which are of particular importance in the proof of *theorems*. They are CP and RA. Their importance lies in the fact that each has the effect of reducing by one the number of suppositions upon which we rely. Thus if we have a conclusion depending upon only one supposition and we can apply either of these rules to it then we obtain a conclusion depending upon no suppositions, that is, a theorem. To illustrate this, I give two proofs of simple theorems.

P1.   To prove: $\vdash (p \cdot q) \supset p$
       Proof:

1	(1)	$(p \cdot q)$	S
1	(2)	p	1, CE
	(3)	$(p \cdot q) \supset p$	1, 2, CP

This was proved as D14 by the axiomatic method. Since line (2) was derived from only one supposition and line (3) was derived from lines (1) and (2) it depends only upon 'the remaining suppositions' of which there are none. The blank in its left-hand column indicates this and therefore that it is a theorem.

P2.   To prove: $\vdash p \lor \sim p$
       Proof:

1	(1)	$\sim(p \lor \sim p)$	S
2	(2)	p	S
2	(3)	$p \lor \sim p$	2, D
1,2	(4)	$(p \lor \sim p) \cdot \sim(p \lor \sim p)$	3, 1, C
1	(5)	$\sim p$	2, 4, RA
1	(6)	$p \lor \sim p$	5, D
1	(7)	$(p \lor \sim p) \cdot \sim(p \lor \sim p)$	6, 1, C
	(8)	$\sim\sim(p \lor \sim p)$	1, 7, RA
	(9)	$p \lor \sim p$	8, DN

At line (4) we have an expression of the form $(Q \cdot \sim Q)$ resting on suppositions 1 and 2; RA allows us to derive the negation of one of these suppositions $(\sim p)$ on the remaining supposition 1. At line (7) we have an expression of the form $(Q \cdot \sim Q)$ resting only on supposition 1, i.e. $\sim(p \lor \sim p)$; RA allows us to derive the negation of that supposition. The resulting expression rests on no suppositions and so it is a theorem.

I shall now set out a number of proofs which serve further to illustrate the methods of natural deduction. Not all the expressions proved are theorems but we may obtain theorems by the device of taking the conjunction of the suppositions to imply the formula proved. Thus, if we write 'S₁', 'S₂', ... for suppositions and 'C' for the conclusion proved, our proofs are for expressions of the form

$$S_1, S_2, \ldots \vdash C$$

which become theorems if we write

$$\vdash (S_1 \cdot S_2 \cdot \ldots) \supset C.$$

This is known as 'the deduction theorem' and can be formally proved.[13]

P3.   To prove: $(p \supset (q \supset r)), p, \sim r \vdash \sim q$

Proof:

1	(1)	$p \supset (q \supset r)$	S
2	(2)	p	S
3	(3)	$\sim r$	S
1,2	(4)	$q \supset r$	1, 2, MPP
1,2,3	(5)	$\sim q$	3, 4, MTT

P4.   To prove: $\sim p \supset q, \sim q \vdash p$

Proof:

1	(1)	$\sim p \supset q$	S
2	(2)	$\sim q$	S
1,2	(3)	$\sim \sim p$	1, 2, MTT
1,2	(4)	p	3, DN

P5.   To prove: $p \supset (q \supset r) \vdash q \supset (p \supset r)$

Proof:

1	(1)	$p \supset (q \supset r)$	S
2	(2)	q	S
3	(3)	p	S
1,3	(4)	$q \supset r$	1, 3, MPP
1,2,3	(5)	r	2, 4, MPP
1,2	(6)	$p \supset r$	3, 5, CP
1	(7)	$q \supset (p \supset r)$	2, 6, CP

This corresponds to part of D22 of the axiomatic method. In the course of this proof we assumed p and q, whereas we set out to prove the conclusion on the supposition of $p \supset (q \supset r)$ only. The two applications of CP have the effect of removing, in turn, these suppositions, so that the conclusion depends only upon the supposition intended.

[13] See I. M. Copi, *Symbolic Logic*, pp. 231 and 288 for proofs.

P6.   To prove: $(q \supset r) \vdash (\sim q \supset \sim p) \supset (p \supset r)$
       Proof:

1	(1)	$q \supset r$	S
2	(2)	$\sim q \supset \sim p$	S
3	(3)	p	S
3	(4)	$\sim \sim p$	3, DN
2,3	(5)	$\sim \sim q$	4, 2, MTT
2,3	(6)	q	5, DN
1,2,3	(7)	r	6, 1, MPP
1,2	(8)	$p \supset r$	3, 7, CP
1	(9)	$(\sim q \supset \sim p) \supset (p \supset r)$	2, 8, CP

P7.   To prove: $(q \supset r) \vdash (p \cdot q) \supset (p \cdot r)$
       Proof:

1	(1)	$q \supset r$	S
2	(2)	$p \cdot q$	S
2	(3)	p	2, CE
2	(4)	q	2, CE
1,2	(5)	r	1, 4, MPP
1,2	(6)	$p \cdot r$	3, 5, C
1	(7)	$(p \cdot q) \supset (p \cdot r)$	2, 6, CP

This corresponds to D18 which was proved in the axiomatic system.

P8.   To prove: $q \supset r \vdash (p \lor q) \supset (p \lor r)$
       Proof:

1	(1)	$q \supset r$	S
2	(2)	$p \lor q$	S
3	(3)	p	S
3	(4)	$p \lor r$	3, D
5	(5)	q	S
1,5	(6)	r	1, 5, MPP
1,5	(7)	$p \lor r$	6, D
1,2	(8)	$p \lor r$	2, 3, 4, 5, 7, DE
1	(9)	$(p \lor q) \supset (p \lor r)$	2, 8, CP

This proof needs some explanation. The difficulty lies in the use of the rule DE, which we have not used before. The rule may be put thus:

Given (a) $P \lor Q$
      (b) a proof of R from P
      (c) a proof of R from Q

253

we may derive R as conclusion depending upon suppositions upon which (a) depends, and upon suppositions upon which (b) depends, apart from P, and upon suppositions upon which (c) depends, apart from Q.

In this proof
$$\begin{aligned} P \vee Q &= p \vee q \\ R &= p \vee r \\ P &= p \\ Q &= q \end{aligned}$$

Now, (a) $p \vee q$ depends upon supposition 2 (itself),
    (b) the proof of $p \vee r$ from p depends upon supposition 3 (line (4)),
    (c) the proof of $p \vee r$ from q depends upon suppositions 1 and 5 (line (7)).

Thus we can derive $p \vee r$ on all those suppositions except 3 and 5, that is, on suppositions 1 and 2. Shortly, we proved $p \vee r$ on supposition 3 and, quite separately, on suppositions 1 and 5. DE allows us to replace suppositions 3 and 5 by supposition 2. This is a method of reducing the suppositions upon which we rely by deriving an expression in two different ways. Lines (4), (7) and (8) differ most importantly in the suppositions upon which they depend.

Note that

$$(q \supset r) \supset ((p \vee q) \supset (p \vee r))$$

was taken as axiom 4 in the axiomatic system.

P9.   To prove: $p \supset q, p \supset \sim q \vdash \sim p$
    Proof:

1	(1)	$p \supset q$	S
2	(2)	$p \supset \sim q$	S
3	(3)	p	S
1, 3	(4)	q	1, 3, MPP
2, 3	(5)	$\sim q$	2, 3, MPP
1, 2, 3	(6)	$q \cdot \sim q$	4, 5, C
1, 2	(7)	$\sim p$	3, 6, RA

P10.   To prove: $p \supset q, q \supset r \vdash p \supset r$
    Proof:

1	(1)	$p \supset q$	S
2	(2)	$q \supset r$	S
3	(3)	p	S
1, 3	(4)	q	1, 3, MPP
1, 2, 3	(5)	r	2, 4, MPP
1, 2	(6)	$p \supset r$	3, 5, CP

Note that

$$((p \supset q) \cdot (q \supset r)) \supset (p \supset r)$$

was proved as D17 in the axiomatic system.

We may shorten our proofs by using a further rule—allowing us to use in any proof a theorem already proved. This does not, of course, enable us to prove anything that cannot be proved without it; it is merely a convenience when dealing with long proofs. Other derived rules may also be introduced for the same purpose. For example, we can add the rule that not only any theorem, but also any substitution-instance of a theorem may be introduced in a proof. These two rules allow us to introduce expressions without suppositions.

I now give an example of a proof using the latter rule, which will be called the rule of Theorem Introduction and indicated by 'TI' followed by the number of the theorem and an indication of any substitution that has been made.

P11.   To prove: $p, \vdash (p \cdot q) \lor (p \cdot \sim q)$

Proof:

1	(1)	p	S
	(2)	$q \lor \sim q$	TI, P2, q/p
3	(3)	q	S
1, 3	(4)	$p \cdot q$	1, 3, C
1, 3	(5)	$(p \cdot q) \lor (p \cdot \sim q)$	4, D
6	(6)	$\sim q$	S
1, 6	(7)	$p \cdot \sim q$	1, 6, C
1, 6	(8)	$(p \cdot q) \lor (p \cdot \sim q)$	7, D
1	(9)	$(p \cdot q) \lor (p \cdot \sim q)$	2, 3, 5, 6, 8, DE.

Without the use of the Rule TI the proof would have to be much longer because it would be necessary to include the proof of P2.

It can be proved that every theorem which is provable using our rules is a tautology; thus our rules form a consistent set. This may be shown either by a truth-table method or a formal proof. The system can also be proved to be complete, that is, it can be shown that the rules suffice to prove all the tautologies of the system. There is, of course, no question of the independence of axioms to be considered here.

b. PREDICATE CALCULUS

In presenting a system of natural deduction for the predicate calculus I shall introduce another device which might have been used in the axiomatic system but was not used in presenting it there. This is the device of symbolizing an *arbitrarily selected individual* or, as it is sometimes called, the device of *arbitrary names*. This replaces the distinction between free and bound variables previously used. It is important in connection with inference rules for adding or removing quantifiers. If a predicate can be shown to apply to an arbitrarily selected individual then it follows that it applies to every individual of the appropriate type. This is to say that if *whichever* object you choose has *f* then all objects have *f*.

The following symbols and rules will be used.

(i) *Primitive Symbols*

(a) *Individual Variables:* '*x*', '*y*', '*z*' and, if required, the same letters with subscripts.

(b) *Individual Constants:* '*m*', '*n*', '*o*' ... stand for specific individuals.

(c) *Arbitrary Names:* '*a*', '*b*', '*c*' ... stand for arbitrarily selected individuals.

(d) *Predicate Variables:* '*f*', '*g*', '*h*' ...

(e) *Quantifiers:* '(x)', '(y)' ... shall be universal quantifiers and '$(\exists x)$', '$(\exists y)$', ... shall be existential quantifiers.

(*f*) *Logical Constants:* As before we use the symbols '$\sim$', '$\vee$', '$\cdot$', '$\supset$' and '$\equiv$'.

(*g*) *Brackets:* The same conventions as before are used.

[We shall use the metalogical symbols '*A*', '*B*' ... for any wff and 'α', 'β' ... for individual variables and constants or arbitrary names. '$A(\alpha)$' signifies an expression in which α occurs.]

(ii) *Rules of Formation*

We shall use RF1 of the propositional calculus and, in addition, the following rules. These are similar to the rules used for the axiomatic method except that free and bound variables are not mentioned whereas arbitrary names are.

RF2

(a) A predicate variable of *n* places followed by *n* individual variables, individual constants or arbitrary names is a wff.

(b) If *A* is a wff then $\sim A$ is a wff.

(c) If *A* and *B* are wffs, then $A \cdot B$, $A \vee B$, $A \supset B$ and $A \equiv B$ are wffs.

(d) If A is a wff in which variable α occurs, then $(\alpha)A$ and $(\exists\alpha)A$ are wffs.

(iii) *Rules of Procedure*

We shall use the rules for natural deduction in the propositional calculus, together with the following four rules, also referred to by their initial letters.

(a) *Universal Instantiation* (UI). If A is a wff in which α is an individual variable and if β is an individual constant or an arbitrary name, then given $(\alpha)A(\alpha)$ we may derive $A(\beta)$, which is the wff derived from $A(\alpha)$ by substituting every occurrence of α by β. The conclusion depends upon any supposition upon which the premiss depends.

(b) *Existential Generalization* (EG). Given the same conditions as those under UI and given $A(\beta)$, we may derive $(\exists\alpha)A(\alpha)$. The conclusion depends upon any supposition upon which the premiss depends.

(c) *Universal Generalization* (UG). If $A(\beta)$ is a wff containing the arbitrary name β, and α is a variable not occurring in $A(\beta)$, and if $A(\alpha)$ is the wff derived by substituting all and only occurrences of β in $A(\beta)$ by α, then given $A(\beta)$ we may derive $(\alpha)A(\alpha)$, provided that β occurs in no supposition upon which $A(\beta)$ depends. The conclusion depends upon the same suppositions as the premiss.

(d) *Existential Instantiation* (EI). Given the same conditions as those under UG, then given $(\exists\alpha)A(\alpha)$ together with a proof of some wff C from $A(\beta)$ as supposition, we may draw the conclusion C, provided that β does not occur in C or in any supposition used to derive C from $A(\beta)$, apart from $A(\beta)$ itself. The conclusion rests on any suppositions upon which $(\exists\alpha)A(\alpha)$ depends or which are used to derive C from $A(\beta)$, apart from $A(\beta)$.[14]

We may explain the basis of these rules in a common-sense way as follows.

(a) Whatever is true of every object is true of any arbitrarily selected object. We may compare this with the axiom $(x)fx \supset fy$

---

[14] There has been some controversy over this rule. Lemmon's treatment in *Beginning Logic* is perhaps the clearest but see also Lemmon's notes 'Quantifier Rules and Natural Deduction', *Mind* Vol. LXX, p. 235, and 'A Further Note on Natural Deduction', *Mind*, Vol. LXXIV, p. 594.

in the axiomatic system. It may be thought that this conflicts with what has been said earlier about the lack of existential import of universal statements. However, there is no conflict. If every object is said to have a certain predicate then there must be objects with that predicate. Further, the expression $(x)(fx \supset gx)$ may be regarded as saying 'If any object has f then it has g'; if we conclude from it $(fa \supset ga)$, according to the present rule, we are merely saying 'If any arbitrarily selected object has f then it also has g' so we have not made any illegitimate existential assumption.

(b) Whatever is true of a given object is true of some unspecified object. We may compare this with the axiom $fy \supset (\exists x)fx$. Again, no illegitimate existential assumption is made.

(c) Whatever is true of an arbitrarily selected object is true of every object. We could adopt the expression $fx \supset (x)fx$ as an axiom in the axiomatic system. We in fact used it as a derived rule.

(d) Whatever is true of some object is true of some specified object.

We shall again use the *Rule of Theorem Introduction* (TI) according to which we may use at any stage in a proof any theorem, or its substitution instances, which has already been proved.

Proofs by natural deduction in the predicate calculus are set out in a similar way to proofs in the propositional calculus. Wherever appropriate, the rules of the propositional calculus are used but where necessary the four new rules will be used. A useful method of proof may be summarized in the following way: we symbolize our premisses, then use UI or EI to remove the quantifiers; we apply the methods of the propositional calculus to the result and then use UG or EG to replace the quantifiers.

I shall now give a number of proofs as illustrations of the method of natural deduction for the predicate calculus and, especially, of the use of the newly introduced rules.

S1. To prove: $fm, (x)(fx \supset gx) \vdash gm$

Proof:

1	(1)	fm	S
2	(2)	$(x)(fx \supset gx)$	S
2	(3)	$fm \supset gm$	2, UI
1,2	(4)	gm	1, 3, MPP

S2.   To prove: $(x)(fx \supset gx)$, $(x)(gx \supset hx) \vdash (x)(fx \supset hx)$

        Proof:

1	(1)	$(x)(fx \supset gx)$	S
2	(2)	$(x)(gx \supset hx)$	S
1	(3)	$fa \supset ga$	1, UI
2	(4)	$ga \supset ha$	2, UI
1,2	(5)	$fa \supset ha$	3, 4, C, TI, D17, MPP
1,2	(6)	$(x)(fx \supset hx)$	5, UG

Since D17, that is,

$$((p \supset q) \cdot (q \supset r)) \supset (p \supset r)$$

was proved quite generally it applies to any three statements related in the appropriate way. It therefore applies to fa, ga and ha. This is the basis of step (5), which is also an abbreviation.

S3.   To prove: $(x)fx \vdash (\exists x)fx$

        Proof:

1	(1)	$(x)fx$	S
1	(2)	fa	1, UI
1	(3)	$(\exists x)fx$	2, EG

S4.   To prove: $(x)(fx \supset gx)$, $(\exists x)fx \vdash (\exists x)gx$

        Proof:

1	(1)	$(x)(fx \supset gx)$	S
2	(2)	$(\exists x)fx$	S
3	(3)	fa	S
1	(4)	$fa \supset ga$	1, UI
1,3	(5)	ga	3, 4, MPP
1,3	(6)	$(\exists x)gx$	5, EG
1,2	(7)	$(\exists x)gx$	2, 3, 6, EI

Here, we first derived $(\exists x)gx$ from $(x)(fx \supset gx)$ and fa which last was a supposition which we were not asked to make in the first place. This was the supposition that some object a had property f. The argument, however, did not depend upon our choosing a particular object rather than some other; it was an arbitrary choice. Moreover, a is not involved in the conclusion, which follows just as well from

1 and 2. The rule EI allows us to transfer our reliance upon one supposition 3 to another supposition 2. The last step of the proof depends upon regarding fa as a 'typical instantiation' of $(\exists x)fx$. The numbers cited on the right of line (7) are: the number of the line in which the existential statement occurs (2), the number of the line where its typical instantiation occurs (3) and the number of the line in which $(\exists x)gx$ is obtained as a conclusion from the supposition of the typical instantiation (6). This use of EI is comparable to the use of DE in the propositional calculus (see p. 253).

S5.   To prove: $\vdash (x)(fx \supset gx) \supset ((x)fx \supset (x)gx)$

Proof:

1	(1)	$(x)(fx \supset gx)$	S
2	(2)	$(x)fx$	S
1	(3)	$fa \supset ga$	1, UI
2	(4)	fa	2, UI
1,2	(5)	ga	3, 4, MPP
1,2	(6)	$(x)gx$	5, UG
1	(7)	$(x)fx \supset (x)gx$	2, 6, CP
	(8)	$(x)(fx \supset gx) \supset ((x)fx \supset (x)gx)$	1, 7, CP

This is a theorem. It is instructive to compare this proof with the much longer proof of the same theorem (T9) in the axiomatic system.

It will be remembered that we proved (T10 and T11) the theorem

$$(\exists x)fx \equiv \sim (x) \sim fx$$

by the axiomatic method. We may prove the same theorem using natural deduction or we may prove that on the supposition $(\exists x)fx$ we may derive $\sim (x) \sim fx$ and that on the supposition $\sim (x) \sim fx$ we may derive $(\exists x)fx$. This amounts to saying that $(\exists x)fx$ and $\sim (x) \sim fx$ are *interderivable*. This may be represented, using the symbol $\dashv\vdash$, thus

$$(\exists x)fx \dashv\vdash \sim (x) \sim fx.$$

S6.   To prove: $(\exists x)fx \dashv\vdash \sim (x) \sim fx$
        This must be proved in two parts: we first prove
        (a) $(\exists x)fx \vdash \sim (x) \sim fx$ and then
        (b) $\sim (x) \sim fx \vdash (\exists x)fx$.

Proof:

(a)
1	(1)	$(\exists x)fx$	S
2	(2)	fa	S
3	(3)	$(x)\sim fx$	S
3	(4)	$\sim fa$	3, UI
2,3	(5)	$fa \cdot \sim fa$	2, 4, C
2	(6)	$\sim (x)\sim fx$	3, 5, RA
1	(7)	$\sim (x)\sim fx$	1, 2, 6, EI

(b)
1	(1)	$\sim (x)\sim fx$	S
2	(2)	$\sim (\exists x)fx$	S
3	(3)	fa	S
3	(4)	$(\exists x)fx$	3, EG
2,3	(5)	$(\exists x)fx \cdot \sim (\exists x)fx$	2, 4, C
2	(6)	$\sim fa$	3, 5, RA
2	(7)	$(x)\sim fx$	6, UG
1,2	(8)	$(x)\sim fx \cdot \sim (x)\sim fx$	1, 7, C
1	(9)	$\sim \sim (\exists x)fx$	2, 8, RA
1	(10)	$(\exists x)fx$	9, DN

From (a) and (b) together we obtain

$$(\exists x)fx \dashv\vdash \sim (x)\sim fx$$

As in the axiomatic system, we can derive 'mixed' formulae, that is, formulae containing propositional variables as well as predicate variables. I shall prove one theorem of this kind.

S7.   To prove: $\vdash (x)(p \cdot fx) \supset (p \cdot (x)fx)$

Proof:

1	(1)	$(x)(p \cdot fx)$	S
1	(2)	$p \cdot fa$	1, UI
1	(3)	p	2, CE
1	(4)	fa	2, CE
1	(5)	$(x)fx$	4, UG
1	(6)	$p \cdot (x)fx$	3, 5, C
	(7)	$(x)(p \cdot fx) \supset (p \cdot (x)fx)$	1, 6, CP

This was proved as T6 by the axiomatic method. Once again, the proof by the method of natural deduction is much shorter and easier.

We have so far proved expressions containing only monadic predicates. We may extend these methods to polyadic predicates and, therefore, to expressions controlled by more than one quantifier.

261

Monadic predicates may be regarded as representing properties whereas polyadic predicates may be regarded as representing relations. For example, if '*m*' represents some individual, say Socrates, and '*f*' represents the property of being mortal, we represent the statement

>   Socrates is mortal

by the expression

>   *fm*

and the statement

>   Everything is mortal

by the expression

> $(x)fx.$

Further we can represent the statement

>   All men are mortal

by the expression

> $(x)(gx \supset fx),$

where '*g*' represents the property of being a man. On the other hand, if we wish to represent the statement

>   John is taller than Mary

we may do so by writing

>   *fmn*,

where '*f*' stands for the relation of being taller than, '*m*' stands for John and '*n*' for Mary. Now suppose we wish to represent the statement

>   Everyone is taller than Mary.

We may do so by writing

> $(x)fxn$

where '*x*' is a variable ranging over people.
  We may represent the statement

>   Someone is taller than Mary

by the expression

> $(\exists x)fxn$

where '*x*' again ranges over people.

Extending these devices we can represent more complex expressions by using more than one quantifier. Let us use the predicate-variable 'l' for 'likes'. We may now represent the statement

>Everyone likes someone

by the expression

>$(x)(\exists y)lxy$

which may be read: 'For all x, there is a y such that x likes y'. Similarly, we may represent the statement

>Someone likes everyone

by the expression

>$(\exists x)(y)lxy$

which may be read, 'There is an x such that for all y, x likes y'. It is important to note that the order of the quantifiers is vital since changing the order results in changing the sense of the expression. We may, however, have expressions containing just two universal quantifiers or just two existential quantifiers and then the order of the quantifiers is immaterial.

For example, suppose we wish to represent the statement

>If any man is taller than another, then the second is shorter than the first

regarded as a generally true statement. We may use the expression

>$(x)(y)(hxy \supset iyx)$

where 'h' stands for 'is taller than' and 'i' for 'is shorter than'. This may be read 'For all x and for all y, if x is taller than y then y is shorter than x', and it does not make any difference if we represent this by

>$(y)(x)(hxy \supset iyx)$.

Similarly, we may represent the statement

>Someone is taller than someone

by the expression

>$(\exists x)(\exists y)hxy$

which may be read 'There is an x and there is a y such that x is taller than y'. Again, the order of the quantifiers makes no difference to the sense.

263

We can prove formally

S8.　　$(x)(y)fxy \equiv (y)(x)fxy$

and

S9.　　$(\exists x)(\exists y)fxy \equiv (\exists y)(\exists x)fxy.$

We can also prove

$$(\exists x)(y)fxy \supset (y)(\exists x)fxy$$

but we *cannot* prove

$$(y)(\exists x)fxy \supset (\exists x)(y)fxy.$$

I shall now prove the first of these

S10.　　To prove:

$\vdash (\exists x)(y)fxy \supset (y)(\exists x)fxy$

Proof:

1	(1)	$(\exists x)(y)fxy$	S
2	(2)	$(y)fay$	S
2	(3)	fab	2, UI
2	(4)	$(\exists x)fxb$	3, EG
2	(5)	$(y)(\exists x)fxy$	4, UG
1	(6)	$(y)(\exists x)fxy$	1, 2, 5, EI
	(7)	$(\exists x)(y)fxy \supset (y)(\exists x)fxy$	1, 6, CP

We may use an example to show that this theorem is reasonable but that the implication in the reverse direction is not. If we let 'f' stand for 'knows' then the theorem, S10, may be read 'If someone knows everyone then everyone has someone who knows him'. On the other hand, the expression

$$(y)(\exists x)fxy \supset (\exists x)(y)fxy$$

would have to be read 'If everyone has someone who knows him, then there is someone who knows everyone', which is unacceptable.

I shall finally prove two expressions containing complications of the sort just discussed.

S11.　To prove: $(x)(fx \supset gx) \vdash (x)((\exists y)(fy \cdot hxy)$
$\supset (\exists y)(gy \cdot hxy))$

Proof:

1	(1)	$(x)(fx \supset gx)$	S
2	(2)	$(\exists y)(fy \cdot hay)$	S
3	(3)	$fb \cdot hab$	S
3	(4)	fb	3, CE
3	(5)	hab	3, CE
1	(6)	$fb \supset gb$	1, UI
1,3	(7)	gb	4, 6, MPP
1,3	(8)	$gb \cdot hab$	5, 7, C
1,3	(9)	$(\exists y)(gy \cdot hay)$	8, EG
1,2	(10)	$(\exists y)(gy \cdot hay)$	2, 3, 9, EI
1	(11)	$(\exists y)(fy \cdot hay) \supset (\exists y)(gy \cdot hay)$	2, 10, CP
1	(12)	$(x)((\exists y)(fy \cdot hxy) \supset (\exists y)(gy \cdot hxy))$	11, UG

S12.　To prove: $(x)(fx \supset (y)(gy \supset hxy))$, $(x)(fx \supset (z)(iz \supset$
$\sim hxz))$, $(\exists x)fx \vdash (y)(gy \supset \sim iy)$.

Proof:

1	(1)	$(x)(fx \supset (y)(gy \supset hxy))$	S
2	(2)	$(x)(fx \supset (z)(iz \supset \sim hxz))$	S
3	(3)	$(\exists x)fx$	S
4	(4)	fa	S
1	(5)	$fa \supset (y)(gy \supset hay)$	1, UI
2	(6)	$fa \supset (z)(iz \supset \sim haz)$	2, UI
1,4	(7)	$(y)(gy \supset hay)$	4, 5, MPP
2,4	(8)	$(z)(iz \supset \sim haz)$	4, 6, MPP
1,4	(9)	$gb \supset hab$	7, UI
2,4	(10)	$ib \supset \sim hab$	8, UI
1,2,4	(11)	$gb \supset \sim ib$	9, 10, MTT, C, TI, D17, MPP
1,2,4	(12)	$(y)(gy \supset \sim iy)$	11, UG
1,2,3	(13)	$(y)(gy \supset \sim iy)$	3, 4, 12, EI

The final step has the effect of eliminating the supposition 4, which was not a supposition which we were asked to make in the first place.

4. SOME APPLICATIONS

I now consider some arguments in everyday English and the ways in which they may be formalized. We have seen that some arguments can be treated as simply relating categorical statements; they can be shown to be valid or invalid without considering the internal structure of the statements related.

For example, consider the following argument

> If it is false that John's passing implies that he bribed the examiner, then if the examination paper was fair, the examiner was not impartial. *Therefore*, if John passed and the examination paper was fair, then, if the examiner was impartial, John bribed the examiner.

Here, the conclusion is made up of statements which have already appeared in the premiss or the negations of those statements. There are no differences between the statements which need be marked by using different quantifiers. We can, therefore, represent the argument by the following expression in the propositional calculus.

$$(\sim (p \supset q) \supset (r \supset s)) \supset ((p \cdot r) \supset (\sim s \supset q))$$

I have represented the statements by letters in the following way

p = John passed
q = John bribed the examiner
r = The examination paper was fair
s = The examiner was not impartial.

If this expression is tested by constructing a truth table or by using the short method it will turn out to be valid. We now have an alternative method of establishing acceptability, namely, by giving a formal proof of the expression in the axiomatic system or the system of natural deduction. The disadvantage of this method is that if the expression happened not to be acceptable we might not be able to show this by a formal proof, since failure to prove something can never show that it cannot be proved.

We may deal in a similar way with arguments which, at first sight may appear to need quantifiers for their formalization but which can, in fact, be formalized without using them. For example, consider the argument

> If there is an election then the Conservative Party will win. Any party which wins an election will govern for five years. There will be an election. Therefore, the Conservative Party will govern for five years.

Here, it looks as if the third statement is an existential statement in contrast to the others which are universal. However, since 'there is an election' occurs as the antecedent of the first premiss and since 'Any party which wins an election will govern for five years' can be thought of as the hypothetical statement 'If any party (e.g. the Conservative Party) wins an election then it will govern for five years' we may represent the argument by the expression

$$((p \supset q) \cdot (q \supset r) \cdot p) \supset r$$

where p = There is an election
q = The Conservative Party will win
r = The Conservative Party will govern for five years.

There are, however, dangers in this and we can treat the argument in this way only if it is clear that the validity of the argument does not turn on the difference between existential and universal statements.

The following argument is one which cannot be treated by means of the propositional calculus for this reason.

> All thieves are untrustworthy. *Therefore* if there is someone who is a thief and whom everybody trusts, then there is someone who is untrustworthy and whom everybody trusts.

This may be represented by the expression

$$(x)(fx \supset gx) \supset (x)((\exists y)(fy \cdot hxy) \supset (\exists y)(gy \cdot hxy))$$

where f = is a thief
g = is untrustworthy
h = trusts

and, in consequence,

$(x)(fx \supset gx)$ = all thieves are untrustworthy
$(\exists y)(fy \cdot hxy)$ = there is someone who is a thief and is trusted by x
$(\exists y)(gy \cdot hxy)$ = there is someone who is untrustworthy and is trusted by x.

The universal quantifier indicates that 'x' is to be interpreted as 'everybody'.

The conclusion, here, does not simply repeat statements contained in the premises. The quantifiers are essential and it is important that relations requiring dyadic predicates figure in it. As there is no decision procedure for the predicate calculus, comparable to the truth-table method for the propositional calculus, there is no way of testing the acceptability of the expression except by a formal proof.

In fact, S11, which we have proved already was

$$(x)(fx \supset gx) \vdash (x)((\exists y)(fy \cdot hxy) \supset (\exists y)(gy \cdot hxy))$$

267

and is a sufficient basis for the argument, with the reservations already noted. One more step of Conditional Proof will yield our expression.

Consider now, the following argument

> If anyone is guilty, then anyone who is an accessory is a friend of the guilty man; if anyone is guilty, then anyone who will not be punished is not a friend of the guilty man; there is someone who is guilty. *Therefore*, if anyone is an accessory he will be punished.

We need quantifiers and dyadic predicates again. The argument may be represented by the expression

$$((x)(fx \supset (y)(gy \supset hxy)) \cdot (x)(fx \supset (z)(iz \supset \sim hxz))$$
$$\cdot (\exists x)fx) \supset (y)(gy \supset \sim iy)$$

or by the expression

$$(x)(fx \supset (y)(gy \supset hxy)), (x)(fx \supset (z)(iz \supset \sim hxz)),$$
$$(\exists x)fx \vdash (y)(gy \supset \sim iy)$$

where

$f =$ is guilty
$g =$ is an accessory
$h =$ is a friend of
$i =$ will not be punished

and, in consequence,

$(x)(fx \supset (y)(gy \supset hxy))$ = if x is guilty then anyone who is an accessory is a friend of x;

$(x)(fx \supset (z)(iz \supset \sim hxz))$ = if x is guilty then anyone who will not be punished is not a friend of x;

$(\exists x)fx$ = there is someone who is guilty;

$(y)(gy \supset \sim iy)$ = if anyone is an accessory then he will be punished.

The universal quantifier indicates that 'hxy' is to be interpreted as 'y is a friend of anyone who is guilty'. I have assumed that if x is a friend of y then y is a friend of x and vice versa. The second formalization of this argument has already been proved as S12.

If syllogisms are represented in the predicate calculus, each mood may be represented by a different expression. For example, using 'fx' in place of the middle term, 'gx' in place of the predicate term and 'hx' in place of the subject term we obtain the following expressions.

Barbara:	$((x)(fx \supset gx) \cdot (x)(hx \supset fx)) \supset (x)(hx \supset gx)$
Darii:	$((x)(fx \supset gx) \cdot (\exists x)(hx \cdot fx)) \supset (\exists x)(hx \cdot gx)$
Ferio:	$((x)(fx \supset \sim gx) \cdot (\exists x)(hx \cdot fx)) \supset (\exists x)(hx \cdot \sim gx)$
Fresison:	$((x)(gx \supset \sim fx) \cdot (\exists x)(fx \cdot hx)) \supset (\exists x)(hx \cdot \sim gx)$

Each of the expressions can be derived formally in the predicate calculus: the only exceptions are those moods which have two universal premisses and a particular conclusion, including the weakened moods. Because each expression representing a mood can, with these exceptions, be derived separately using the rules of the calculus there is no need for the traditional method of reduction for proving validity; the rules of the calculus replace the *dictum de omni et nullo* and the general rules of the syllogism. Nevertheless, these expressions in the predicate calculus make it easy to see the connections between different moods.

For example, consider the two expressions for Ferio and Fresison.

Ferio:	$((x)(fx \supset \sim gx) \cdot (\exists x)(hx \cdot fx)) \supset (\exists x)(hx \cdot \sim gx)$
Fresison:	$((x)(gx \supset \sim fx) \cdot (\exists x)(fx \cdot hx)) \supset (\exists x)(hx \cdot \sim gx)$

The conclusions are the same. The second premiss in each expression can be derived from the other, since $p \cdot q \equiv q \cdot p$. The first premiss in each can be derived from the other using *modus tollendo tollens* in one of its forms. Thus the two syllogisms are equivalent.

The moods which cannot be shown to be valid as they stand in the traditional logic may be made valid, as we have seen, by the addition of an existential premiss. The mood *Darapti*, for example, is represented by the following expression

Darapti: $((x)(fx \supset gx) \cdot (x)(fx \supset hx)) \supset (\exists x)(hx \cdot gx)$

This expression cannot be proved in the predicate calculus. However, if we add an existential premiss, namely, $(\exists x)fx$ we get the following expression which can be proved in the predicate calculus

$$((x)(fx \supset gx) \cdot (x)(fx \supset hx) \cdot (\exists x)fx) \supset (\exists x)(hx \cdot gx).$$

The other questionable moods, including the weakened moods, yield to similar treatment.

It should be clear from these remarks about the syllogism, that the traditional syllogistic logic can be regarded as just a fragment of the predicate calculus. It deals with certain types of argument involving just three statements of a very limited variety of forms. The types of statements which can be represented in the predicate calculus are many more than those needed for the syllogism. The predicate calculus is thus a much more general and powerful system than the theory of the syllogism.

5. FURTHER STEPS

My aim in this book has been to introduce the beginner to logical conceptions, principles and techniques over a wide front. I have, however, worked on the assumption that the first requirement is a grasp of principles and I have accordingly aimed to impart this rather than a mastery of techniques. I have also assumed that most beginners will be interested in the connection of logical techniques with the inferences they encounter in everyday discourse and in other academic studies. I have therefore stressed the origins of logic in everyday discourse, whether technical or untechnical, and developments in logic which have resulted from attempts to deal adequately with such discourse.

In pursuit of these aims, and in the interests of brevity, I have sometimes had to sacrifice rigour and attention to detail. Anyone who wishes to study logic seriously and in depth will be required to pursue further most of the matters discussed. Essential reading falls conveniently into two groups: philosophical logic and techniques of formal logic. I give below some reading under these headings in the form of books and articles to which I am indebted and to which the serious student of logic is advised to proceed immediately. The first group is mainly relevant to matters raised in the first three chapters; the second group is mainly relevant to matters raised in the last two chapters.

I. PHILOSOPHICAL LOGIC AND THE PHILOSOPHY OF LANGUAGE

J. L. Austin, *How to do Things with Words* (Oxford, 1962).

J. L. Austin, *Philosophical Papers* (Oxford, 1961).

*S. F. Barker, *Induction and Hypothesis* (Ithaca, N.Y., 1957).

*A. G. N. Flew (editor), *Logic and Language* I and II (Oxford, 1951 and 1953).

J. A. Fodor and J. J. Katz (editors), *The Structure of Language* (Englewood Cliffs, N.J., 1964).

G. Frege, *Translations from the Philosophical Writings of G. Frege*, P. Geach and M. Black (Oxford, 1952).

G. Frege, *The Foundations of Arithmetic*, trans. J. L. Austin (Oxford, 1950).

P. Geach, *Reference and Generality* (Ithaca, N.Y., 1962).

L. Linsky, *Referring* (London, 1967).

L. Linsky (editor), *Semantics and the Philosophy of Language* (Urbana, Illinois, 1952).

*W. V. Quine, *From a Logical Point of View* (Cambridge, Mass., 1953).

B. Russell, *Introduction to Mathematical Philosophy* (London, 1919).

*G. Ryle, 'Formal and Informal Logic' in *Dilemmas* (Cambridge, 1954).

*G. Ryle, 'Ordinary Language' in C. E. Caton (editor), *Philosophy and Ordinary Language* (Urbana, Illinois, 1963).

*G. Ryle, " 'If', 'So' and 'Because' " in M. Black (editor), *Philosophical Analysis* (Ithaca, N.Y., 1950).

*P. F. Strawson, *Introduction to Logical Theory* (London, 1952).

P. F. Strawson (editor), *Philosophical Logic* (Oxford, 1967).

A. Tarski, *Logic, Semantics and Metamathematics*, trans. J. M. Woodger (Oxford, 1956).

*S. E. Toulmin, *The Uses of Argument* (Cambridge, 1958).

*F. Waismann, *Principles of Linguistic Philosophy* (London, 1965).

L. Wittgenstein, *Philosophical Investigations* (Oxford, 1953).

P. Ziff, *Semantic Analysis* (Ithaca, N.Y., 1960).

The works marked * contain material which is less advanced or technical.

II. TECHNIQUES OF FORMAL LOGIC

This is arranged in two subsections: (a) traditional and (b) modern. The books are arranged, within each subsection, in the order in which they might profitably be read.

(a) *Traditional*

H. W. B. Joseph, *An Introduction to Logic* (Oxford, 1906).

J. N. Keynes, *Formal Logic* (London, 1884).

L. S. Stebbing, *A Modern Introduction to Logic*, 2nd edition (London, 1933).

W. E. Johnson, *Logic* (Cambridge, 1921–22).

J. Łukasiewicz, *Aristotle's Syllogistic* (Oxford, 1951).

(b) *Modern*

A. H. Basson and D. J. O'Connor, *Introduction to Symbolic Logic*, 2nd edition (London, 1957).

E. J. Lemmon, *Beginning Logic* (London, 1965).

I. M. Copi, *Symbolic Logic*, 3rd edition (New York, 1967).

A. N. Whitehead and B. Russell, *Principia Mathematica*, especially the Introductions (Cambridge, 1910 and abridged, in paperback, Cambridge, 1962).

THE CRITICISM OF ARGUMENTS

W. V. Quine, *Methods of Logic*, 2nd edition (New York, 1959).

D. Hilbert and W. Ackermann, *Principles of Mathematical Logic* (New York, 1950).

P. Suppes, *Introduction to Logic* (Princeton, N.J., 1957).

S. C. Kleene, *Introduction to Metamathematics* (Princeton, N.J., 1952).

A. Church, *Introduction to Mathematical Logic* (Princeton, N.J., 1956).

P. Suppes, *Axiomatic Set Theory* (Princeton, N.J., 1960).

W. V. Quine, *Set Theory and its Logic* (Cambridge, Mass., 1963).

Useful articles on logic and more specific topics will be found in

P. Edwards (editor), *The Encyclopedia of Philosophy* (New York, 1967).

APPENDIX

A Note on Other Systems

The systems dealt with in Chap. V are not suitable for dealing with statements which contain, and arguments which depend upon, such words as 'possible', 'impossible', 'necessary', 'may', 'can' and other words which logicians call *modal*. A variety of systems of *modal logic* has now been developed; indeed, this has been, in recent years, one of the most lively developments in formal logic. Much recent work springs from the earlier work of C. I. Lewis. Pioneering books in the field are

> C. I. Lewis, *A Survey of Symbolic Logic* (Berkeley, Calif., (1918)

and

> C. I. Lewis and C. H. Langford, *Symbolic Logic*, 2nd edition (New York, 1951).

Features of these systems are the introduction of *strict implication*, a tighter relation than material implication, and *modal operators* for 'possibly', 'necessarily' and related words. A short account is to be found in Paul Edwards' *Encyclopedia of Philosophy* (art. 'Logic, Modal') and fuller treatments of some of the problems in

> G. H. von Wright, *An Essay in Modal Logic* (Amsterdam, 1951)

and

> A. N. Prior, *Formal Logic*, 2nd edition (Oxford, 1962).

Another important development, related particularly to the study of the foundations of mathematics, is *intuitionist logic*. Most mathematicians probably accept what is known as a *platonist* view of mathematics. This is a variety of philosophical realism concerning mathematical objects, that is, the view that mathematics deals with objects which are not mind-dependent and that mathematical statements are either true or false independently of our knowledge of them and of our decisions and conventions. Mathematical truths are descriptive of some reality. This view essentially involves *the law of excluded middle*, according to which any mathematical statement must be true or false, no other possibility being open.

Almost throughout the history of mathematics there have been objections to this view; some recent ones are to be found in the *intuitionism* of L. E. J. Brouwer. They lean heavily on the notion of *construction*. According to intuitionism a mathematical object can be said to exist only if a constructive proof can be given; a constructive proof is one that either gives an example of such an object or gives a method of finding an example. As a consequence, it is not permitted to talk of an 'actual' infinity; one may talk only of a 'potential' infinity, since an infinite collection cannot be constructed. It also follows that no mathematical statement can be true unless it is *known* to be true through an acceptable mathematical method of proof.

Intuitionist logic involves an unusual view of negation and a criticism of the law of excluded middle. The fact that p cannot be proved does not show that $\sim p$ is true. It is necessary to prove $\sim p$ and the only way to do this is to show that from the assumption that p is true (i.e. can be proved) a contradiction follows. It is a consequence of this that in intuitionist logic $p \equiv \sim \sim p$ is not generally true. That is, we cannot prove p merely by proving $\sim \sim p$. The law of excluded middle is questionable because there is no reason to suppose that for any statement p we will ever be able to prove p or to prove that a contradiction follows from the assumption of p. That is $(p \lor \sim p)$ is not generally true since our inability to prove p does not imply the truth of $\sim p$ and our inability to prove $\sim p$ does not imply the truth of p.

Alonzo Church in his *Introduction to Mathematical Logic* (Section 26), gives a brief account of intuitionist propositional calculus and characterizes it as a 'partial system' of propositional calculus; it embodies 'the part of propositional calculus which may be said to be independent in some sense of the existence of a negation'.

It is important to note that if we accept an intuitionist logic in connection with the foundations of mathematics we are forced to make some basic changes in classical mathematics, since certain proofs and theorems will then be unacceptable.

An account of various views about the foundations of mathematics is to be found in

S. Körner, *The Philosophy of Mathematics* (London, 1960).

Important works on intuitionsim are

A. Heyting, *Intuitionism, An Introduction* (Amsterdam, 1956).
A. Heyting, *Mathematische Grundlagenforschung. Intuitionismus. Beweistheorie* (Berlin, 1934).

and, in an expanded French version,

Les Fondements des Mathematique. Intuitionisme. Theorie de la démonstration (Paris, 1955).

Index

Abstraction, 65, 88, 130, 200
Ackermann, W., 237, 239n.
Adams, J. C., 59
adjunction, 232
affirmative, 73
algebra, Boolean, 160ff.
'all', 73ff., 137ff.
alternation, 98ff.
alternations, denial of, 113f.
ambiguity, 24
ambiguous name, 216, 256
analogy, 124, 132
'and', 91ff.
  asymmetrical use of, 94
  symmetrical use of, 92
antecedent, 115
apodosis, 115
arbitrary names, 216, 256
argument, 4f.
  analysis of, 27f.
  conclusive and non-conclusive, 30, 31ff.,
    46ff., 54
  deductive, 30
  form of, 30, 31ff.
  frequency, 55
  from particular to particular, 58f.
  hypothetical, 44
  inductive, 30, 48ff.
  interpretative, 59ff.
argument-place, 237
Aristotle, 38n., 168, 180, 222, 224
article, definite, 69
  indefinite, 69
asserting, 79
assertion, 9, 69, 75
assuming, 79
assumption, 246
'A' statement, 72
Austin, J. L., 8n., 29n., 64n.
axiom, 224
axioms, independence of, 228
  for predicate calculus, 240
  for propositional calculus, 232
  and rules, 246

Barker, S. F., 58n.
Basson, A. H., 187n., 229n.
Bernays, P., 232

bi-conditional, 131
Bird, O., 154n.
Boole, G., 155, 160, 187
brackets, 204ff., 225, 230, 238, 256
Brouwer, L. E. J., 273

Calculus, class, 65, 201
  functional, 193
  predicate, 65, 193, 201, 236ff., 256ff.
  propositional, 11, 65, 91, 124, 201,
    229ff., 248ff.
Caton, C. E., 64n.
causal relations, 94
Church, A., 218n., 239n., 274
circles, Euler's, 115ff., 156
class, complement of, 160
  defining property of, 155
  empty or null, 155, 166
  inclusion, 163ff.
  member of, 155, 163ff.
  membership, 163ff., 193
  unit, 166
  universal, 166
classes, 65, 78f., 154ff.
  algebra of, 160ff.
  in extension, 155
  identity of, 165
  in intension, 155
  relations between, 160ff.
completeness, 228, 255
compound statements, 90ff.
conditional proof (CP), 248
confirmation, logic of, 120
conjunction, 91ff., 248
conjunction elimination (CE), 248
conjunctions, denial of, 110ff.
conjunctive function, 96
connective, 98, 202
  main, 206
consequent, 115
consistency, 228, 255
constant, binary, 230
  individual, 165, 237, 256
  and variable, 32, 64, 225, 230
constants, ranking of, 230n.
construction, 273
contradiction, 20, 23, 103ff., 107, 196
  and terms, 108f.

275

contradictory function, 109
contraposition, 146f.
contrapositive, 146, 149f.
contrariety, 104, 105, 106f.
  and terms, 108f.
conversion, 139ff.
  per accidens, 142
  simple, 141
Copi, I. M., 228n., 229n., 252n.
copula, 72

Decision procedure, 226
definition, 225
  explicit, 69
definitions, for propositional calculus, 232
demonstratives, 78
DeMorgan, A., 155, 161
denial, 89, 101ff.
  of compound statements, 109, 113
  of simple statements, 101ff.
derivability, sign of, 247
'derivable', 223ff.
Descartes, R., 84n.
detachment, 232
dictum de omni et nullo, 168, 170, 177, 180
discourse, universe of, 108f., 161
disjunction, 98ff., 249
disjunction elimination (DE), 249
disjunctions, denial of, 112f.
distribution of terms, 74, 136ff., 157, 170f., 197, 223
double negation (DN), 143, 248

Eaton, R. M., 187n., 192n.
Edwards, P., 273
'either . . . or', 98ff.
Encyclopedia of Philosophy, 7n.
entailment, 26
equivalence, 105
  material, 130, 132
'E' statement, 72
Euler, L., 115
evidence, going beyond the, 56, 139
excluded middle, law of, 273
existence, 67ff., 198
  not a predicate, 70f.
  presupposition of, 152ff.
existential import, 79ff., 151ff., 156, 195
extension, of a term, 179

Fallacy, of affirming the consequent, 119
  of denying the antecedent, 119
  of four terms, 177
  of illicit major, 178
  of illicit minor, 178
  of undistributed middle, 178
falsity, 12ff.
Faris, J. A., 219n.

figure, of the syllogism, 169
formula, accepted, 225
  allowable (wff), 225
  well-formed, 225

Geach, P. T., 137n., 157n., 185n.
generalization, 30, 51
Gentzen, G., 224
geometry, non-Euclidean, 228
God, 68, 70, 71, 84
Gould, J. A., 228n.

Hare, R. M., 29n.
Hart, H. L. A., 61n.
Heyting, A., 274
Hilbert, D., 237, 239n.
Hobbes, T., 56n.
'horseshoe', 123
hypothesis, 115

Identity, 67, 69f.
'if and only if', 69, 132
'if . . . then', 114ff., 218f.
implication, 15ff., 114ff., 160
  material, 126ff., 218f.
  'paradox of', 126ff.
  strict, 133f., 273
'implies', 123
implying, 75
individual, arbitrarily selected, 216, 256
induction, eliminative, 57
  enumerative, 57
  summary, 57
inference, 15ff.
  immediate, 83, 135ff.
  mediate, 135
inference pattern, 32ff., 246
infinity, actual, 274
instance, 194
inverse, 148
inversion, 147ff.
'is', of existence, 67ff., 87
  of identity, 69f.
  of predication or attribution, 70ff., 87
'I' statement, 72

Jevons, W. S., 155
Johnson, W. E., 57n.
Joseph, H. W. B., 179n.

Key words, 43ff, 64, 67ff., 124
Kleene, S. C., 224n.
Kneale, W. C. and M., viii, 134n., 168n., 223n.
Körner, S., 274

Langford, C. H., 134, 273
language, and reasoning, 21f.
  rules of, 62ff.

laws, logical, 64
Lemmon, E. J., viii, 257n.
Leverrier, U. J. J., 59
Lewis, C. I., 130n., 134, 273
Linsky, L., 137n.
logic, extensional, 134
  formal, 43
  and foundations of mathematics, 1
  intensional, 134
  intuitionist, 273f.
  modal, 133, 273
  as normative, 5f.
  as philosophy, 1
  and poetry, 6f.
  and science, 3
  scope of, 1ff.
  symbolic, 65
  systems of, 6
  traditional, 38n., 65, 88, 130f., 168ff.
'logically impossible', 151
Łukasiewicz, J., 179n., 185n.

Mace, C. A., 64n.
major premiss, 169
major term, 169
Mates, B., viii
mathematics, 132, 273
meaning, 10ff., 12ff., 64
  and equivalence, 122ff., 132
  theories of, 14
mention and use, 9
minor premiss, 169
minor term, 169
Mitchell, D., 12
modus (ponendo) ponens, 117f., 194f., 248
modus (tollendo) tollens, 118f., 195f., 248
mood, of the syllogism, 169
  weakened, 174

Name, 157
Nagel, E., 228n.
necessary condition, 67
negation, 89, 196
negative, 73
Newcomb, S., 59n.
Newman, J. R., 228n.
'no', 101ff.
'not', 101ff.

Obversion, 139, 143ff.
O'Connor, D. J., 187n., 229n.
Oliver, J. W., 221n.
'only', 89
opposition, contradictory, 103ff., 144f.
  contrary, 104f., 144f.
  square of, 104ff.
'or', exclusive use, 98, 113
  inclusive use, 99, 112
'O' statement, 72

Particular statements, 71, 73ff.
Peirce, C. S., 155
Peter of Spain, 174n.
Plantinga, A., 71
Popper, K. R., 48n., 105n.
predicate, 65, 70, 192
  monadic, 262f.
  polyadic, 262f.
predicate calculus, axiomatic, 236ff.,
    natural, 256ff.
predication, 67, 70ff.
premiss, 17
presupposition, 69, 71, 84
Principia Mathematica, 132n., 224
Prior, A. N., 133n.
product, logical, 162
proof, 26, 227, 232
property, 70
proposition, 7ff.
protasis, 115

Quantifier, 84ff., 167f., 214ff., 237
  existential, 86f.
  particular, 86f.
  universal, 85f.
Quine, W. V., viii, 165n., 201n., 214n.,
    224n.

Reductio ad absurdum, 249
reference, 14, 69, 179
relation, 33ff.
  asymmetrical, 159
  converse of, 158f.
  dyadic, 158
  intransitive, 37, 159
  non-symmetrical, 159
  non-transitive, 37, 159
  relative product of, 35
  square of, 35
  symmetrical, 159
  transitive, 37, 159
relations, logical properties of, 158ff.
replacement, 231
Rescher, N., 29n.
Rosser, B., 218n.
rule, for bound variables, 240
  of deduction or derivation, 225
  of existential generalization, 257
  of existential instantiation, 216, 257
  of formation, 225, 238, 256
  of inference, 64
  of procedure, 225
  for quantifiers, 240
  of universal generalization, 257
  of universal instantiation, 216, 257
rules, for class algebra, 188
  for predicate calculus (axiomatic),
    238ff.
  for predicate calculus (natural), 256

rules, *(contd.)*
  for propositional calculus (axiomatic), 230
  for propositional calculus (natural), 248f.
  semantical, 63ff.
  of the syllogism, 170f.
  syntactical, 62f.
Russell, B., 37n., 129, 132n.
Ryle, G., 19n., 64n.

Sampling, 54
Schilpp, P. A., 129n.
scope, of connective, 206
self-contradiction, 204
sentence, 7ff., 63
  simple and compound, 11
singular statements, 73ff., 77ff., 165, 194
Smart, J. J. C., 60n.
'some', 73ff., 138
statement, 7ff.
  analytic and synthetic, 20f.
  categorical, 90
  compound, 90
  form of, 23
  hypothetical, 83, 114
  and non-statement, 28f.
  particular affirmative, 137f.
  particular negative, 137f.
  relational, 180
  simple, 90
  singular, 73ff., 77ff., 165, 194
  universal affirmative, 137f.
  universal negative, 137f.
stating, 47
Stebbing, L. S., 37n., 57n., 66n., 105n., 160n., 172n.,
Strawson, P. F., viii, 2n., 10n., 64n.
subalternation, 104, 106f.
subcontrariety, 104f., 107
subject-matter, 37, 46, 51
subject-predicate form, 169
substitution, 231, 239
sufficient condition, 67
suggesting, 75
sum, logical, 162
Suppes, P., viii, 250
support, 5, 22ff.
  conclusive, 23ff.
  inconclusive, 26f.
supposition, 246, 248
syllogism, 42, 65f., 87, 135, 168, 223, 268f.
  categorical, 169
  class interpretation of, 157
  hypothetical, 169
  reduction of, 171ff.
  as relating classes, 186ff.

syllogism *(contd.)*
  as relating predicates, 192ff.
  as relating propositions, 183ff.
syllogistic proofs, 171ff.
  theory, criticisms of, 179ff.
symbol, 114, 123
  metalogical, 230, 238, 256
  primitive, 225, 229f., 237, 256
system, axiomatic, 224ff., 229ff.
  elements of, 225
  logical, 43, 65, 200, 222ff., 273f.
  of natural deduction, 224, 225, 246ff.

Tautology, 203, 226f., 255
term, 65, 156
  middle, 66
  predicate, 66, 137
  subject, 66, 137
testing, mechanical, 218
theorem, 223ff., 247, 251
  introduction (TI), 255, 258
theory, scientific, 120
'to be', 67ff.
topic-neutral words, 43
truth, 17, 198
  column, 97, 207
  conditions, 92
  factual, 19ff.
  logical, 19ff.
  row, 97, 207
  table, 96ff., 100, 109, 111, 112f., 123f., 125, 201ff., 232
'truth-functional', 130, 132f.

'Undetermined', 105
unicorns, 67f.
universal statements, 71, 73ff.

Validity, deductive, 18
  and invalidity, 218ff.
  short method of testing, 209ff.
  testing of, 201ff.
  and truth, 17
variable, free and bound, 238
  individual, 165, 237, 256
  predicate, 237, 256
  propositional, 229, 248
Venn diagrams, 161ff.
Venn, J., 155n.
von Wright, G. H., 133n., 273

Words, 63
Whitehead, A. N., and Russell, B., 132n., 224, 232
Wittgenstein, L., 2n.

Ziff, P., 2n., 63n.

GEORGE ALLEN & UNWIN LTD

Head office:
London: 40 Museum Street, W.C.1

Trade orders and enquiries:
Park Lane, Hemel Hempstead, Herts

Auckland: P.O. Box 36013, Northcote Central, N.4
Barbados: P.O. Box 222, Bridgetown
Beirut: Deeb Building, Jeanne d'Arc Street
Bombay: 15 Graham Road, Ballard Estate, Bombay 1
Buenos Aires: Escritorio 454–459, Florida 165
Calcutta: 17 Chittaranjan Avenue, Calcutta 13
Cape Town: 68 Shortmarket Street
Hong Kong: 105 Wing On Mansion, 26 Hancow Road, Kowloon
Ibadan: P.O. Box 62
Karachi: Karachi Chambers, McLeod Road
Madras: Mohan Mansions, 38c Mount Road, Madras 6
Mexico: Villalongin 32, Mexico 5, D.F.
Nairobi: P.O. Box 30583
New Delhi: 13–14 Asaf Ali Road, New Delhi 1
Ontario: 81 Curlew Drive, Don Mills
Philippines: P.O. Box 4322, Manila
Rio de Janeiro: Caixa Postal 2537–Zc–00
Singapore: 36c Prinsep Street, Singapore 7
Sydney, N.S.W.: Bradbury House, 55 York Street
Tokyo: P.O. Box 26, Kamata